The Terminology of Bon Vivant Life and Other Sociological Insights: Collected Essays

By L. Larry Liu

Table of Content

Acknowledgment

Though I am the sole author of the present work, it goes almost without saying that this work would not have been possible without studying for a year in Oxford. My course has been in comparative social policy, and was made possible by the fortuitous decision of the Jack Kent Cooke Foundation to sponsor a scholarship for a student to attend Lincoln College, Oxford. This relationship was made possible by the fact that the new executive director at the foundation, Harold Levy, a Lincoln alumnus, was a good friend of the Lincoln rector, Henry Woodhuysen. Harold wanted to make sure that Cooke Scholars would have the opportunity to burnish Oxford credentials and have that experience. I have gotten to know the two of them quite well, and thank them for their foresight and generosity.

The greatest intellectual debts go to my friends in Oxford, with whom I consumed too many pints of alcohol but shared great memories, nonetheless. I have no doubt that all of my friends, whom I was sad to see go, will do great things in life. Oxford did not disappoint me with their talent pool.

Mustafa Aydogan has been a faithful and helpful flat mate with whom I fondly remember making awesome Kofte, the Turkish national dish. He is a busy biologist, whose preference to wear a suit with bow tie has made me aware of what a bon vivant can be. He dragged me to his book shopping tours in Oxfam, where obscure titled books can be gotten for a few pounds. I had been ordering most of my books on Amazon previously and only occasionally went to used book stores, but I now very strongly appreciate the value of acquiring obscure books. Mustafa's goal is to build a personal library, which scientists doing research can use. He wants to be the book patron in Istanbul, while I am happy to amass my much smaller personal library. While we both were bibliophiles, he regarded books as a shrine to be treasured and not defiled, while I consider it merely as a store of knowledge, and we had one of our rare arguments when he caught me scribbling on the inside flap of my books, where I kept my summary notes of the book. How can I defile the precious book pages? I most fondly remember our kitchen table conversations (there was no living room in our modest flat) which ranged from politics, philosophy to his beloved history of sciences.

Jozef Kosc is perhaps the incarnation of the bon vivant, because he was the first to use that term, and the term instantly clicked with me. He took me out to the Chabad House lectures, introducing me to Jewish philosophy and thought. On our intellectual chats on the rooftop next to our flat, he lectured me about the value of traditional conservatism, the Straussian resistance to socio-economic modernization, which creates cultural and political instability. Rather than basing his ideology on liberalism, which seeks to elevate individual freedom above other values, he insists on the need for society to be regulated by traditional virtues surrounding the family, the nation-state and religion. While I don't disagree that the common people need some philosophical guidance, I think he is too pessimistic about human nature, which reveals a somewhat libertarian streak in my own thinking. Where we clearly agree is that neoliberal capitalism is a threat to current society, though his focus is more on society and culture and mine on the political economy. In any case, our discussions had been continuously inspiring.

Alistair Leitch is a rare intellectual talent, who is the most well-read person that I know. He is an intellectual omnivore and traverses the social sciences widely with degrees in social policy and social and economic history. He is from Scotland, and very much follows the traditions of Hume and Smith. He is a true incarnation of the bon vivant by constantly overdressing (tweed jacket and tie in classroom), enjoying good savory meals, intellectual discussion and music of all stripes, consuming an inordinate amount of Scottish whisky and being the first to go to an event and the last to leave. Our full day discussion sessions, ranging from the importance of nationalizing strategic industries, the malaise of modern capitalist economies plagued by low growth, work insecurity, poverty and failed social policy, the lack of a forward-looking vision by the contemporary socialist left, the importance of T.H. Marshall's social citizenship rights to social science methodology, philosophy, history, the history of sciences and the determinants of a good life.

Lars Gladhaug strikes me as a very talented and brilliant US-American historian with a strong preference for the status quo as the "best of all available options". We would easily get into debates, and he forced me to defend my position to more justly distribute the proceeds of capitalist society, the practical difficulties of a basic income, and the question of Marxian dialectics in history. Oliver Fleisch is an incredible thinker and does not reveal his ideological position easily (he turns out to be a fan of Hayekian, Austrian economics), but he is capable to deconstruct my argument in a logical, Socratic manner, such that I have to justify myself (which reminded me somewhat of my brother). He is very pedantic and detail-obsessed, as can be expected from a good German. The nightly kitchen conversation with him that went until 5am will remain unforgotten.

There have been numerous other friends and acquaintances that I have made in Oxford, but they are too numerous to list, and I am mortally afraid of forgetting to mention some. I have substantially benefited from conversations and company with them. Phoebe Ai, Skaiste Aleksandraviciute, Yussef Al-Tamini, Lewis Arthurton, Arutyun Arutyunyan, Danny Avraham, Ruba Awadallah, David Baker, Rens Bakker, Ali Bargu, Selcuk Beduk, Rowan Border, Eli

Brackman, Emma Brunskill-Powell, Jennifer Cassidy, Shan Chang, Cheryl Chen, Vinton Cheng, Hormuz Dadabhoy, Gabe Delaney, Henry-Martin Demasco, Jay Reynolds Der, Blair Ding, Agnes Ebenberger, Scott Greenhalgh, Zach Gross, Fabian Gunzinger, Olya Homonchuk, Jamie Hirst, Nidhi Joshi, Caspar Kaiser, Shrochis Karki, Abe Kenmore, Tanya Khan, Tanyah Khan, Eugina Kim, Joobong Kim, Younga Kim, Franziska Kirschner, Hans-Jochen Kockert, Marisol Lang, Chieh-hsiu Liu, Ting Liu, Xi Liu, Elizabeth Lui, Sorina Maciuca, Melis Meier, Severin Meier, Stefan Mirza, Gabrielle Newell, Karen Ng, Cherry Ni, Christian Niederhuber, Abhishek Parajuli, Tristan Parker, Dipal Patel, Jay Patel, Julia Poenit, Ertugrul Polat, Lauge Rasmussen, Constantin Reinprecht, Risha Roy, Saroj Saurya, Clara Schmidt, Tom Scott, Gil Selby, Josh Simpson, Nidhi Singh, James Snowdon, Lukas Sprenger, Adam Steel, John Sullivan, Shouji Sun, Yoichiro Tamanyu, David Tedone, Trang Tran, Nhat An Trinh, Michael Wang, Stefan Witschen, Pauline Wu, Michael Yehuda, Xixi Yu, Yuxi Zhang, Ching Zhao. Chris Wilson was my favorite teacher, a passionate demographer, who enjoyed listening and explaining his subject to students. Erzsebet Bukodi was my thesis supervisor, and substantially helped me on my academic research, even though we have different methodological backgrounds. I benefited from insights in social policy from Stuart Basten, Mary Daly, Paola Mattei, Robert Walker. My undergraduate adviser, Randall Collins, is reflected in my ruminations of sociological theory, which is always relevant to social reality and life. Among relatives, I thank my parents, Kuo Chun and Mei Ling Liu, my brother Nicky Liu, my uncle Patrick Huang, aunt and uncle Ai Ling and Tien Jui Chang, cousins Sylvia, Vincent and Tiffany, and cousin-in-law Norman Korompis.

Philadelphia, PA
September 2016
L. Larry Liu

The Terminology of Bon Vivant Life and Other Sociological Insights

One of the major perks of living in Oxford and studying with very distinguished and rather intellectual students with many interesting and enjoyable discussions is to recycle very valuable ideas about social life, personal identity, and what it takes to have a "bon vivant" lifestyle. Oxford contains a university city, where thousands of bright students get together in limited space and just get on with it. The fact that it is full of elitism and fame results in the best and brightest bothering to apply to attend the university and for speakers from all over the world to be willing to stop by for a talk or seminar. There are many opportunities to hang out in pubs, cafes, social rooms in colleges, go out on a boat ride (punt), walk in the university park, bicycle across town, study in the library, watch the birds along Christ Church meadow, attend cheap concerts on the top seats of the Sheldonian theatre, and see students dressed in weird gowns during exam season.

What follows is a definition of the terminology, which I- in conversation with fellow bon vivants- have developed during my time in Oxford. (Not all my bon vivant fellows will agree with all that I write here, but the reflections would also not have come about without them.)

The list is not meant to be exhaustive, and it may be supplemented as time goes on. They are not presented in alphabetical order, but ad hoc. Not all concepts are strongly related to bon vivants, and there are many broader sociological reflections on which I dwelled on for a longer time. The goal is to show as many people as possible the contours of how good life can be structured, and how society can be understood. None of the terms and ideas are original, and we merely see ourselves as inheritors of the tradition of great thinkers. As Marx says, "The ruling ideas are the ideas of the rulers." But it is the task of every new generation to come to understand and cherish the valuable elements of the past, and appropriate some new ideas for the present and future.

Bon Vivant

What does the word in the title suggest? The literal French translation would be "someone who lives a good life". Wiktionary agrees with this definition, and adds the enjoyment of good food and drink to it. If one were to take it to extreme levels, it would imply people, who eat and eat, and get so obese because they can't stop eating. That is a possible interpretation, but not the one that I favor. Of course, food and drink are essential to a happy life, but one can eat good food and drink good drinks without having very intellectual and stimulating conversations. In intellectual life, those stimulating conversations are the pre-requisite to also enjoying the food and the drink. The intellectual conversations can only happen among intellectual people, and they share certain key features:
(1) curiosity about the world,
(2) vast accumulation of knowledge in different fields,
(3) interest in finer things like female beauty (for males), music, art, food, dress, literature etc.,
(4) enjoyment of leisure reading,
(5) deconstruction and critique of social reality and mainstream ideas (the much touted "critical thinking").

Brain Bullshiting

The first realization of the intellectual is not necessarily that his ideas are the greatest, but quite possibly the opposite. The wisest man in history is considered to be Socrates, because he among all the philosophers was the only one who knew that he knew nothing. It is very difficult to gather expertise over even just one subject matter even if we devote thousands and thousands of hours to deepen our knowledge in that subject. It is questionable why one should only become the expert in one topic, and not strive to be a polymath, i.e. someone, who knows about many different topics. But even as we gather all this knowledge, and present to peers in scientific journals and conferences about how much understanding we have of an aspect of social and natural reality, do we really know for sure what we know?

Every quantitative researcher knows that he/she uses certain assumptions to prove their hypothesis, but there are thousands of lurking variables that are too numerous to capture and difficult to comprehend, thus destroying the credibility of any finding. For qualitative social science researchers the situation is even worse, because their assumptions to make their claims are not often transparent, so it is easy for skeptics to question the "evidence" of an argument, simply because "I say so". Whole books are, of course, written by scientists about how to create "rigor" in their field, and establish boundaries that can make them represent reality better, but how successful are they really?

This does not mean that it is not possible to theorize and uncover the truth, but we have to say goodbye to the notion that such enterprise would be easy. What makes the intellectual certainly very much different from the rest of the species is his unstoppable capacity to produce "brain bullshit", and one look at peer-reviewed research quickly convinces one of this fact. Sometimes I wish I was born as a sheep, who could graze in the vast grass fields of rural England, chewing my grass in peace, not being bothered about anything else in the world. Or as Emily Dickinson writes, "How happy is the little stone..."

90-10-1 Rule of Intellect

Every intellectual person has to realize that he belongs to a rare breed creature. No reading of Nietzsche is required to understand this (though helpful). As soon as he strikes up a conversation with another person, he can immediately measure the level of intellectual curiosity that that person has. In most cases, he will have to realize that most people do not share a great intellectual passion, are not curious individuals, and are "**empty toothpastes**". (Have you tried to squeeze an empty toothpaste very hard and almost nothing comes out?). The 90-10-1 rule of intellect says that 90% of the people are normal people in that they lack intellectual curiosity, need to be told what to do, how things work, and enjoy the simple pleasures of life (pop culture, fashion design, sunbathing, television, relaxing, traveling etc.); 10% of the people are relatively intelligent, can be taught how complex ideas, concepts and computations can be made, can hold their own in a modest amount of intellectual conversations, but are happy to pursue the simple pleasures of life and still blend in well either way (think of most government bureaucrats or lawyers); and 1% of the people belong to the intellectual class and exhibit the features listed in the "Bon Vivant" term. Their mind gets easily bored, and they crave permanent intellectual stimulation via pondering, reading and conversing. They have what Pierre Bourdieu (1986) called ample "cultural capital".

Another way to categorize the three groups of people is by the content of their conversations. The vast majority of people talk about other people (think of gossip) and little else. (We exclude everyday statements and questions like "where is the toilet?", "where is Tesco?", which are mundane and common to nearly all human beings in modern civilization.) A small group of people enjoy talking about events, such as political news or even the sports column of the newspaper. And an even smaller group talks about ideas, which may be broad scholarship (e.g. Esping-Andersen's welfare state typology or Einstein's theory of relativity) or high-level philosophical ideas (e.g. Hegel, Marx, Kant, Aristotle). The three groups of categories are like a pyramid with steps. The lowest step are talking about people, the next highest step are events, and the highest step are ideas (whereby I think that philosophy is ranked higher than both social and natural science ideas). If one can talk about ideas, it won't be difficult to talk about events and people, but if one only knows how to talk about people, it is unlikely that one can talk about events or ideas.

Some people will now object that 90-10-1 does not add up mathematically and is not empirically true. How do I know that these percentage distributions are correct? Well, I don't know whether they are correct, and it does not matter whether the true value is 80-19-1 or 85-14-1 or 89-10-1. I also don't know whether the real distribution is just like in the Bell curve where there are different shades of intellect, and it is not possible to neatly define a cutoff between the three categories. But the point of typologies is to create a simple enough pattern for the mind to understand underlying social phenomena. The mathematical incorrectness of 101% is for me a rough rule-of-thumb, which is more pleasing to the brain than 89-10-1 or 90-9-1 or 91-8.5-0.5 and any other brain-confusing combinations. Someone suggested to me that 100% belong to the lower intellect categories and 1% belong to the top, and are outside the "regular" public. That is another way of looking at this mathematical "problem".

50-50 Conversation Rule

It can be quite intimidating at first to initiate conversations with perfect strangers. But there is no reason for a bon vivant to be deterred, because 50% of the time a conversation can be quite enjoyable, provide light entertainment, and can sometimes even result in serious intellectual engagement (as happened to me several times). The other 50% of the time, the conversation partner is boring and/or anti-social. These kinds of conversations drain mutual energy, as there is nothing much to say, and can only be salvaged by a retreat. (This would be a "failed interaction ritual" in the words of Erving Goffman 1967.) You must have encountered that during dinner parties and social events. The fear of meeting the poor conversation partners often deters one from approaching any strange person, but that fear is not really necessary, because one should not preclude oneself from having a potentially useful conversation with another person.

The critical mind will now again ask whether there is any empirical basis for the 50-50 rule? Why is it not 60-40 or 70-30? Why do I not differentiate the Oxford context from the general public context? Again, I am willing to sacrifice empirical precision for typological certainty. Even if it were true that the number of interesting conversation partners is much less than the number of uninteresting conversation partners, for the *next* person that one talks to the heuristic choice pattern should be treated *as if it were* a coin toss. Any other more pessimistic perspective would result in the decision not to engage, and to never find out whether that person could have been interesting. In other words, a 1 in a 100 chance (engaging) is still a higher chance than a 0 chance (not engaging) of finding interesting conversation partners.

Knowledge as Pollen

If the society is structured in a 90-10-1 way does it mean that non-intellectual people are forever lost to the intellectual cause? Not necessarily. It is true that it would be difficult to teach much to mentally challenged people, but the overwhelming majority of people can still substantially benefit from being exposed to more intellectual people. How can get one better at things? By hanging out with people superior to oneself, and minimizing contact with people inferior to oneself. (Of course, in order to replenish the stock of superior-skilled people, one also needs to hang out with inferior-skilled people and teach them.)

There clearly is a learning effect, because one can study what the person good at math or languages knows, and one is pushed to perform better and learn quickly to keep up with the superior group. There clearly is a negative knock-on effect if one hangs out too much with people with inferior skills. If you want to learn Spanish, a Spanish tutor will help you more than your classmates, who know as little as you and quickly switch back to the comfortable native language in personal interaction. That is quite understandable, because communicating with ease is an intrinsic human tendency, but it won't help you with the foreign language.

To borrow from biology, teaching, lecturing and explaining may be compared to pollen from the flowers. Flowers have two ways to reproduce themselves: the wind or insects carry the pollen. There is a multitude of pollen and only a small percentage makes it to the final destination and lead to the creation of new flowers. One may also make a comparison with mammal sperms of which multiple millions get transmitted via ejaculation, but only a few hundred are eligible to compete for the ovum, and usually only one sperm can merge with the ovum to produce new life.

This biological principle can be easily transferred to education and knowledge. Every professor knows that only a handful of students in every undergraduate class show interest in the subject material that is taught. Those are the same students, who not only perform well in exams and assignments but also ask many questions and make many comments in class. Some professors then consider themselves as a failure, because they have not been able to reach out to more students. But that is not true, because to the extent that they have created or increased the curiosity among some students, they have been very successful. I take enormous pleasure in lecturing other people about the things I know about. My intimate hope is that I get critical feedback or get a lecture on their expertise, but even if not, even if the listener will forget everything that I have said, and the listener nods along merely to be polite, it still gives me an enormous amount of pleasure to see that other people have learned something or are exposed to it. The greatest gratification is when your listeners repeat, recycle and reapply your ideas elsewhere.

Knowledge, Wisdom and Freedom

It is an old cliché that knowledge is power, but it is true. The more you know, the less likely you can be tricked. Think of the gullible old people, who pick up the phone and reveal their bank account number to fraudulent callers, who wrongfully say that the old people have won money, and then have their life savings stolen from them. Think of insider trading in the financial markets, which creates outsize profits for a few financial market participants like members of Congress during the financial crisis immediately after they voted to bail out the banks. Think of people with a higher education, who tend to exercise more and eat healthier food, and thus are less likely to become obese and sick than their lesser educated fellows. Knowledge is power.

But knowledge coupled with wisdom is freedom. It is the freedom from oppression by others, and freedom for selecting what is the best for oneself and others. It, therefore, makes sense to maximize wisdom for as many people as possible, though conservative rulers have always been afraid of what would happen if the masses knew too much. Charles Binderup (Congressman) used to say that if people knew how the financial system worked, there would be a revolution the next day. School systems are ironically not designed to allow people to maximize their freedom, maybe to increase knowledge, but more textbook knowledge rather than knowledge about what matters in life (wisdom). Compulsory schooling was introduced so that people follow the hierarchy in the factory and office in their careers. The teacher is the authority figure similar to the CEO and the line manager. The libertarian, anti-authoritarian education perspective is wonderfully summarized in Pink Floyd's "Another Brick in the Wall" song.

In the ideal society, of course, it would be absurd to demand schools to be abolished, because there are advantages to have central institutions where people can learn to be socialized and integrate to society. But there are different ways how to bring the best out of students. One example is Noam Chomsky's educational history, which is reported in Barsky's (1998) biography of him: he went to a Deweyite school, where he and his classmates were free to explore whatever topic interested them. There were teachers and they provided some structures, but they would be supportive rather than directive. There were no grades and no ranking, so there was no external competitive pressure. Students competed with themselves. How much more do I know today than yesterday? That was done rather than competing with other students. He then went to a public high school, where there was competitive pressure, rankings, GPA, exams. He found out that he was a good student, but he hated his high school experience.

The good grades got him into the University of Pennsylvania, which he also hated. He was teaching Hebrew school and considered dropping out of university until his mentor Zellig Harris convinced him to stay. He pulled him out of the regular classroom experience, invited him to his house, where he and other linguists and graduate students would lounge around, and have stimulating discussions and seminars. Because of Harris' influence, Chomsky received his BA in linguistics without administrative hassles. He got his doctorate also at UPenn, but received a four-year fellowship in Harvard, where he was buried in the stacks of the Harvard library and pursued his own passions while doing research. What comes out of this unique educational experience are his great linguistic theories and his prolific political activism. It is a rare experience, but one that serves as an inspiration for what human experience is possible.

A teacher was once asked by his student, "Professor, what material are we going to cover in class?" His reply was, "It doesn't matter what we cover. It matters what you *discover*." (quoted from Chomsky, "The Purpose of Higher Education"). I can tell you my argument in all the papers that I wrote, but I have probably forgotten most of high school math. I had a little Chomsky-style experience not at UPenn where everything was competitive, but at the community college, where I attended a liberal arts honors program. But rather than honors being a club where kids with high grades sit around and congratulate themselves, it was a serious program, where we read a lot of literature, history and philosophy, and had intense, thought-provoking seminars. One of the fabulous teachers in the program said to us in all frankness, "You all already have A's. Now, contribute to the discussion and take away as much (or little) from it as you see fit." I have never had this kind of educational experience ever again.

Rituals

Confucius stuck to the iron rituals that one has to behave well, especially to superiors. He said that the relationship between the son and the father is as strictly regulated as the relationship between citizen and ruler. What Confucius, of course, was concerned with was to have a stable hierarchical society, where most people did what the leaders wanted (loyalty), while in return the ruler was obliged to be protective of the people's interests (good governance). Whether or not Confucius was right, I take the point from him that one needs to have solid rituals to live a stable and fulfilled life, and to remind oneself of the things that one ought to do or are worth doing. I, for instance, do my laundry every Saturday morning. My breakfast alternates between jam, chocolate spread and peanut butter on wheat bread, and between oatmeal and Cheerios. My lunch and dinner alternate between rice, noodles and potatoes, between chicken, beef, turkey, lamb, pork, salmon and cod, and between cabbage, spinach, broccoli, kale, mixed vegetables and spliced green. This forms a nutritional balance, which I have called the "**trinity**". (Have you noticed that many good ideas come in threes? See Wikipedia, "Rule of Three (writing)")

There are many great trinities, and public speakers who can drill down their messages to threes tend to be very impactful and easy to remember. The reason why I love tea, for instance, is because of the (1) smell/taste, (2) the warmth, and (3) the time that it takes to cool down, steep and drink (reflecting a more slow and perceptive pace of life). The reason why I like cooking with other people is (1) sociability, (2) education/ learning effect, and (3) ritual solidarity that such activity creates.

Many people can have a chaotic daily schedule, but they are devout Sunday churchgoers. More interesting and fateful are the rituals with friends and other people. Mencius, one of Confucius' followers, says **"eat, drink, men, women"**, which means that the two essential human pleasures are sex and food/drinks. Leaving sexual pleasures aside for the moment, lunch or dinner rituals are quite powerful mechanisms to maintain friendships, because essential daily activities are combined with a social atmosphere, which are essential for personal well-being and a good life (Aristotle's view of friendship is summarized by me in Liu 2016). But the ritual can involve anything else like cooking, doing sports, going to a concert etc. It was Emile Durkheim (1912), who noted that religious rituals exist in order to remind followers of the "sacred", and the sacred is nothing else but the collective belief in the maintenance of community life. Rituals keep the solidarity alive. That is the case even as religions are myths, i.e. invented stories, but to create a collective identity and steer people's action.

Confrontation

Most cultures and most people have a strong aversion to confrontations. What might happen in authoritarian regimes when we criticize the government? Get caught, lose our job, have our reputation ruined, have our family members abducted and possibly get killed? In the worst of all situations, it might not make much sense to confront, but run and hide. If an organization is declining or deteriorating, we have the choice between exit, voice and loyalty, as Albert Hirschman (1970) described. We can choose to flee the situation, we can voice our opposition and seek change, or we can put up with the status quo and hold onto the existing form of organization as long as possible. When should we choose voice, i.e. confrontation? Luckily, most of us don't live in the most repressive states in the world, and there are different more harmless situations for life and limb, where some confrontation can actually pay off.

For instance, I was supposed to receive scholarship money from the college, but they had decided not to transfer the funds to me, because they don't care or just forgot. I wrote an email to the secretary asking about when the transfer would happen. She said it would happen soon. Almost three more weeks pass, and I decided to confront her in the office in person. I was nice and pleasant, but firm, and she said that the transfer will happen as soon as the sick accountant was back in office. I nodded, and said that I will be back next week if I had not received the stipend by then. It came in a few days later. A friendly confrontation often works wonder. Who really takes the bother to advocate for you? Within big bureaucratic organizations we are just a piece of scribble on the file. If we show our faces, we can accomplish much more. The point is that one never knows what one is entitled to unless one asks for it. And sometimes a rejection should not be treated as permanent, such as was the case when Ghandi pushed for India's independence from Britain, or when Martin Luther King pushed for black civil rights in the US. A direct confrontation can also relieve tensions in relationships (imagine a deflating balloon after one releases the opening), but battles must of course be chosen wisely because we only have limited resources and time.

In the words of Confucius, "A scholar must be thus earnest, urgent and bland. Among his friends, earnest and urgent. Among his brethren, bland."

Leisure

During an average life, there are many organizations and people, who capture much of one's attention space. The boss wants us to work longer hours. The colleagues want us to produce another report, so we look good in front of the boss. The college professor demands us to write another paper, which he only half-heartedly reads anyway, but still expecting us to love his subject as much as he does. Some of what other people demand us to do absolutely make sense, and can improve us or our knowledge. For instance, I would never be good at teaching myself statistics or a language, because I lack the discipline. While I have no problem reading an endless amount of history, philosophy and social science texts, there is a limitation as to how many hours I will invest in studying how to input a statistical software. Having someone else impose structure on your life, then makes absolute sense.

On the other hand, there is no doubt that a good life cannot be led without sufficient leisure. Why is that the case? Let us recall, what makes up the bon vivant intellectual: he is curious about everything surrounding him, and continuously wants to learn new things. He has certain passions and he wants to pursue them. But these passions will not be pursued as long as he has to do things that *others* want him to do. The ability, therefore, to retreat from the demands from other people, and live like a monk, therefore, counts for much.

In modern life, in the absence of having rich parents, there are principally three means by which a life of leisure can be led: (1)

priest, (2) scholar, (3) unemployed, welfare recipient. As a priest, one can sit in the ivory tower and philosophize about the human condition. In churches, one can read the Bible and interpret it, but supplement it with some more secular reading. In more Protestant churches, the pastors are often required to not only give weekly sermons (which can also draw very broadly on contemporary topics, such as the one sermon I attended, where that pastor cited Obama's drone wars), but also build relationships with the church community, and care for their material welfare. I personally could never contemplate a life as a priest or pastor, because the requirement to believe in God makes it difficult for me to adhere to its principles. The Bible is certainly a hugely important book for many people, but why should we make one book the focal point of personal inquiry? Other than that, there are very few formal obligations on the life of a priest, and one should admire the prolific writings of Pope Francis, who condemns capitalism, which is something that most investment bankers, who are busy exploiting the system, would not do.

Being a scholar at a well-funded university with tenure is another option. One can publish papers on any topic that interests one, and carry out book projects, which allow a level of creativity, which most lawyers, accountants and other corporate drones don't have. To pursue one's research agenda also means plenty of time to consume the literature of one's choice. Lecturing students and leading seminars, while talking about the things one is interested in, are other important perks. Going to academic conferences, where one can become more knowledgeable about one's field, is inherently more interesting than working on boring excel sheets in Goldman Sachs or going to a company cocktail party with small-talking colleagues. Star professors at elite universities are also better remunerated than any priest. The extent of freedom is greater in academia than even among clerics.

But a few caveats are in order too: Life as an academic is very much time-consuming. One has to spend a lot of time in mindless committees; chair administrative positions, which distract from research; supervise some mediocre students beside the brilliant students; read and review colleagues' journal articles, which might be boring or uninteresting; apply for grants and rewrite proposals to find the right language to please the donors; and most importantly, have the publication pressure make one strategic about what and how to research, which substantially reduces freedom.

That leaves us with the welfare recipient. The stigmatized "lazy" people sit around at home, and have absolutely no obligations. Unlike for the scholars and priests, there are really no obligations and time constraints on the welfare recipient. Getting up whenever he wants to, sleeping as long as he wants to, watching TV as long as he wants to, then going to the library and studying much of the day, going to public university lectures and seminars, and destroying any speaker with harsh criticism, because one has so much free time to think, develop ideas and read. Many academics admit that they don't know much outside their area of expertise, and that is because they spend so much time researching their own subject that they can't look at the bigger picture ("Fachidioten", as the Germans call them, or specialist idiots). Someone, who has spent all his life, outside of formal structures like the university or the church, does not have to adhere to any jargon, and can freely draw on his own ideas and perspectives.

I have a relative, who has taught me many valuable insights on Marx and Spinoza, and he turns out to be a middle-aged guy living on disability benefits (suffering from substantial physical impairment due to a kidney disease), renting a rent-subsidized modest apartment, spending many hours in the public library and living a rather undisciplined life. He does not write much, and he has virtually no concrete material aims in life. One does not have to be a welfare recipient to be a philosopher, but having a guaranteed source of non-work income can really help. I am personally quite sympathetic to the "high life" of the long-term unemployed. As Bertrand Russell (1932) writes in his 'Praise for Idleness', "Modern methods of production have given us the possibility of ease and security for all; we have chosen, instead, to have overwork for some and starvation for others. Hitherto we have continued to be as energetic as we were before there were machines; in this we have been foolish, but there is no reason to go on being foolish forever."

But as with most things in life, there are substantial restrictions with the welfare recipient existence in today's world. One has to constantly deal with the welfare bureaucracy, because the state is enormously suspicious of people, who live on the dole rather than work and pay taxes into the system. State officials have, therefore, developed complex bureaucratic requirements, which can often be quite time-consuming just so people keep their entitlement for benefits. In Austria and Germany, one needs to constantly search for jobs to continue collecting long-term unemployment insurance, which means a weekly encounter with the bureaucrats in the labor market agency. In the US, the slightest change of income can lead to cuts in Medicaid and Food stamps, which will force people to stand in line for 5-6 hours to have their paperwork for welfare benefits processed again. Welfare there is also limited to 5 years of one's lifetime. The politics of welfare state retrenchment shows that welfare recipients tend to be among the weakest constituency, and they can have their benefits slashed the most, unlike social programs with stronger veto points (e.g. pensioners). Being a welfare recipient, one is at a very low social status with very limited funds to enjoy sensual pleasures (or even something as essential as buying books) unlike priests and scholars, and those restrictions can diminish any bon vivant experience. In the worst case scenario, one feels trapped in Jeremy Bentham's (1843) panopticon. A panopticon is an institution, where prison inmates are told that they are being observed all the time by a single person, and they never know when they are observed, so they behave as if they were being watched all the time.

One may conclude that outside of coming from an affluent family or winning the lottery, there are many constraints for living a genuine life of leisure. The capitalist system knows how to encroach on one's freedom, and the relevant policymakers and powerful actors are still less than enthusiastic to support a basic income scheme, which can make Keynes' (1930) dream of a universal leisurely existence reality. Some people would claim a life of leisure is a threat to the moral fabric of society, which has always revolved around work. This opinion is full of conservative-authoritarian biases. The truth is that most humans will be creative in what they do, and that is even more likely to be the case for intellectuals, who have always done what they enjoyed doing whenever they can withstand the pressures and demands of their environment.

Objectives

Life is full of uncertainty. Though we operate with many constraints, we do have the ability to make choices within certain parameters. One choice can often have cumulative effects, creating a path dependence, which is difficult to reverse. This condition of uncertainty and the possibility to make negatively fateful choices, make it all the more important for the bon vivant intellectual to make clear choices about how he should spend his time and effort. Developing clear objectives in life is a very daunting and challenging project, and most of us don't want to picture what we are going to do even the next day. But it is important to set objectives.

We can blame neoliberalism for much of this confusion and uncertainty. In a much simpler world, people were hunter-gatherers. Life was simple and communal. Our ancestors worked together to build weapons and instruments, hunt for food, pick up berries, cook the food, eat, sing songs, tell stories and recite poems in the camp fire, have sex, raise children, fight wars with other tribes, and do a few other things (see Diamond 2012 for traditional society practices). Even if there was uncertainty about what one should do when growing up, it didn't matter, because life was lived intensely in a community setting, and one will be taught the values and ideas of that community in due time. Even under feudalist and agriculture-based societies, there was communal certainty, which came from the mutual dependence relation between the serfs and the masters, and within the family, which ensured the hereditary transfer of social status. If your father was a peasant, you are a peasant. If your father was the landlord, you will be the next landlord.

There is no doubt that these old regimes of social systems were much more oppressive than much of what we would find in today's world. The liberal capitalists are right to say that individual preferences and characteristics are best lived out in the individualist liberal-capitalist societies of the developed world. It is better to be a woman or homosexual or disabled person in a liberal capitalist society than in, say, Iran or North Korea. So there is no need to romanticize certain aspects about the past (Simmel 1922).

But let us not forget what modern society is losing: the certainty of identity, which creates a life in flux. Our parents have worked jobs that are now becoming increasingly obsolete (my parents were postal workers for instance), so we children have to scramble hard to retrain for another position that might still exist. Given the accelerating automation trend, I do not expect that many good job opportunities will be created, unless there is a concerted political effort a la Franklin Roosevelt to ensure such outcome (or one modeled on shorter work weeks and a basic income). The moral glue which bound us together is evidently non-functional and collapsing, as laid out by Erik Ringmar (2005). The family, religion, and the nation-state were the principal social institutions, which would guarantee that people have something to fall back on. All of these institutions doubtless still exist. I am sure that there are many people, who argue that they will always play an important role in anchoring our identity, and we could scarcely survive otherwise. But the point is that to the extent that they are weaker than before there is the limited ability of social protection for individuals, who are exposed to what Ulrich Beck (1992) referred to as the "risk society".

The family structures are broken up by increased divorce rates (compared to earlier periods), the decline of three-generation households (weakening the role of the family patriarch, the grandfather), the rise of gender equality and children's rights, and higher female labor participation rates, which makes the coordination of family life much more unstable (though some welfare states, which provide generous parental leave laws do better than the less generous welfare states). Rather than taking one's parents as the reference group, most teenagers orient themselves to their age peers, which weaken family bonds.

Religion is a powerful glue that holds society together, which even Emile Durkheim had realized a long while back. But it cannot be denied, that in Europe the churches are getting emptier and emptier, and that the fastest growing religious conviction is atheism and agnosticism. In a much more individualist society, a church group can be quite an important social network, but people can create networks outside of churches as well. The church's' heyday was when the people were more obedient to the demands of their clerical leaders, but such authoritarian appeal often falls on deaf ears, especially among more skeptical younger people.

The nation state has resulted from many years of national struggle somewhere in the mid-19th century. When World War II extinguished the European empires, many African leaders rallied their people around the banner of African nationalism. This is strange insofar as the boundaries of those nation states were the legacy of European conceptions of national sovereignty and territoriality, but the point is that Africans now thought for the first time since the Europeans conquered their lands, that they could rule themselves (though most leaders still adhered to their tribal norms as opposed to national norms, which creates resource and ethnic conflicts between tribes, sometimes resulting in war and even genocide) (Zuberi's documentary in 2013). Millions of men were sent into the trenches in Europe during WW I and later in Asia, when the Japanese made their conquest in WW II. Soldiers were fighting for every piece of their country's territory, and their families were supporting the war effort by supplying more children (future warriors), taxes, and labor in the weapons manufacturing industry.

But just as much as people were aroused by the nation state to die and fight for a worthy cause, the absence of war kills any fervor and passions that people may have about the nation state. In some sense, the government share of GDP has been creeping up and up in the recent past, mainly because of rising welfare expenditures, so the state delivers tangible results for people, but people don't tend to get roused by welfare benefits as much as if they are slitting the throats of men in other countries' uniform. In the UK, the NHS (national health service) is considered to be a national religion, and it would be hard to privatize it, but it is also true that people take it for granted when they need medical treatment, and don't make it such a big deal in their everyday life, which is very different when the country is engaged in a war.

In the neoliberal and postmodern world we are retreating toward social enclaves, and hope that those can give us any meaning in life. Some examples include social networks, Islamist terrorist groups and right-wing groups, to take three interesting or extreme examples. I would call them a pseudo community, because they give a certain group of people a sense of security, but it cannot compare to the three big institutions (family, religion and state) in their scope of coverage, and the unified narrative which holds society together (the "unified narrative", community orientation and the good Aristotelian life is laid out in MacIntyre 1981). Islamist radicalism considers itself to be a religion, but to the extent that they practice terrorism, they have no genuine mass appeal. Mark Zuckerberg thinks that his service connects over 1 billion people with each other, even though Facebook really reinforces the fragmentation of society, because we will only mix with people that we care about and whose views we tend to share.

Neoconservatives argue that if we want to restore a good society, we need to restore the strong institutions (family, religion, state) that we have lost. I call this the "neoconservative pipedream", because even though there are some desirable features with returning to social stability, it is questionable whether such an outcome is achievable under current circumstances, and whether it is desirable to subject people with torment and guilt. There has to be some other kind of moral compass, which guides people's action, which is, of course, more necessary for the general public than for the intellectual, who finds consolation easily in ideas and books. But I will concede to neoconservatives that I have not yet found another stone of wisdom.

This discussion returns me back to the importance of setting objectives. As Nietzsche (1891) noted, the Ubermensch does not believe in a God, and sets his objectives, his moral compass and his values. Ubermensch shall live in the present rather in the other-world, trying to escape it. But the catch is that not many people are Ubermensch, i.e. above human, but simply Mensch, or human. In a world without strong family, religion and state, you will sense that people have few convictions; they don't know what they should do with their lives. They don't even know what to eat the next day. Decisions are made spontaneously. The choices are far and wide. In the chaos of life, only internal willpower can create order.

I am spending my year here in Oxford, and wonder how to most efficiently spend my time here. But here are two exciting insights: (1) It doesn't matter what I do here, whether I attend five public lectures a week or one, one or two concerts a week, meet two or four friends a week. Life will continue regardless of what I do, and it is foolish to think that doing anything means automatically that time is wasted. (2) Because it doesn't matter what I do, I have to consciously remind myself of why I am here in Oxford. When I confront the question whether I should go to another lecture or stay home, I often opt for the lecture, because I thought that coming to Oxford means that I could learn as much as possible, while hanging out in the room doing readings (which I still do here), I can do anywhere else in the world too. When I sacrifice another afternoon to have discussions with friends, colleagues and bon vivants, I tell myself that the objective of being in Oxford is to have interesting conversations with interesting people. Another goal is to gain female friends, which I have tended to neglect in my earlier years. Learning French, Mandarin and statistics are other concrete learning objectives. Getting out a journal article would be even better. These are only small objectives, but if you picture the goal and the actions to get there, you have run half the marathon. As Antonio Machado writes, "Wanderer, your footsteps are the *road*, and nothing more; wanderer, there is no *road*, the *road* is *made by walking*."

There is a distinction that one can make between different goals. There are what I call *ornamental objectives* and what I would call *fundamental objectives*. The former is nice to accomplish but not essential, while the latter goals are absolutely essential and should receive the first priority. Is there a rule of thumb for what fundamental objectives in lives should be? Yes, there clearly are important life decisions, which can substantially shape our future, and much of it- for young people especially- has to do with becoming an adult. When is somebody an adult? One might say that if you reach the age of majority, which is commonly perceived to be 18 years of life, you are an adult. That is a good rule of thumb for letting someone into a bar and expect that they will get drunk "responsibly", but the physical age is not necessarily related to important life choices and objectives that one has to reach. The age is simply what nature and the passage of time give you without your own input. (Unless you consider it is a huge objective to reach the physical passage to adulthood, because one lives a very dangerous lifestyle, like being a Syrian refugee trying to cross the sea between Turkey and Greece.)

The other definition of adulthood consists of three very tangible factors: (1) a job (2) a house, and (3) a family. Following that definition, the picture becomes more complicated. I have anecdotally heard of cases, where the parents die when one is still quite young, possibly even before the age of majority, or the parents or foster parents kick one out of the house when one reaches 18. There is no faster way to become an adult than under those trying circumstances. In less developed societies, it is quite common to work and marry young. Education tends to be much shorter and dire poverty forces early labor participation. But the average situation in the more developed world is very different. It is not very uncommon for 25 year olds and sometimes even 30 year olds to hang around in their parents' basement, and maybe have a life partner, but certainly no kids and no marriage. They may have a job, but the hours are so unpredictable and the pay is so low that it would not be worth it to move out into a separate apartment. In that case, the three objectives which mark the rite of passage into adulthood remain unreached, which can be quite frustrating. But the point is that fundamental objectives involve the rite of passage to adulthood.

Trying to work on reaching fundamental objectives will always have first priority in terms of time commitment and effort as compared to ornamental objectives, but one should not forget what those ornamental objectives are, and how important those can be to live a desirable life. Someone can live a life reaching all his fundamental objectives (e.g. earning a good income), but never being able to read books, write poems, play their favorite instruments, do painting, perform dances, play sports, meet new friends, learn a new language or travel the world, because they had been too absorbed in their paid employment. Ornamental objectives take various forms, but they are no less important to live a life like a bon vivant than the fundamental objectives.

How important is it to accomplish objectives? I would say it is enormously important. Consider lying in your deathbed, whenever that might be. Can you say with confidence that you have accomplished your objectives or did the best you could given the circumstances you were facing? As mortal creatures we will inevitably end in a deathbed, and then realize that the most valuable commodity of all (time) is no longer available to us. Young people have a lot of time ahead of them, whereas older people have very little time ahead of them. Making big mistakes as a young person carries fewer penalties than making mistakes as an old person. There is less time to make up for mistakes during old age. The question in one's deathbed will be whether one can look in the mirror and not feel any regrets for what happened in the past. We make very fateful choices during our younger age, and we are path dependently linked to the decisions of the past. The outcomes are often beyond individual control. Are we the unfortunate people, who get hit by a car, lose important family members early in life or get struck by cancer?

But what matters for self-reflective purposes are not the things that lie beyond our control, but those that lie very firmly in our control: our objectives. Have I done the things that I set out to do? I still regret to this day that I have not stopped Jürgen Habermas, while he was strolling around in the Vienna Museum of Modern Art. He was standing at the window, looking outside, and then moved toward the exit, while I just stared at him and could not bring myself to talk to him. What an honor it was, but I have clearly failed in attaining my objective. On the other hand, my most important objective in Oxford was to have great conversations with great minds and people, and there is no better place to do that than in Oxford, and I am happily achieving this objective.

What was most disturbing to me was to hang out with people, who had no clear objectives in life. They might be working at a job, but they are not sure whether that work is purposive. There are people, who are raising children without a clear idea of what their kids should know and appreciate. For people without sufficient wisdom and without clear objectives, it is easy to regret things. I was hanging out with a relative, who would make one decision and regret it the next moment. He ordered spinach, but then decided to order beans. He ordered fish, but then decided to order beef. He left a girl behind, and then regrets not having gotten around to screw her. Life for him is a constant bouncing between different internally incoherent positions, which makes him structurally regret his decisions. Without unifying the internal Jekyll and Hyde, we cannot hope to feel accomplished and content. Set yourself clear goals. Work hard to accomplish them. Don't expect too much as a result. Life goes on after a bad defeat, and so it will after a big victory.

Charisma, Leadership and Aura

One of the key insights in Weberian sociology is that leaders possess certain features that distinguish them from the everyday crowds. They possess charisma, which the dictionary defines as "compelling attractiveness or charm that can inspire devotion in others" and "a divinely conferred power or talent". Weber (1978: 241) writes that "The term 'charisma' will be applied to a certain quality of an individual personality by virtue of which he is considered extraordinary and treated as endowed with supernatural, superhuman, or at least specifically exceptional powers or qualities. These are such as are not accessible to the ordinary person, but are regarded as of divine origin or as exemplary." What is the rule of thumb for someone possessing a lot of charisma, and thus being able to rule the organization with the least amount of resistance from the followers? When he walks into the room and everyone turns their head toward him. A woman can also be a charismatic leader, and one may think of Joanne of Arc. But the examples are far and between. Empress Dowager Qixi preferred to rule the Chinese Qing empire from behind via her sons (Chang 2014), so one can't speak of much charisma. Angela Merkel is one of the most boring politicians, yet the most powerful leader in Europe. What the Germans like about her is precisely that boring quality which confers stability to the country. Hillary Clinton is nowhere near as charismatic as her hyper-charismatic husband Bill (on gender and power see Liu 2015).

So what makes people turn their heads toward the leader? There is a blend of clothing style, manners, body language, and speech, which creates rhythmic entrainment. Randall Collins (2005a) has an example with a sexual context and writes that this rhythmic entrainment is the excitement, which is created when two people intensify each other's body movements as they are both caught in a rhythm. I don't see why such entrainment and captivation cannot also happen with leaders, who walk into a room. Collins further theorizes that the goal of individuals is to maximize their level of "emotional energy" (see Collins 2005b), and that can happen by having a satisfying conversation, going to a great party or listening to a fascinating, charismatic orator. The leader is certainly well-groomed, but good clothing and dress are not sufficient. The good leader approaches people the right way. Take say Bill Clinton. He could look a person in the eye with a narrow gaze while talking to them (without being creepy). He would lean over and be physically close to the person, and make him/her feel like they are the only person that exist on planet. He would lift his eyebrows occasionally to emphasize his points. The people that he would be talking to would be so baffled and impressed, and nod along as in a rhythmic entrainment. When Clinton was about to wrap up, he would step back but continue maintaining eye contact for a little while longer, which is a nice way of saying goodbye. (See the video High Existence.com.)

Loizos Heracleous (2014 paper reported in 2015 article) studied what rhetorical strategy made Steve Jobs, the Apple founder, so charismatic. He first noted that Jobs did not rely on a single rhetorical strategy, but changed it from audience to audience. Aristotle's ethos (credibility), pathos (emotions) and logos (logic) were decisive in picking the right rhetorical strategy. Jobs was very skillful in using amplification, repetition and reframing of the discussion to captivate his audience. He used figurative language and metaphors instead of numbers and statistics to dazzle his audience. His overall message to promote his brand and his central themes was constantly present for the viewers. Jobs' mentality was also rather restless, because he pretended that every day was his last, so he wanted to do what was worthwhile (Gunawardana 2015). Jobs had a strong company vision, which he thought would change the world, not just to make money. One of his employees said that if he stood next to Jobs, he felt the energy from him, his vision, and so his employees were willing to work for him for many hours. Jobs also employed rather aggressive language and metaphor, characterizing his business competitors as "mortal enemies", and that Apple needs to "survive", which riled up the employees (high level of emotional energy). He talked with certainty about his goals rather than in possibilities revealing his conviction, e.g. "we will release the new Mac by this date", which also boosted employee morale (Charisma on Command, Youtube; a good study on the charisma of Napoleon, Jobs, Alexander the Great and Jesus can be found in Collins and McConnell 2015).

What is important to note is that not everyone can be a leader, not only because of different levels of ability and charisma, but also because the definition of a leader is to direct others to do things, and if everyone is a leader, then there are no followers to direct orders to. Emerson (1962) defines power as a dependence relationship, where the follower is dependent on the leader, and where the leaders can overcome the resistance of the follower to get things done in the leader's way. Resistance can be overcome by brute force, but that is often ineffective, because the followers will find ways to undermine the leader in some other way, like sabotage. It is better to charm the followers into doing things not only in the leader's interest, but in the follower's interest or even broader in the national interest. In Napoleon's words, "A soldier will fight long and hard for a bit of colored ribbon."

Sexual Charisma

Charisma is not only used to advance to the top of an institution (political charisma), but can also be used to make sexual conquests. Someone with a very high level of sexual charisma will have no problem to attract the desirable sexual partners. While sexual charisma is not specific to one gender, social traditions and biological constraints fixate sexual charisma with males, while the expectation for women is that they don't have to be so charismatic and wait to be conquered by men. There clearly is no point for a woman to be so sexually charismatic, and, in fact, what is more common is their great extent of sexual caution. In an experiment, where a man and a woman go out independently on the streets and ask the opposite gender for having sex, it is the woman asking the man that is more likely to succeed than the man asking the woman. A woman carries the greater burden of childbearing, and needs to be very cautious in mate selection, while the male objective to spread their genes allows them to be more indiscriminate with their mate selection. There is clearly a double standard in how society views men and women, who are sexually daring. While the man, who sleeps around and has a mistress, is only "following his biological instincts", a woman, who does the same, is derogatorily seen as a "slut" or "bitch". Female sexual charisma tends to be associated with looks rather than action. Looks involves biology for which I lack the expertise, while action is deeply sociological, so I focus on it.

Because of these sex differences, I restrict my analysis of sexual charisma exclusively to men. What creates sexual charisma? What makes certain men so irresistible for many women? (1) The look and smile, (2) the curiosity and conversation style, (3) the compliments, (4), the persistence, (5) the mimicry, and (6) the touch. Let's go through each of these factors.

Picture a casual dinner party, which has a roughly equal gender distribution. What you will notice is that most people have a very low level of charisma, which you can tell, because most people stay within their own crowd and don't venture beyond it. I find it rather boring to go to an event with dear friends, because it will be impossible to get to know strangers, but getting to know strangers is not what most people are looking out to do. But there are a few people (including bon vivants) who think it is their objective to strike up conversations with people of the opposite gender, specifically men initiating the conversation with the women. The first impression is the last impression. The charismatic man knows this. But he also knows that there is no point in being too shy about taking the first step, because how else is he going to find out that the next encounter is going to be so interesting?

The strongest impression in the eyes of the woman is what is happening on the man's face. The two parts of the face, which convey feelings in the strongest way, are the eyes and the mouth. Eyes are fixated at the woman with only occasional glances away to ensure that the full attention is paid to her. Every person likes to receive attention. The mouth usually forms a non-threatening and inviting smile. Most people prefer happy feelings over sad feelings, and feelings tend to be rather contagious, so sad people tend to be avoided, while happy people are good to be around with. Here there is a slight distinction between a powerfully charismatic person and a sexually charismatic person. A powerful man tries not to smile too often, because he wants to project his authority and influence. A sexually oriented man will smile as often as possible to put the woman in a good mood.

But looks and smiles alone will not cut it. It then becomes merely awkward. Humans are quite unique in that effective social interaction does not merely involve the showing off of muscles or various other body parts, but also speech. A charismatic person is a great conversationalist, because he can easily speak about any subject in the world. Here it is important that the man does not endlessly lecture resulting in the woman's boredom, but that the man gets the woman to carry much of the conversation. In the ideal conversation, every partner carries roughly an equal share of what is spoken. But that may very well be the case for mundane conversations. Remember we are still at the dinner party, where the charismatic man is going for a hunt. He wants to ask questions, which get her to open up and talk about herself. He will need some level of curiosity to keep the questions coming. I don't have a clear guideline as to what questions need to be asked, but they certainly need to be more creative than the mundane questionnaires that only have rather short answers (e.g. age, place of birth etc.).

The charismatic man also plays a more offensive part in the interaction, and that takes the form of compliments. Most women like to hear compliments. This can revolve around an event which they organized or a paper which they wrote (for more academic types). But the simplest forms of compliments, which are often quite effective, revolve around clothing and other visible body parts. Compliments include the hair, glasses, eyes, make-up, shirt, pants, skirts etc. Effective flirters do not stop complimenting the woman. They exhibit a very persistent feature, which is comparable to artillery fire. The military example of 'conquest' is not very far off from the reality of getting a date or getting laid. As I said earlier, the woman has to be very careful in her mating choices, so she has the tendency to elevate barriers, and it is the responsibility of the man to destroy these barriers. When watching sexually charismatic men in action, their persistent flirt strategies are equivalent to unbreakable and uninterrupted heavy artillery fire. The uncharismatic man will not even try to fire his cannon, and will quickly retreat in the face of the stable barrier. But it is only uninterrupted pounding that can destroy the barrier.

There are other important elements to the interaction: mimicry and touch. People like to hang out with people, who are similar to themselves. We like people who are on "our wavelength". But how can we make sure that somebody is on our wavelength? One can find similarities via hobbies, common friends and enemies, and common interests. But these similarities are established via conversation. However, there are also more subtle means of establishing similarities, and that is via the mimicry in the body language, replicating what the other is doing. Touch is also quite important, though the charismatic man will not drive it too far or else he will be labeled a pervert, which won't necessarily make him succeed in the cause of doing perverse (sexual) stuff later that night. It is only during the act of sexual intercourse or after rapport has been established (husband-wife, boyfriend-girlfriend etc.) that all body regions are fair game. During the hunting season, the charismatic man will restrict himself to her hands, her arms and her shoulders. The point of sexual conquest is to be able to touch all the relevant body parts, but there is a hierarchy of escalation, which may be climbed only at opportune moments and when she signals the willingness (often non-verbally).

There are certainly other factors to be very sexually charismatic. The charismatic man will have naturally internalized all these steps, and considers them to be of second nature. It is the uncharismatic man, who struggles with these basic principles.

Network Analysis

In the first edition of Granovetter's and Swedberg's (1992) edited book titled "Sociology of Economic Life", I found a chapter by Melville Dalton on *Men who Manage*, which is the classic study of how enterprises and organizations are actually run. Rather than having a company flow chart, where the highest manager is drawn at the top, and the lower managers are drawn at the bottom, it is more accurate to observe precisely where the different managers are located within the organization based on (1) the number of ties to other people within the organization, and (2) the level of network centrality of individuals (i.e. who is the go-to or point-to person for decisions, problems, challenges and everyday interactions?). In Dalton's study, it was the deputy director rather than the director, who made most of the important decisions and was central in the network. Think of families where it is the father, who is supposedly in charge as the formal figurehead, who receives and entertains guests, but it is the mother, who decides what socks her husband will wear, what books the children should read, and what food should be consumed, and so forth. I know quite a few families, where the women are de-facto leaders of their family, and are central in the network.

My former adviser, Randall Collins (1997) had theorized powerful intellectual networks of philosophers throughout history and throughout time. Whether it is Buddhist monks, ancient Greek or German philosophers, who created abstract ideas that had universal appeal, all idea creation is a collective effort based on a web of networks. Collins produced a nearly 1,000 page tome on this subject, laying out in detail the personal relations of philosophers within the network as well as the intellectual ideas that mattered in their respective time. He distilled three basic findings: (1) Knowledge is created in networks. (2) Knowledge is created when there are conflicts and contradictions between different schools of thought. (3) Every important idea can have between 3 and 6 main thinkers (think of Marx, Weber and Durkheim in sociology). He called this the "law of small numbers". If it gets to more than that, the field becomes too crowded, while public **attention space** is limited. In addition, there is a limit to how many new ideas one can produce within a field or subfield, and so every new addition becomes more of a commentary than a seminal work. I am typing this post in the social science library, and next to the computer desks there is a book shelf on the history of economic thought, and countless books in that section carry the word "Marx", "Hayek" and "Keynes" in the title. The amount of commentary can be endless. The amount of key thinkers is limited.

Stanford sociology, which is at the heart of Silicon Valley, and the tech industry, is also at the center of network analysis, which means using the fancy computer simulations to predict exactly how many nodes there are in organizations and groups and how strong they are. For us, it is super interesting to study actual networks, because we want to get a promotion, and we are always told how important networking is. We don't need a sociology PhD or knowledge of computer models to know this, but can qualitatively know this from our firsthand experience in the workplace or in school. If one wants to be powerful one needs to be connected to power. Senator Harry Reid (2009), the son of a poor, rural family, would not have become senate majority leader without his mentor governor Mike O'Callaghan, who gave him the recommendation to study in law school, get a job as a Congressional cop, become his lieutenant governor, and get connections to run for Congress and Senate. O'Callaghan got to know Reid in high school, where O'Callaghan had taught him as a student. That's about as full-scale of a mentorship as one can imagine.

Networks often make the difference in terms of how much we can get away with. Think of the rich son, who crashes his rich daddy's Ferrari, has his father intervene to cover his ass in front of law enforcement officials, and gives his son another Ferrari as a reward. Or think of the bank bailouts in 2008 provided by former Goldman Sachs chair Hank Paulson, then the US treasury secretary. I can tell another little story from my own life. I went to the school counselor to have my transcript filled out and had to pay a nominal 10 dollar fee for that. I had to go back a second time a few months later to request another transcript. This time one of my teachers, a good friend of mine, walked with me to the transcript office, and the teacher and the counselor exchanged a few words of pleasantry, then the teacher left. The counselor processed the paperwork, and I was about to pull out my wallet, and the counselor waved his hands and said, "Don't worry about it. You know the teacher. So it's for free." What a surprise.

So, we should ask ourselves who is really in charge in an organization, and don't take official titles for granted. For personal success, networks are the lifeblood. Or as Aristotle says, "Man is a political animal." Wherever there are people, there is politics.

Deconstruction of Social Reality: Sociology as Zoology

One of the most formative moments in my undergraduate experience was the one class I took in ethnographic fieldwork. There was one student, who wanted to do research on a child welfare agency, and she had spent most of her presentation time outlining the goals of the agency, which one could also read from the website if one wanted to. She was speaking as if she was the employee of the organization. The teacher, a young sociologist and assistant professor, noticed it right away and criticized the student for not being "critical" enough, and gave us a lesson that the whole point of sociology was to be "critical". What a teaching lesson that was. In that example, let us imagine what being critical means: does the welfare agency really promote child welfare? What are the goals of the individuals and the leaders in the organization? How committed are the staff members about the goals of the organization? How does the child welfare agency profit from child abuse or a public narrative of such?

So what is the best way to conceptualize society? To be a good sociologist, one has to imagine that one is an observer of the animal world. (Isn't it ironic that one of my Penn professors, David Grazian 2015, wrote a book about the sociology of zoos?) Of course, that is easier said than done. A marine biologist does not need much convincing that the fishes, octopuses and whales that they study are indeed animals. He cannot just go up to the sea creatures and speak English to them. He has to observe their behavior for a long time. He has to capture them and size them up to study their internal organs. They will partly always remain a greater mystery than humans because of the communication barrier (on the other hand, greater human intelligence, the capacity to tell lies and obfuscate make humans more of a mystery), but the biologists' mind is alerted. When we go to a zoo, we look at the monkeys and how they interact with each other, and might draw similarities to humans who are also mammals. But there would be a clear conception of difference. Most people (mostly children) go to the zoo just to have a fun experience. But there are certainly also many people, who go to the zoo just so they can study animal behavior.

Sociologists do the same with society, but with different methods. Unlike for the biologists, our subjects can communicate in the same language as we do. The human animal is also different in that social norms influence and constrain both the researcher and the subject, which create various complications, which the bureaucratic hurdles of ethics forms reveal rather clearly. But the point is that sociologists have to imagine that what they are studying are animals roaming around, and the insights one may get are clearly enlightening. When I walk on the streets, I observe how people talk with each other, how they are using inanimate objects to communicate (called cell phones), how they are angrily hurling abuses at each other, how they are kissing, how they are telling lies and so forth. Then I shake my head, and say "look at these ridiculous animals".

Of course, I cannot do that in all situations, because sometimes we have to act the way we should following societal norms, or otherwise it will be difficult to survive in society. That was a painful lesson to the ethnomethodologists around Garfinkel (1984; see article and references in Wikipedia, "Ethnomethodology"), who told his students to respond to mundane questions via deconstruction. "How are you?"- "What do you mean how are you?"- "I mean, how are you?"- "Do you mean my body, my soul, my mind, my day? What exactly" Evidently, the students brought themselves in big trouble, because people expect that social codes can be quickly read by the other side. In the absence of norms, there would be no society. But we can only know about society after having questioned its norms. It's the same with health. We can only come to appreciate health after having been injured or becoming sick.

A final classic sociological example is included in my first sociology reader in the community college: Horace Miner's (1956) classic study of the "body rituals of Nacirema". One is introduced to, for instance, the weird oral hygiene practices of a strange tribe until one realizes that what is meant by that is the dentistry in modern day America (reverse spelling of Nacirema). It's like Jared Diamond's (2012) use of the term WEIRD people as referring to Western Educated Industrialized Rich Democratic people. This is a classic example of social deconstruction.

But a critical perspective is not confined to sociology at all. To deconstruct, i.e. question, challenge, social reality is something, which anyone, who does not accept the status quo, can do. Intellectuals have a higher likelihood of doing so. The word deconstruction unfortunately has been appropriated by Jacques Derrida, who claimed that words have no intrinsic meanings in themselves. There are no greater ideas, but all words link to some other word or a sign. Meaning is created via the contrast among the different signs. In literary and postmodern theory, deconstruction is extremely popular, as any text can be taken and multiple interpretations be applied to it. For me literary and postmodern theory is insofar disturbing, because I have a hard time understanding anything that they write. It cannot be a mark of intelligence to obfuscate meaning instead of clarifying. Postmodernism is the worst kind of brain bullshiting one can imagine, but it has kept some intellectuals nicely occupied and employed. The same can be said of Picasso's art.

But I take the point that deconstruction of social reality (not just text) is what we intellectuals should be engaged in, and even if we did not want to, we could not resist, because our minds are so full of ideas, and it never stops. I have caught myself many times standing in the mirror, mumbling rhetorical attacks against people with whose points I disagree with. Even for scholars, who want to be productive, there is no other way to discover new research ideas without questioning old assumptions. When that stops happening toward middle age, and one begins recycling old claims without many new insights, then one knows that the good times are over.

Flowers vs. Wine: Long-Term Contentment

If humans were to always follow their instincts, they would pursue their short-term gratification and neglect long-term contentment. Think of the experimental psychology experiment with rats, where the rats were in a cage and given the choice to push a button and receive an exciting electric shock, which felt amazing, so they kept on pushing the button until they dropped dead. We can think of the short-term pleasures associated with the lust for power, prestige, sex and money. Gordon Gekko said famously in the Wall Street movie that "greed is good". Many of these elements are, unfortunately, promoted by our neoliberal political economy, where capital accumulation is pursued for its own sake. Marx (1848) wrote in awe and condemnation, "The bourgeoisie, by the rapid improvement of all instruments of production, by the immensely facilitated means of communication, draws all, even the most barbarian, nations into civilization. The cheap prices of commodities are the heavy artillery with which it batters down all Chinese walls, with which it forces the barbarians' intensely obstinate hatred of foreigners to capitulate."

The homo oeconomicus in the most ideal form has abandoned impulse control and self-constraining social norms like valuing the family and the community. Fortunately, few of us are true homo oeconomicus, and most of us are just alienated cogs in the wheel, who don't identify with work, but with private passions like painting, sports or family life.

The ancient Greeks have intensely thought about the good life, though there were three distinct perspectives on it: (1) Hedonists thought that the goal in life is to maximize pleasure and not accept boundaries to desires for material and experiential goods. (2) Epicureans also want to increase pleasure but by limiting desires, minimizing pain, maximizing tranquility and constantly gaining new knowledge in the world. The simple life and the absence of pain are the greatest producers of pleasure. (3) Stoics also thought that one had to limit desires, but to have a good life means that even under the most adverse circumstances (poverty, homelessness, sickness etc.) one can lead a good life. They did not like the fluffy idea of pleasure, and instead man shall pursue reason and be free of silly passions and worry.

It becomes clear from the discussion about long- and short-term pleasures that it is the Epicureans and the Stoics, who believed in the pursuit of long-term contentment. The pursuit of Christian theology can also produce long-term contentment, because the essential message is that as long as their followers pay respects to a holy figure, who has taken all the sins upon himself to spiritually cleanse his sinful followers, they should be content at heart. Christians are told that they should not follow current passions like gambling or sex, but should wait for the heavenly kingdom after death and do good deeds during life. (Needless to say, Christianity is a myth, but to the extent that a placebo has a real effect on people's well-being religion is no less "real" than other real things.)

Think of Pope Francis, the pope of the poor, who does not collect a salary, and happily leads his crusade against global capitalism while washing the feet of poor worshipers (though he has all expenses paid for by the Vatican, including airfare, lodging and food). There are, indeed, studies that show that religious people take less time to heal in the hospital than non-religious people (reported in Serwach 2004). On the other hand, one can twist it back and claim that religious people tend to be more depressed than secular people, which studies show as well (reported in Persaud and Bruggen 2013). Having been a previously regular churchgoer myself I can confirm the contradictory experience of feeling the salvation and the guilt trip of being labelled a "sinner".

What has the pursuit of long-term contentment have to do with wine and flowers? When we take a walk in a garden, we admire the beautiful flowers, take photos of it, and praise the garden owner for his meticulous work to create these flowers. So we should all like flowers, right? That is exactly what western society is saying, because there is a tradition of equipping weddings and other festivals with flowers, and if a man arrives at a date, he should not forget to bring flowers for the woman. But what is the problem here? The problem is that the beauty of the flower is a fleeting phenomenon. We can keep it for a short time before it turns bad, losing leaves and color. A flower is like the candle in the wind, as Elton John mourned the early death of Princess Diana (who died with her lover shortly after having divorced the crown prince). How long can the fire survive the wind, and if there is no wind, how long can the candle burn until it has melted completely?

Wine obviously also has an expiration date, but you might have noticed that the same brand wine that has been stored longer costs more money, and that is because the taste becomes more refined after storing it for a longer time. Rather than getting worse, the wine gets better the longer we keep it. Wine represents long-term contentment, while the flowers represent short-term pleasures. We are better off with the wine than with the flowers. I conclude with the analogy of finding a marriageable partner: should we select beauty or should we select intelligence and maturity? While beauty is an important criterion at the beginning, it is the least enduring, while intellect is something that gets better over time (unless that person gets a brain disease). For the maintenance of the species, intelligence is to be preferred over beauty if both cannot be gotten at the same time.

Moderation

In passionate moments, when one is young, going to extremes is considered perfectly acceptable. Young people have few stakes in society. When they confront inequality and social problems, they are rather unhappy about them. They blame the pre-existing power structure of which they are no part. In more developed societies, growing up implies that one distances oneself from the values and ideas of one's parents, and develop a more independent ideology. On the other hand, young people are very dependent on their peer group, and those peer groups themselves might be influenced by TV commercials and shape their consumer preferences. As people get older, they develop a substantially more conservative mind, because they have a stake in the political system. They also do not think that they have as much free time as previously. The accumulating demands of family and work make participating in anti-war protest rather unlikely. In a political sense, people are becoming more moderate as they age.

The above description is not meant to defend the current political and economic order. I am merely describing the most dominant life narratives for most people. Of course, even old aged people have to detest the current economic order if they seriously contemplate a situation where increasing shares of the national wealth are concentrated in ever fewer hands, while most working people are getting by on insecure and temporary jobs if they are lucky enough, and if not they have to rely on the dole. This kind of extreme political economy is everything but an exercise of moderation, and requires a political upheaval to change. But leave that aside, and one notices the importance of moderation in many aspects of life.

As far as personal consumption patterns are concerned, one is told that it is necessary to consume alcohol to be a full member of the social group. At the same time, most doctors agree that consuming too much alcohol is damaging to health and well-being. When consuming no alcohol, while everyone else does it, it can result in social exclusion, which negatively impacts on mental health. The right solution in this dilemma is certainly not to choose either complete abstention from alcohol or binge drinking, but to consume alcoholic drinks in moderation. If red wine is consumed in moderate amounts, it might even have a positive health impact. Even if alcohol had mostly negative influences on the body, they would not be so bad as long as only small quantities are consumed.

Researchers in Carnegie Mellon University tested the claim whether doubling the amount of sex that couples had would increase happiness. Their finding was that increasing the frequency of sex does not increase happiness. In fact, it lowered their satisfaction, because being told to have more sex does not create the romantic frame of mind and spontaneity, which is necessary to have an enjoyable sex life (Rea 2015). A General Social Survey study found that the average amount of sex that is the most desirable is about once a week (Dillner 2015). However many times the optimal amount of sex is, it is limited. Having too little makes life not so great, and having too much of it would make life quite miserable as well.

This principle of moderation can be expanded to many aspects of life, such as earning money, climbing the career ladder, becoming a powerful and influential person, becoming a famous and well-respected person. All of these things may still be pursued (and as I argued in a previous passage, good leadership matters), but the question is how intensely they are pursued. Earning a lot of cash may be justifiable if that money is used to allow one's children educational and economic success, but earning too much cash, when it requires so much time that it allows one to never bond with one's children is probably quite problematic.

Great philosophers of all stripes have known the importance of moderation. I will restrict myself to Aristotle and Confucius, the two great towering figures of intellect in human history. Aristotle called moderation the "Golden Mean" (Wikipedia). Aristotle was highly critical of excess and deficiency, which are both undesirable features. Only the mean contains virtue. Being bold without being careless makes one courageous, which is a desirable quality. But being very bold is reckless, and being too self-restrained is cowardly. These are both undesirable features. A Cretan tale reveals the importance of the moderation principle: Daedalus and Icarus intended to escape the clutches of King Minos by using feathered wings to fly away. Daedalus told his son Icarus to avoid flying too high, where the sun burns the feathers, and results in crashing into the ocean, while flying too low would make one drown in the water. Icarus ignored his father's advice and kept on flying higher. His feathers were burned, and he drowned to death.

Confucius had developed what may be called the "Doctrine of the Mean" (Wikipedia). He noted that moderation was a feature that was rarely found among people, "The Master [Confucius] said, The virtue embodied in the doctrine of the Mean is of the highest order. But it has long been rare among people." (Analects 6:29). There are three guidelines that ensure the attainment of the mean: self-watchfulness: includes permanent self-questioning, self-disciplining and self-cultivating; leniency: understanding, concern and tolerance toward others, doing unto others as one would have liked others to do unto one; and sincerity: being truthful and creating a bond between the heaven and humans. The old philosophers knew that a good life required moderation.

The Discontents of Modern Academic Life

Academic specialization is a rather novel phenomenon. We can say with great confidence that biology was formalized over the last 400 years, sociology has perhaps half that lifespan, and if we go into the foray of literary theory or gender studies, we cannot speak of more than the last 60 or 70 years (instructive summaries of the "history of science" in Wikipedia and Collins 1994). The strengthening of independent academic institutions and universities certainly help to facilitate the division into many different disciplines. We could also argue that the sheer amount of collective knowledge which humans have produced over so many thousands of years makes it simply impossible for a person to have much knowledge about many areas of life. A polymath today would have a much harder time being a polymath, because there are just so many things to know.

Literacy and book printing certainly helped people to spread knowledge. Not too long ago, there was no script, and there was no way to critically assess any knowledge. Societies were heavily reliant on old members of the community, who would recite poems and songs to transmit the limited wisdom of the community. Such limited wisdom could never be questioned or substantially modified, because it would risk being forgotten. Script changed all that. It first made bookkeeping and the settling of debts possible. Then it made chronicles and histories possible. No more reliance on old people's memory. Then people, who were interested in philosophical ideas, were also able to formulate their ideas (on the difference between oral and literate societies, see Ong 1982; Havelock 1988). But creating script and teaching a few priests how to read and write is no panacea. Public administration and philosophy had now been made possible with script, but most people simply could not read. Illiterate people are masses that are easily controlled.

The next innovation was book printing, which is what really destroyed church authority in Europe. The classic story prioritizes on Martin Luther's challenge to Catholic authority, and his 95 theses, which he placed on the church door in Wittenberg. But his ideas would not have been able to be spread widely without print. The printing press had just been developed by Johannes Gutenberg (who was ironically bankrupted because he borrowed so much money to create his Gutenberg Bible and could not repay his debt). Book print allowed Luther to spread his message across the continent. The popularity of the Protestant idea is what offered him the political protection against papal assassins, who would not have minded to kill him otherwise.

School instruction was the next great frontier of innovation. It relied heavily on the capitalist requirement for educated workers, who could follow instructions, and the desire to give peasants and workers a chance to participate in society. As more people are educated, credential inflation started to happen, where more and more people get an education without receiving much validation in the labor market (Collins 2011). Initially, only very few people imagined they would complete more education than secondary school. But the post-World War II expansion of higher education to the masses, once again helped in the spread of knowledge to people in the previously less educated classes.

The most recent frontier has been the computer and the internet, where all kinds of information can be easily transmitted online and does not require physical paper or book copies. It is very easily possible to write multiple hundreds of thousands of pages of writing without absorbing more than a few megabyte on the server. A lot of information is easily accessible on the web, and it would be hard to imagine what one would do without Wikipedia.

Now what has the spread of knowledge got to do with academic specialization? If knowledge spreads, then more knowledge gets created, but because we only have a limited amount of time in each individual lifetime, we have to block out most of the knowledge that exists in the world, and instead concentrate on the knowledge that we are interested in. We specialize. When we think back to our primary and secondary school days, we remember how the teachers are trying to cram so much knowledge into us. Reconsidering it we notice that the teachers were only scratching the surface and merely picked the canonical texts and the canonical knowledge for teaching. Individual humans only have a limited capacity to receive information. Even the smartest academics now have to admit that they only have a rather limited knowledge about the world, let alone their own subject. In a more ignorant time, we would praise Aristotle and Confucius as the wise men of the world, who could just about tackle any subject that they came across. Even if we need to laugh today at their simplistic insights, we have to recognize that they did not have many peers in their era who could criticize them.

But today, there are many academics and there are many scholars out there, who are spending most of their waking life on pursuing research. But does the proliferation of academic texts really produce qualitatively greater insights than what the scholars in the old days were capable of producing? Not necessarily. One thing that is for sure is that as academia became institutionalized, and the job market became much more competitive, the requirement for multiple publications in a short span of time has massively increased. This is what is referred to as "**publish or perish**" academic environment. This is felt most acutely among young academics today, who are trained in these major graduate schools so they can put out a publishable paper after their second year in the PhD program, another 2 or 3 papers by the time they finish their PhD (maybe chapters from their dissertation), 3 more during their postdoc, and then 6 more as assistant professor before they come up for tenure review.

Whenever quantitative requirements take overhand, research results suffer. Why might that be the case? Think of the frequency of sex example: if couples were told to double the frequency of sex, their happiness and satisfaction decreased. Sex may be something great, but only if it happens at the frequency that is desired by that couple. Research is also great, but forcing academics to push out so many papers in so little time, makes the researchers less careful about their research content, and more careful about what can get published. It makes it more difficult for young researchers to walk along the research path, which they are truly passionate about.

Now let us briefly consider the factors which contribute to the predicament where young researchers are very exclusively focused on methods:

1. Measureable impact factor on journals
2. PhD glut
3. Fewer tenure-track positions among professors
4. Reliance on outside funding

5.   Young researcher's inexperience with methods makes them focus more on methods

6.   Path dependence and changing norms about good research

Parallel to the rising publication pressure is the fact that there are only a limited amount of top journals in a given field, such that most academics are only inclined to publish their papers in a few very reputable, 'high-impact' journals. Given that Google Scholar and other online profiles make it easily possible to track citations, there is much less ambiguity about what a high impact factor is. I have heard of an anecdote of one assistant professor, who almost had his career ruined because he refused to submit the dozen or so working papers that he had ready to submit to secondary journals, because he insisted on having them published in the top journals that had rejected his drafts in peer review.

There is an explosion in submissions, which results from the scarcity of high impact factor journals, the easy identification of such, and the glut of academic PhDs eager to have their research recognized somewhere (the glut itself being a reflection of the lack of availability of tenure-track positions). This explosion then induces editors and reviewers to increase the criteria requirements on the articles (often using young academics as reviewers, who are obsessed about methodology- more below). Now you have so-called "sloppily" researched papers thrown out during peer review. That should be good, right? Because reputable journals should only publish reputable papers. No, because a rejection of a powerful finding with unpopular methodology (which is by itself not bad) makes young researchers pay more attention to 'proper' methodology rather than pursue their research interests and their findings. (Older researchers already have tenure and feel less stress publishing in top journals. They also have a lot of experience in what it takes to get it published.)

Donors (governments and private foundations) also create the expectation to produce findings that have some relevance to them and to larger society. To the extent that the corporatization of higher education makes professors more reliant on outside sources of funding, these outside donors' wishes naturally shape the path of research, and the kinds of questions and methods, which researchers are using.

Whether it were the fascists or the communists, each authoritarian government knew that they could assert the greatest political control over the country when it controlled the hearts and minds of young people, because they are the most easily influenced demographic. They have very few preconceived notions about society, and it is the easiest to indoctrinate them in any desired ideology. The same logic applies to researchers. Even though, researchers and scholars belong to the higher echelon of society, they are not all intellectuals, who can easily deconstruct propaganda. A young undergraduate student, who enters a PhD program with little knowledge about the esoteric language of senior academics, has almost no preconceived notions of what is "proper" research. He or she relies on the "wisdom" of his older peers to tell that person what "proper" research is.

In today's PhD programs, there not only is an increased pressure toward publication (resulting from the PhD glut and lack of tenure-track positions), but also an increasing emphasis on methods, so young researchers often internalize what is being expected of them, which is to adhere to research guidelines. Their lack of experience makes them adhere more strictly to proper methods than is the case for older researchers. When these young researchers go on to peer-review articles, their trained technician eyes scrutinize the methodology rather than reflect on the insightfulness of the finding. Young, methodology-driven researchers taking on editorships and peer-reviews create a massive change in norms and a path dependency against which only old faculty with tenure seem to be immune to. This process within the social sciences has been the worst in economics, where historical and political-based researchers have long stopped publishing with the mainstream economics journals, but it starts affecting political science and sociology journals as well.

I don't want to make the argument that researchers today are no longer able to pursue their own research agenda. But the formalization of academics and the heavy emphasis on methodology substantially reduces the original joy of being a researcher. This joy is comparable to being a wanderer at night on the street, who is amazed by the formation of the stars, and why they are arranged in such order and not in any other way. I am also not making the argument that methodology does not matter in scientific research, because any finding relies on some kind of method. But the method should be flexibly chosen and needs to appear sound, and should then be tried without fear and get published somewhere.

I need to make a note of the difference between older and younger academics. What is interesting to note is that formerly academics who were still training in graduate schools received much less training in methods. That is partly because methods were not so sophisticated in the past, and so there were not so many fancy methods that needed to be taught to students. But the job market was more relaxed, when a limited number of people trained in a PhD program, and the expansion of postsecondary enrolment implied that there would be an increasing demand for college professors. So it was easily possible to land a tenure track job without a single publication fresh after submitting the dissertation. A few publications were also sufficient to land tenure, and then life was generally much more relaxed.

As an undergraduate and now graduate student, I have noticed that it was not only more fun to talk with older, more experienced faculty, but they were also better to work with than younger faculty, who are much more steeped in developing, using and critiquing methodology (for the reasons mentioned above). With older faculty, you would walk into their office, and waste half an hour on small talk, which is linked with what one has read in the newspaper, or reporting on interesting bits of research findings. Then the second half of the conversation would revolve around one's research project, and they would give very helpful advice about what books to read and which people to talk to. As they are older, they generally have developed an extensive network, which are useful as interview subject for social scientists. They also tend to be rather agnostic about the methodology as long as it sounds sound, while they are very curious about one's findings. Contrast that with younger faculty members, who don't hide their rushed appearance, their need to spend time on doing their research and publishing their own work, and their meticulous attention to methodology. They spend much less time talking about findings and implications, and are much more concerned to talk about things that one can do to increase the likelihood of having the paper published in a journal.

This behavior is not surprising given that they need these publications for their own career success. But to the extent that their emphasis is so methodology-heavy, they are more technicians rather than academics or intellectuals which they thought they would be when they entered the academic profession. Talking with many younger faculty is like going to the dentist, and having your teeth fixed. It is a formality which needs to be done rather than an intellectual journey that can be enjoyed. "Don't forget to brush your teeth properly", then becomes indistinguishable from, "Don't forget to include this variable in your regression." Like a hamster in a wheel, the proletarianization of the academic class is getting completed.

Let me list a few examples: I went to a young professor and then an old professor to ask them for a research job. It was the old professor who gave me the job, not only because we talked about all sorts of things (research, politics, history, education etc.), but also because he did not care about my methodological background. He was a fairly qualitative researcher, who was interested in what happened in the world, and was happy to let me do literature reviews which he did not want to do himself. He was quite perceptive, and genuinely curious. The job interview was more like talking to an old friend. And I never ever got a job so effortlessly again. The young faculty member, however, treated it like a real job interview, and asked me about my knowledge of Stata. Of course, I did not do any statistics in the past and said so. He replied to me that once I had acquired some statistical and software knowledge I should come back to him to ask for the job again. That was it for me then. It was only the method which mattered, not my persona and not my interests. And that was not the only example.

The other example is the difference between two classes that I have taken here, one of them was taught by a young professor (in his mid-30s) and another by an old professor (in his 60s). During the last class, the young professor discussed possible exam questions, and what the things are that we should add into our writing to get a distinction on our diploma. He was teaching us the formal methods to receive a grade, and the content of what we had learned in class was totally secondary to achieving the grade. In the last class with the old professor, he did not even talk about the exam. He had placed his entire focus on asking insightful questions about his research subject, sharing anecdotes of encounters he had with other people, and inviting students to make their own observations of the world. He was clearly only interested in the content and the findings in his subject, and not about formal requirements to steer student behaviour. The old professor pursued the intellectual principle of projecting with confidence his fascination about his subject, and then expecting that a few people pick up the knowledge and become inspired. This is knowledge as pollen. Even if he inspired a few people to research in his area, his teaching would have been a resounding success, while the young professor, who wanted us to do well in the exams, can expect nothing more out of his students than to perform well on the exam, and then hopefully forget as much as possible after they completed the exam.

With the older faculty, I would talk about God and the world. With the younger faculty, I could only communicate on the level of methodology. Also it was interesting that the older faculty were much more relaxed about the broad range of research interests, while the younger faculty preferred a rather narrow research focus and being an expert in only one area. No polymath, no bon vivant for the young scholars.

I will end on some solutions for this hamster-in-the-wheel predicament of the academic class:

1. Found more journals
2. Increase higher education funding
3. Grant more tenures

The major underlying factor for the changing norms in academia is the lack of resources. Methodological sophistication has to shift upward, because we are facing a scarcity of high-impact journals, a scarcity of higher education funding, and a scarcity of tenures (being the flipside of the PhD glut). The best way to reduce the anxiety among young academics in the academic labor market is to remove the conditions of scarcity. Scarcity is the single factor, which makes lives for many people very miserable. While I sit very comfortably in the library and in a computer room and dwell on my thoughts without having to worry about a stable supply of electricity, food and other relevant inputs, the homeless people on the streets, who lack all of these things, could not care less about the academic predicament that I have described above. In Maslow's hierarchy of needs, the homeless people are located so low in the hierarchy that they cannot begin to appreciate the more complex challenges in the world. If you did surveys of what people of different socio-economic classes are interested in or concerned about, you will find that working class people are more interested in bread and butter issues (wages, benefits, social spending), while middle class people are more concerned about broader concerns (environment, health, lifestyle, women's rights etc.).

Returning back to the academic context, we have to imagine the impact of increasing the availability of resources in higher education (which would also result in more tenure and more journals if these resources are well managed) on the current methodological obsession. For a start, the plentiful availability of tenure-track positions would immediately downgrade the requirement to publish at a highly-ranked (high 'impact-factor') journal. The point of publishing a paper with a highly ranked journal is not vanity, but the desire to land a tenure-track position. But if these positions become easily available there also is no need to publish at journals with high methodological threshold criteria. By massively increasing the supply of journals, there will be a market niche for only lightly reviewed journals. Of course, any academic journal will have minimum standards (e.g. length, grammar or formatting requirements), but the methodological requirement will be sharply reduced on average. With that we might also see more interesting research findings and topics.

More tenure and fewer restrictions on journal publications is certainly good for professors, but is that good for the quality of the research output? We cannot know for sure, but it cannot be much worse than today, when overt methodological focus and permanent publication pressure produce plenty of poor research papers, which do not have exciting findings, because of the pre-set constraints on what is a 'publishable' paper. 'Be fruitful and multiply' might, in fact, be a strategy that will increase the quality of research, because novel ideas that do not get vetted can then be read by other researchers, who can then push the knowledge frontier even further. If Hegel, Marx or Kant had to submit their writings to journals, they would have been torn to shreds by peer review. But the fact that we are still using their ideas, they were among the greatest thinkers of all times. Every intellectual still owes a great debt toward them. In today's academic environment, it is hard to come up with great thinkers of such kind.

As more papers get published, logically there will also be more rubbish that gets published. But the rubbish does not compete with the high-quality material, and should be of no concern to good researchers, who produce good findings (because the total number of journals is not capped). The pond should be large enough to feed everybody. Academic stratification will not be dissolved for the same reason that other human organizations do not lose their stratification. Academics of like-mind will get together and set their own standards of research, and have their fellow researchers publish within that journal. So the higher-ranked journals where most scientists continue to congregate will still exist. We will just have made lives easier for more academics.

Simplicity

The value of being an expert is that most people cannot and do not acquire the knowledge about a particular subject as the expert does. Procreation as an act requires no expert knowledge, because all humans are hard-wired to prefer sexual activities. Instead, experts are necessary in a highly technocratic world, which places a priority on rational procedures (see Wikipedia, "rationalization (Sociology)"). Imagine going to an airport without air traffic controllers. Airplanes would be crashing down all the time, because no one coordinates these airplanes during takeoff and landing. The benign view of experts is that these are the very gifted and talented people, who develop their expertise to benefit the society. We only need some people who know how to land airplanes safely, so that not all of us have to do it. The less benign view is that these gifted and talented people use the same expertise to maintain their high status in the hierarchy and exploit less knowledgeable people, who are ranked lower in the overall hierarchy. In that sense, experts use language that is complicated to understand to explain concepts, which are, in essence, fairly simple and straightforward. This behavior is precisely the opposite of what science is in the most ideal form: Ockham's razor. In other words, the goal is to express science in the most simple words possible without dumbing down.

I was once told the anecdote of a mathematician, who went to a conference, and explained his research in the most simple terms possible. He was not taken seriously at all by his colleagues, who ridiculed him for the weak methodology. I have no idea whether this anecdote reflects a broader reality, but to the extent that only jargon makes one acceptable to the wider academic community, those scientists are violating the Ockham's razor principle. They maintain their exclusivity, privilege and power at the expense of public benefit. The heavy use of complicated jargon is a social norm that is gradually created, and most people, who enter the club and want to be accepted by the other members, gladly accept these norms. During my undergraduate days, one would read about the initiation rites to Greek letter societies, which, in the best case scenario, just means embarrassing oneself (running around naked) and in the worst case can result in death (becoming alcoholically intoxicated). A young person rarely questions these norms if they want to be part of that community.

But returning back to simplicity, in more physically harmless adult settings, jargon is deliberately developed to create a barrier between the insider and the outsider. Being a scholar creates substantial barriers to the outside and non-scholarly world. Rarely will one find academics, which are loved by scholars and the general readers at the same time. Either one writes with sufficient complexity and depth of knowledge to be liked by fellow scholars, but can be hardly understood by the public. Or one writes in relatively simple prose while condensing too much complexity in the world, which will appeal to the masses, but will be criticized severely by academic crowds. There is fairly little crossover between the two.

What oftentimes happens instead is that there are some people, who become the "translators". These are people, who have a fairly good understanding of expert knowledge, but can use relatively simple language to convey that expert knowledge to the public. These translators play an important role in somewhat reducing the cartel-like power of the experts, who consider exclusivity of knowledge as part of their self-interest. Some scientific disciplines like sociology, politics or history are somewhat closer to lived reality, and can be rather easily explained. As an expert of society, I don't find it particularly challenging to explain social concepts to the broader public. The natural sciences often are structured in a somewhat more difficult manner, because their knowledge is not so intuitive. The human world is the one in which we live and observe all the time, but the natural world is somewhat distant and apart. That does not mean that natural sciences are impossible to understand for the lay person. It just takes some people, who are skilled in breaking down these concepts and use simple language without dumbing it down. Bill Nye and Neil Tyson come to mind.

In a genuinely democratic society it becomes less acceptable to create barriers to knowledge. In the old days, the priests read their script in Latin, and no one in the lay public could understand anything that the priests were saying, and yet people had to accord them the greatest amount of respect. Mass education allows people to challenge authority. In today's world, Wikipedia, social networks and online classes facilitate more opportunities for acquiring knowledge cheaply and easily. They should be more widely used, though it is obvious that the most educated classes benefit from new innovations much more disproportionately than the common masses, which is one meaning of the term 'new digital divide'.

There is an obvious utilitarian case to be made for expressing knowledge more simply aside from democratizing knowledge and power. If we are interested to extend the borders of human knowledge then it is absolutely important to share knowledge as widely as possible. 10 brains are smarter than 1, 100 are smarter than 10, and so forth. Authoritarian societies hate innovation, because it could challenge the social order. People rarely want to just know about what the healthiest foods to consume are or which computer operating system to install. They will also want to know whether the current social and political order is the most optimal once they freely access, evaluate and contribute to knowledge. By reducing the jargon and making knowledge as widely accessible as possible, more people can work on a problem and contribute better to society.

Definitional Power

How should an individual judge whether one position is better than another? I have said how important it is to create objectives in life and then try to live by them. It is not easy to answer the question what our objectives should be, but it is important to know that when we define a position and believe in it, we have definitional power. Sociologists developed this concept called "social constructionism" (Berger and Luckmann 1966). In other words, society creates constructs with which we view the world. The traditional construct of homosexuals in most society is that they are not only marginal to society, but are also quite bad for society. What happened over time is that society has become more tolerant of homosexuals and created new social constructs, which are more accepting of homosexuals. We oftentimes do not know where the power to define reality comes from, but we should be aware that it exists.

A similar term is the famous 'self-fulfilling prophecy'. In other words, we believe something to be true, and it will be true in its consequences. We believe that we will not get the job offer, and our negative thinking results in us not bothering to apply. But not bothering to apply makes it impossible to even be considered for the position. I recommend people to be very conscious of their odds. The odds of success will always be higher when they try it than if they didn't. Another example is that we think that the person we are speaking to is an evil crook, so we behave in front of them in a manner, which elicits evil behavior from that person. If we conversely think that the person is nice and inviting, we will also act such that the behavior of the person reflects nice behavior. This is a rough rule of thumb and will not always be true, but it is true in most cases.

When I traveled to Amsterdam, I visited the Rijksmuseum, as most tourists would have done. The collection was amazing, and had something for every lover of Dutch portraits. But there were only two portraits in the entire museum, which received most of the attention of the visiting public: Rembrandt's "Night Watch" and the Van Gogh "Self-Portrait". There is no doubt that these are two of the greatest of all Dutch painters. But why are these two particular portraits so popular? I am not an artist or art expert, but I did not find anything intrinsically beautiful about their paintings, which could elevate them from the rest of all paintings. What happened over time is that there were some art critics who claimed that these two are the best portraits in Dutch painting, and other critics concurred with that. Once that catches on, then the masses just follow that. Now when I walk into the museum, and I see this huge crowd assembling in front of the Night Watch, then I will also join the crowd, and pay attention to the details in the painting, even though my noob eyes cannot detect the intrinsically special feature in that painting.

Definitional power is not exclusive to art, but can easily be applied to other realms of life as well. Charismatic leaders in organizations like businesses or politics know that the words, demeanor and gestures they are using, very much define how the subordinates in the organization view the issue. Fashion designers rely on the applicability of definitional power. When you watch one of these fashion designer shows, you can see these designers, who speak about the bright colors on the model's skin and how it emphasizes a certain part of their body, and how it is aesthetically pleasing and so forth. But upon closer consideration, there is no reason why this color should be more popular than another, or why this shape should be in fashion. These are indeed aesthetic choices for which there can be no right or wrong.

Having definitional power is something very special, and should be valued. I remember when I was in secondary school, taking an art class. We had to create a painting on a big sheet of paper. To draw straight lines, we could not just rely on our small 30 centimeter rulers. We needed to use the big 150 centimeter ruler of which there was one in the class. Someone had decided to refer to this ruler as "mammut ruler", as in a huge mammal to indicate the big size of the ruler. There would be no reason to call this ruler as such, but once it was called that, everyone else, who borrowed that ruler, was referring to it as the "mammut ruler", and not just a big ruler. Children attach meaning to vowels and words based on what they are taught by their parents and people around them. Language is the cultural rules that encompass definitional power.

But definitional power should not be restricted to the sociological world. Is the individual free to impose some decisions? Yes. Aristotle argued that even though there are some guidelines as to how to live a good and desirable life, there is no authority other than the individual conscience, who can make the important decisions resulting in a happy life. Should I break up with my partner? Should I quit my job? Should I travel now or later? We are faced with a choice, and have to rely on our own voice in making that decision. Now, we can go back to sociology and claim that as creatures of habit, we will go back to our friends and family members and ask for advice. We will also strictly go by what the people close to us have to say. But even if we made the decision to rely on the people close to us to seek guidance, the initial inclination to seek for help is still that of an individual. We can also choose to ignore other people's advice if we think that we have some better considerations.

And here we have the weakness of sociology. Because all that sociology can say is that the Brussels, Ankara and Paris suicide bombers were socialized in the environment, where radical preachers told them that they serve their faith the best by blowing themselves up and killing as many innocent people as possible. These are the valid proximate factors to explain these suicide attacks, but they cannot explain why there are many similar people, who are thrown in such an environment, and do not end up blowing themselves up.

I will not deny for a minute that the society has plenty of space for imposing its definitional power, which my previous description hopefully makes more than clear. But I also want to emphasize that there is some definitional power that ultimately rests with the individual. We have to decide whether we want to wear blue pants or black pants. We have to decide whether we want to be an engineer or a lawyer. We have to decide whether we become socialists or liberals or conservatives. To not make those decisions is still a decision, even if they are poorly chosen ones.

References

Barsky, Robert F. 1998. *Noam Chomsky: A Life of Dissent.* Cambridge: MIT Press.

Beck, Ulrich. 1992. *Risk Society: Toward a New Modernity.* London: SAGE Publications.

Bentham, Jeremy. 1843. *The Works of Jeremy Bentham, vol. 4 (Panopticon, Constitution, Colonies, Codification).* Edinburgh: William Tait.

Berger, Peter, and Thomas Luckmann. 1966. *The Social Construction of Reality: A Treatise in the Sociology of Knowledge.* Garden City: Anchor Books.

Bourdieu, Pierre. 1986. 'The forms of capital." In J. Richardson (Ed.) Handbook of Theory and Research for the Sociology of Education, New York, Greenwood, 241-258.

Chang, Jung. 2014. *Empress Dowager Cixi: The Concubine Who Launched Modern China.* London: Random House.

Charisma on Command. 2016. "Steve Jobs Leadership Skills Breakdown - How To Motivate People." Youtube. https://www.youtube.com/watch?v=dVLERJ5IdrA

Collins, Randall. 1994. *Four Sociological Traditions.* New York: Oxford University Press.

Collins, Randall. 1997. *The Sociology of Philosophies: A Global Theory of Intellectual Change.* Cambridge: Harvard University Press.

Collins, Randall. 2005a. "Review Forum The Sociology of Almost Everything Four Questions to Randall Collins about Interaction Ritual Chains." *Canadian Journal of Sociology Online.*

Collins, Randall. 2005b. *Interaction Ritual Chains.* Princeton: Princeton University Press.

Collins, Randall. 2011. "Credential Inflation and the Future of Universities." *Italian Journal of Sociology of Education* 2: 228-251.

Collins, Randall, and Maren McConnell. 2015. *Napoleon Never Slept: How Great Leaders Leverage Emotional Energy.* E-Book.

Confucius. *Analects.* https://archive.org/details/chineseclassics02legggoog

Diamond, Jared. 2012. *The World Until Yesterday: What Can We Learn from Traditional Societies?* New York: Viking Press.

Dillner, Luisa. 2015. "How Much Sex Will Make Me Happy?" *Guardian*, November 30.

Durkheim, Emile. 1912. *Elementary Forms of the Religious Life.*

Emerson, Richard M. 1962. "Power-Dependence Relationship." *American Sociological Review* 27(1): 31-41.

Garfinkel, Harold. 1984. *Studies in Ethnomethodology.* Cambridge: polity Press.

Goffman, Erving. 1967. *Interaction Ritual: Essays on Face-to-Face Behavior.* New York: Anchor Books.

Granovetter, Mark, and Richard Swedberg. 1992. *The Sociology of Economic Life.* Boulder, CO: Westview Press.

Grazian, David. 2015. *American Zoo: A Sociological Safari.* Princeton: Princeton University Press.

Gunawardana, Gamini Nanda. 2015. "Charismatic leadership style of Steve Jobs." *Daily Mirror.*

http://www.dailymirror.lk/73763/charismatic-leadership-style-of-steve-jobs

Havelock, Eric A. 1988. *The Muse Learns to Write: Reflections on Orality and Literacy from Antiquity to the Present*. New Haven: Yale University Press.

Heracleous, Loizos and Laura Alexa Klaering. 2014. "Charismatic Leadership and Rhetorical Competence An Analysis of Steve Jobs's Rhetoric." *Group Organization Management* 39(2): 131-161.

Heracleous, Loizos. 2015. "Why Steve Jobs Was Such a Charismatic Leader." University of Warwick. http://www.wbs.ac.uk/news/why-steve-jobs-was-such-a-charismatic-leader1/

Highexistence.com. "This Is the Secret to Bill Clinton's Charisma." http://highexistence.com/secret-to-bill-clintons-charisma-eye-contact-video/

Hirschman, Albert. 1970. *Exit, Voice and Loyalty: Responses to Decline in Firms, Organizations and States*. Cambridge: Harvard University Press.

Keynes, John Maynard. 1930. "Economic Possibilities for our Grandchildren."

Liu, Larry. 2015. "Are Men and Women Different?" Mr. Liu's Opinions, November 29.

Liu, Larry. 2016. "Aristotelian Friendship and the Importance of Making Clear Choices." Mr. Liu's Opinions, January 13.

MacIntyre, Alasdair. 1981. *After Virtue: A Study in Moral Theory*. Notre Dame: University of Notre Dame Press.

Marx, Karl. 1848. "The Manifesto of the Communist Party."

Miner, Horace. 1956. "Body Ritual among the Nacirema." *American Anthropologist* 58: 503-507.

Nietzsche, Friedrich. 1891. *Thus Spoke Zarathrustra*.

Ong, Walter J. 1982. *Orality and Literacy: The Technologizing of the World*. London: Routledge. http://dss-edit.com/prof-anon/sound/library/Ong_orality_and_literacy.pdf

Persaud, Raj and Peter Bruggen. 2013. "Being Religious or Spiritual Is Linked With Getting More Depressed." *Huffington Post*, September 15.

Rea, Shilo.2015. "Carnegie Mellon Researchers Find More Sex Doesn't Lead to Increased Happiness." Carnegie Mellon University.

Reid, Harry. 2009. *The Good Fight: Hard Lessons from Searchlight to Washington*. New York: Putnam.

Ringmar, Eric. 2005. *Surviving Capitalism: How We Learned to Live with the Market and Remained Almost Human*. London: Anthem Press.

Russell, Bertrand. 1932. "In Praise of Idleness."

Serwach, Joseph. 2004. "Research Religious faith shortens hospital stays, aids recovery." University Record Online, University of Michigan.

Simmel, Georg. 1922. *Conflict and the Web of Group Affiliations.* Translated and edited by Kurt Wolff, Glencoe, IL: Free Press.

Weber, Max. 1978. *Economy and Society, Vol.1.* Berkeley: University of California Press.

Zuberi, Tufuku. 2013. "African Independence." Documentary film.

Preface to my Collected Essays

In the following section, I reprint my commentary that regular readers of my blog have encountered and will be familiar with. I have been writing a blog since November 2006. I was a young teenager in Austria, and still wrote in German. By that time I had a few years of library experience infused in me, and for some reason an avid reader turned into an avid writer. Naturally, I hope that over this past decade my views have become sharper and more mature, as my writing experience and reading knowledge of diverse subject matters has increased.

The blog was a free and simple venue where I could enter my reflections about politics and current events that I read about in the newspaper. Rather than have a teacher or a reviewer judge my work, the blog was the most unrestrained and unfiltered way to express my opinions. Writing in a free-floating way has not only helped me to communicate my ideas, thoughts and beliefs to the readers out there, but also helped me to clarify my own political views. Before writing about a topic, my thoughts on the issue were there but rather incoherent and inarticulate. After writing about it, I had a much clearer perspective and can explain it to people on the street.

Someone had explained to me that talk is cheap, but writing is really the difficult task. In a heated conversation with a friend, we can make ad hominem attacks or distract from the issue and possibly get away with it, because the spoken word lends itself to dynamism, allowing frequent changes of topic. It does not make someone a good debater to duck the issue, but one does not necessarily have to confront the logical inconsistency in argumentation. In the written form, such a faux pas would be inexcusable. In written conversations, it is impossible to obscure from the issue, because confusing statements can be re-read an infinite amount of times and pointed out by the readers. We hope the essay that we read is pleasing, logical and coherent, and if it fails to accomplish that task, we consider it a bad piece of writing. It is in writing and in scholarship where serious debates occur ("you said on page 34, paragraph 2, sentence 1 that..."), and not in the bar at night with friends (though the latter affair is more emotionally rousing and memorable perhaps).

It was apt to entitle my blog "Mr. Liu's Opinions", as it was nothing more or less than my opinion. There is the natural danger that uncorrected work will result in views that are too narrow and styles that are too extravagant. But thoughts that are unhinged by others also has the advantage of portraying my views and sentiments. As long as they are well-articulated, well-researched and reasonable, I think blogs deserve a hearing as well.

In the digital age, it is encouraged to operate blogs and share opinions. They contain interesting insights if they are well written and researched. There is an understandable danger that much of what we find in the world wide web is rubbish. We know that there is a lot of conspiracy theory, poorly researched pieces and detestable world views. The internet, while opening the world to more input, carries its own risks. The advent of the internet does not obviate the need for prudent judgment, and we still need to teach young people how to develop their critical thinking skills when approaching online content. That has been true in the past and it is so today.

My blog posts (from January 2015 to August 2016) jump from one issue to another without an apparent thread tying it together. My interests range from conflicts in international relations among countries to conflicts in the workplace, the logic and dynamic of the capitalist economy, the use of prudent social policy (especially the universal basic income), income and wealth inequality, debt crisis, austerity, health care reform, transportation and housing policy, educational philosophy, the history of Chinese civilization, and many more issues. I do not hide my own political biases and preferences, and start with the premise that everyone deserves the right to a good life and that political and economic institutions should facilitate that these ends are, in fact, accomplished. I am a democratic socialist. So perhaps, there is a common thread in my blog posts. I have an undiminished desire to live in a world that serves the needs and interests of the people at large rather than a few privileged classes, and where our grandchildren will look back at our generation to condemn the idiocy and failure of our current political choices.

Libertarianism and Right-to Work Laws

Posted on January 3, 2015

Today, my talk (Youtube video) will be about libertarians and their views on right-to-work laws, which prohibit unions from requiring all workers within a given company to join the union. First we should begin with the types of libertarians that exist. This is a really Orwellian choice of language, don't you think?

In my view, there are two types of libertarians:

1. Left-wing libertarians (or libertarian socialists; some even call them anarcho-syndicalists like Noam Chomsky).
2. Right-wing libertarians, i.e. Koch brother types.

What both sides have in common is their avowed support of "freedom", and usually freedom from state coercion and things like that. But the left-wing is on the side of the workers and the general public except the powerful, and the right-wing is on the side of the rich and powerful, mostly capitalists. It is obvious that the left-wing libertarians will favor unions and oppose right-to-work, and right-wing libertarians oppose unions and support right-to-work.

The early enunciation of this split in libertarianism can be read in John Locke, whom I would consider a right-wing libertarian, because he defended the liberty of the capitalists against that of the laborer. Adam Smith is somewhere in between, because he liked free markets benefiting employers, but he was also highly sympathetic of the cause of the workers and trade unions. Marx was clearly a left-wing libertarian, because he made some negative statements about the state, which under the highest form of communism would "wither away".

In principle, one could say that one is a political centrist libertarian with no partisan preference on either side. But we could only do that if we kept the debate highly abstract and within philosophical debate club circles. But we are talking about problems in the real world, and here you have to choose on whose side you are on. Whose freedom should we advocate? Given the worker-capitalist conflict it is not possible for both sides to have an equal amount of freedom. If you are for "right-to-work" laws then you are in favor of diminished workers' rights and for increased employers' rights. Individual workers (not in a union) are screwed against capitalists unless they have rare and needed skills. But that is always a tiny minority of the workforce, and cannot be national policy. It can only be individual advice ("get more education").

Even if we accept a framework of union coercion restricting workers' individual freedom, one is also implicitly endorsing the increase of employer coercion in the form of lower wages, longer hours, fewer benefits and harsher working conditions. In that case union coercion is much better than employer coercion. So most Americans understand the freedom fallacy and support unions, which poll after poll shows.

But some libertarians bypass the industrial class conflict argument by siding with consumers ("consumer sovereignty" etc.). But that is not realistic to mitigate industrial class conflicts, because customers generally don't care whether a shirt is produced in a sweatshop in Bangladesh or in a decent company. They care about price and product quality only.

Some libertarians might even acknowledge class conflict but counter that workers can always choose to leave their abusive employer and find another job or open up their own company. My response is "good for you". But we are not talking about individual advice, but about the experience of the average worker who is either better off in terms of wages, benefits and rights on the job or worse off under right-to-work, and they are clearly worse off. Even by libertarian economists' own admission if workers do find a better job, they will go for the better job. The fact that many workers don't do it indicates the terrible nature of the job market, which really is a restriction on the freedom of workers. The capitalist has the freedom of movement, and blackmail workers with redundancy, but the worker is tied to his locality in most cases and has no similar method of blackmail against their abusive employers.

Some libertarians might argue that if unions are good for workers then they would voluntarily and on their own accord choose to join a union. We don't have to force them. The Volkswagen Tennessee story is one example of that. Workers had a unionization vote and a majority voted against it, albeit with only a small margin. Right-wing libertarians will beat their chest and proclaim that we should accept workers' choice. Unions are not good for workers, the clever VW workers recognized, so the right-wing libertarian says.

But there are several problems with the argument

1. Mostly Republican politicians (senators and the governor) led a misinformation campaign about how VW will allegedly move the plant to Mexico if they voted in favor of unionization. This is bullshit, because VW management in Germany implicitly supported the unionization vote, because in Germany unions are represented in the corporate boardroom, and they were highly enthusiastic about it.

2. These politicians also threatened that if VW unionized all tax incentives for the plant will be repealed. This is blackmailing and has nothing to do with giving workers "free" choice.

3. Even if one thinks that the first two points do not matter, it does not mean that workers are well-informed about their choices. Libertarians assume that people have the freedom to decide but also that they have all the available information at their disposal. But we have a strong anti-union culture in the South as a result of business/politician propaganda, so information for workers is not as widely available as suggested.

4. I want to diverge with left-libertarians on one more point though they would agree with my first three points: I don't mind having to "force" workers to join a union if I were a dictator, even if a slight majority of workers opposed joining the union right now. I assume they will grow to like the union once they are in it, just like with social security, which the rich try to destroy, but were not successful (yet).In addition, I have no moral qualms to coerce people to embrace higher wages, better working conditions, better taking care of their families and their pursuit of happiness. I will try everything I can to convince them of it, but if they don't oblige then the state still has the power to impose the "common good". But let me give you an example before you go take out your Hayek and quote Road to Serfdom passages.

My favorite example of soft paternalism are pensions: most workers obviously like pensions, so no convincing work and direct government coercion is necessary. But let us assume that libertarians even (!) them to save for the future. But having pensions, i.e. coerced savings, is still a good idea, because most workers are not careful enough with money and will end up with no savings at age 65 and become too oppose pensions, which robs workers of their current labor earnings by forcing weak and unfit to continue working or have to work until they die. Libertarians might argue "Tough luck. Make better decisions!" But I would find that view crazy. Why would we let seniors starve and work themselves to death just so we can enjoy some hollow form of "liberty". Where is my freedom, when I am poor?

Sanders Is Not a Left-Wing Radical Socialist But a Social Democrat

Posted on January 12, 2015

The popular portrayal of Bernie Sanders, independent US Senator from Vermont, is that he is a left-wing radical socialist, who represents political positions that are way to the left of the American people. He wants to have government ownership of all industries and endangers the American way of life, freedom and capitalism. But as a European, I find this popular depiction very questionable. He is at most a Social Democrat, and I should explain below why I think so.

There is confusion in America what socialism really is. For starters, socialists don't always agree among each other what the content of socialism is, but at the very least it contains the state control of the means of production, such as factories, offices, resources and firms. In the more advanced form of socialism, ownership is transferred to the workers. Bernie Sanders has sympathies for it as part of his 12-point proposal for the country, where he pushed for the opportunity for workers to set up worker-owned cooperatives (Sanders 2014). But it is questionable how far he will push it. When push comes to shove, he is a supporter of a social democratic Scandinavian-style welfare state in the form of better education, health care and social service provisions for the general population (Leibovich 2007) rather than the confiscation of companies from the private sector. So where does the fear-mongering about Sanders' policies come from?

The fear-mongering about the left has roots in the anti-communist fear of the 1920s, when the Palmer raids targeted Communist sympathizers right after the end of World War I. Another bout of anti-communism happened after World War II, when the Cold War with the "evil" communist Soviet Union occurred. Senator McCarthy targeted several filmmakers and academics, who had left-leaning sympathies, and that created this image that communism was something to be feared and hated in the US (Powers 1998). Another blow to left-wing ideas happened with the end of the Cold War in 1991, when thinkers like Francis Fukuyama (1992) proudly proclaimed the end of Communist ideology. Since Communism as it played out in Eastern Europe was a failure, and since China became rich after shedding its communist legacy in the late-1970s, we seem to be living in a world, where we no longer have to worry about the fear of socialism making a comeback.

But this is, of course, ideological nonsense of the worst kind. If there is anything that will help revive socialist ideas among the public, then it is the hubris of neoliberal ideology followed by neoliberal policies, which deregulate markets and hammer working people with lower wages, more unemployment and worse working conditions. The Occupy Wall Street movement developed on the heels of the Great Recession, when the governments bailed out the banks, while passing austerity measures on the population. Attacking the "1%" all of a sudden became part of legitimate discourse, and polls are beginning to indicate that young people, who have not been indoctrinated during the Cold War era, look at the term socialism quite favorably (Democratic Underground 2013).

This policy environment then favors somebody like Bernie Sanders to come in and think about running for president in 2016. Whether he is going to become president or not is not so important as the fact that with his insistent focus on the problems facing America (inequality, poverty, global warming, poor infrastructure, education, pension and health care system etc.) he can force the political class to pay attention to the things that the American people really care about.

Sanders has been the longest-serving independent member in the history of the US Congress. The fact that he has been an independent, and does not fall into the Democratic and Republican Party framework has made him so unacceptable in American politics. But Sanders is, nonetheless, widely popular in his constituency by driving very issue-focused elections, providing excellent constituency services and running on a consistently progressive agenda on behalf of workers, women, minorities, poor people, veterans, children etc. to increase voter turnout. Conservatives know that in order for their policies to succeed, the voter turnout has to be as low as possible. That is what the voter ID laws are all about: preventing poor people from going to vote. For progressives like Sanders, the logic is precisely the other way around. He needs a high voter turnout to enable him to get elected, since his policies are so widely popular.

Sanders most important philosophy is that he does not find it fair to live in a society where so few people have so much power and wealth and so many people own so little. How can a society call itself democratic if almost all of the income gains flow to the richest people? But does that position make him a radical communist? I would tend to say no. His proposals to increase Social Security funding, implement a single-payer health care system, invest in the national infrastructure and break up the big banks, to name a few, are fairly moderate social democratic policies that would have been considered very common during the Eisenhower era of the 1950s. Those ideas appear radical only in today's context, when the national discourse, the news media and the wealth in society is so deeply controlled by the nation's oligarchs.

Is Sanders really to the left of what most American people believe in? This is nonsense. Polls show that many people believe in a single-payer health care system, affordable higher education, a massive jobs program, renewable energy and more Social Security. The major problem is not the policy content, but the practical feasibility of getting these policies implemented.

Americans are generally willing to embrace real change. But the problem is that in the current political configuration not much change is possible. Obama may be a progressive at heart, but in terms of policy he is a pragmatic conservative, who does not want to rock the boat. The health care reform and stimulus package has used up his entire political capital, and he gave up to the Republican Congress for most of the remainder of his presidency. Some people would argue that Republican obstructionism prevents him from accomplishing better results for the American people, but that is a cheap excuse. If Obama wanted he could use the bully pulpit of his presidency to challenge Congress to take on a more progressive agenda and call out the Republicans for not moving on that agenda.

In the meantime, as Congress is obstructing progressive change fewer people are going to vote, because they don't feel like they can be part of the political process. It may be true that many people are angry and fed up about declining real wages and more income inequality, but they feel like their vote does not count for anything anyway, so they will end up staying home during election time. And as I pointed out, lower voting turnout benefits the elites.

The difficulty of any progressive agenda is that the power structure in the form of the corporate media (which only report horse races like Jeb Bush vs Hillary Clinton) and the billions of dollars of lobbying money to politicians holds the political system in a very comfortable gridlock. Among the rich, there might be a few sympathetic billionaires that will use fairly left-leaning rhetoric, like Nick Hanauer (2014), who warned his fellow plutocrats of pitchforks that are coming their way. Warren Buffett thought that he should not pay less taxes than his secretary (Isidore 2013), and Bill Gates was sympathetic to Thomas Piketty, the premium scholar on wealth inequality. Those relatively progressive billionaires might be allies of the left, but they are unreliable. Gates (2014) liked Piketty's critique of inequality but did not want to pay more taxes. Buffett and Hanauer are willing to be critical of their unrestrained wealth accumulation, but would they fund political candidates to impose higher taxes on them as eagerly as the Koch brothers and the Waltons would do to lower their taxes? No, the power of self-interest generally works stronger than the enlightened self-interest, which is good for publicity, but never part of a serious agenda.

The political cash of right-wing billionaires, on the other hand, is quite staggering thanks to the Citizens United and McCutcheon Supreme court decision to allow unlimited sums of money to be spent on elections and candidates (e.g. Kennedy 2013). Workers, seniors, students or environmental groups have no ability to match these extreme contributions. The top players are picking their referees, and Americans are clearly worse off for it, and we may expect voter turnout to decrease to even lower levels.

Implementing more socially just policies require a strong grassroots movement. Ralph Nader (2014) wants about 1% of the population to organize local activism in front of Congressional offices to achieve progressive pushback. The Occupy Wall Street movement of 2011 has shown that once there are people, who occupy a physical space, there are opportunities to build a bigger movement out of this, because people can have a sense of not being alone about their skeptical views on inequality and capitalism.

Where does that leave Bernie Sanders? He needs to take advantage of the popular mood of dissatisfaction in this country and provide the needed alternative voice of the country. Whether he wants to run as a Democrat or as an independent candidate is not as important as the fact that he runs and the ability to have a national discourse about real issues and problems that are facing the American people. Sanders argued that he is only willing to run if he sees the huge grassroots support, since he is not relying on the support of the billionaire class that he wants to take on (Easley 2014). But just waiting for the grassroots support will also not have energetic outcomes if there is a lack of leadership. If he were to provide progressives with the leadership they need, then a grassroots movement could emerge out of this, and deliver reforms that Americans so desperately need.

Why Is Wealth Concentrating at the Top?
Posted on <u>January 13, 2015</u>

An important Facebook question that was posed to me was:

Steven Brooks: What is it about extreme wealth that causes the rest of us to fall behind? Is it that money is a finite resource and so earning profit is a zero-sum enterprise? And what is driving the concentration of wealth into an ever tightening range of the population? Is it lack of regulation, or the wrong kinds of regulation, or both? And finally, if a wealth tax could solve the problem, what would that world look like? Norway? Norway's utopia is built upon global income inequality. Wouldn't we just be pushing the problem further downstream?

L Larry Liu: These are great questions. Here my attempt at answering it. There are several factors: as the poor and middle class people see their wages stagnate, those of the rich 1% keep on increasing. Wages are tied to the collective bargaining power of the workers (i.e. unions), the level of investment in the productive-sector economy (i.e. market confidence), the level of employment (the higher the rate, the higher the wages), which in turn depends on other factors like technological displacement of wage labor and/or outsourcing decisions from rich developed countries into poor and less developed countries. Well, we know that all of these values are trending downward, which means there is a constant downward pressure on wages, the primary means of income for little guys like us. Little guys like us then take out enormous loans so we can go to college, buy a house or a car, and make the wealthy creditors really rich.

The wealth of the 1% is not tied to wages, but to the profits of privately-owned companies and other asset values, most importantly housing and real estate. We know that these values have increased. As productivity of individual workers is growing leaps and bounds, but their wages are essentially flat, the corresponding profit share increases. We also know that international real estate speculation from wealthy investors drives up the price of housing and the cost of living higher, which is again reflected in the rising fortunes of the 1%. We also know that the governments and central banks of the world have dumped billions and trillions of dollars to save the financial system from complete meltdown. This is nothing else but the bailout of creditors, who are already rich and fat. The government is then piling up huge amounts of debt, and then turns around to cut government programs for working class people like college funding and health care, so that we have to go to even deeper debt to purchase the services that were once provided by the government.

You would think that democratic elections would make a difference and can mitigate extreme inequality, but that has thus far not been the case, as the poor and middle class are still distracted and divided, while the rich control the media, the education system, and quite frankly the political system. Thanks to Citizens United and McCutcheon Supreme Court decisions, the rich can spent unlimited sums of money into political campaigns. The Koch brothers own $100 billion and are sure to use some of it to buy politicians, set up right-wing think tanks and their media channels.

Greece Anti-Austerity Vote: Viva la Syriza

Posted on February 2, 2015

"Don't go gently into the night; rage, rage against the dying of the light", wrote the new Greek finance minister, the academic economist, Yanis Varoufakis, quoting the poet Dylan Thomas.

Greece has overwhelmingly voted for an end to austerity. After being hammered brutally by the IMF, the EU and their European partners to stick to their budget cutting promises and "structural" reforms the Greeks have finally decided to throw off the yoke of the oppressive financial and economic regime by electing the left-wing Alexis Tzipras and the Syriza government, which had been in complete political oblivion just a few years ago before the crisis blew up. No, the Greeks are not natural communists, but they do listen to their interests, once they are so recklessly driven into a corner. And the new government is in part delivering on some of its promises by canceling the next austerity moves, stopping further privatization, rehiring government workers that were fired, reinstating the minimum wage (which was hopelessly slashed in the previous administration), and by throwing out the strict debt repayment schedule. Now it is time to negotiate with their foreign creditors, and hopefully seek an amicable solution with them.

By following austerity policies so faithfully under the previous conservative administration (Antonis Samaras) the country plunged itself into the largest economic depression it has since in a long time. Wages and living standards were reduced by 30% in short order, and the economy tanked. The European partners say that Greece has taken out too much debt and has to bear the full cost of fiscal adjustment. Every party has to come to an end, we are being told. Austrian and German taxpayers are furious at their governments for rewarding taxpayer bailouts to those "lazy" Greeks.

Is that all that we have to know about the crisis? Let us step back for a moment. Most observers will agree that one of the root causes of the crisis is that the Greeks were members of the eurozone, and either never should have been part of it, or if it were part of it, it had to accept much more restrictive fiscal policies. But there was no mechanism in the EU, which could guarantee such restrictive fiscal policies. I am by the way a supporter of a EU fiscal union. We should keep in mind that with the accession into the eurozone one of the two major policy tools for the national governments, namely monetary policy, is surrendered to the larger political entity, the European Central Bank. That leaves countries with only fiscal policies to adjust to the economic needs of the country.

It is true that the Greek government then went out to borrow a lot of money from other European countries, especially from Germany, France and other countries up north. But one should not forget that the loans were pretty much given to them without any lender restrictions. The common currency had given the banks the green light to lend enormous sums of money without the currency devaluation threat, which could reduce the debt pile significantly (if the money had been lent in the drachma, if it is in D-mark, then the story is less favorable for the Greeks). The Greeks were able to take out the loans due to low-interest policies, and with that German money they bought... you guessed it, German goods. The story of the EU is a complete tragedy: Greece had price and wage growth that was far above productivity rises, while Germany had price and wage growth far below productivity rises. If there was no trade, there would have been adjustment at some point, because the former would have run out of money, and the latter would see its economy falter due to lack of consumption growth. But the situation was maintained by having the Germans produce for export, and the Greeks importing those goods with German money. Germany thus produced 2 trillion euros in export surpluses over the last 15 years, and is defending that with tooth and nail. No wonder this system had to implode.

Once the financial crisis of 2008 hit, the Greeks could no longer hide their debts, and the speculators quickly tried to sell off the Greek bonds. But that makes the situation worse, because now the interest on the Greek bonds increase dramatically, and a recession-battered economy now had to go into deeper debt while at the same time not being able to take counter-cyclical steps to pull the economy out of recession.

The German government and others now realized that their banks were in big trouble, because if the Greeks stopped paying up, then the German banks would collapse too. The Europeans then got the idea to organize a bailout for the banks, which had been sold as a bailout for the Greeks. But it was NOT a bailout for the Greeks, but a bailout for the banks through the backdoor. The German tax money was funneled via the Greek government back to the foreign creditor banks in the form of debt service, and only a small portion (10% or so) was actually used to run other current government expenses. Blaming the Greek people or their government is completely overblown, and at the end the quiet bankers are laughing their way to the bank (what an incestuous description!). Now that the Greeks are negotiating with their new foreign creditors, mainly IMF and EU, the private banks have mostly disposed themselves of their liability. Any losses on defaulted loans would fall on EU taxpayers.

But default is now the only option. Let us examine why. Greek debt now stands at 180% of GDP, and is now unsustainable. The creditors say that the Greeks have to cut their debt nonetheless. But how? By austerity measures, raising taxes on working people and lowering government services to them. The government could have also attacked the assets of the wealthy, but they were clever enough to run away with their assets and hide them from the Bermudas to Switzerland, and the corrupt tax authorities let them get away with it, so they attached the taxes to working people, mostly in the form of sales tax, property tax and income tax. These are the easy targets. Working people can't run away and hide their assets quite as easily as the rich. So there is a lot of tax evasion in Greece, no doubt, and the new Syriza government wants to fight that.

But let us think about the implications of austerity policies. The implication is to remove demand from the economy. You have fewer people employed (25% unemployment rate and 60% youth unemployment), those fewer people pay more taxes and buy fewer products, their wages are reduced to almost nothing. You have a humanitarian crisis in the form of rising emigration, rising suicide rates, more diseases, people becoming homeless and picking up food from the trash can, in short, a humanitarian disaster in the midst of the richest continent on the planet. Now what happens when the economy shrinks? Your debt burden becomes heavier, not lighter. With austerity the income with which to repay the debt shrinks. The debt to GDP ratio itself goes up when the denominator (GDP) decreases. It's math! So working people in Greece are screwed with the stupid carrot that at some distant point in the future their deprivation will have paid off with a reduction of the debt. Yes, an angel that looks like the devil is going to come down and save them! I wish somebody could save the Greeks from these nonsense neoliberal preachers! Syriza, anybody? The Greeks are also being told the nonsense that with the "structural" reforms (basically cutting wages and prices and destroying labor unions) they are going to export their way out of the mess. But where are they going to export their products? Their current account deficit is much lower than it used to be, but it is hard to imagine where the big buyers are going to come from, because the Germans are certainly not doing it. The overwhelming majority of the economy is still driven by domestic consumer purchases of ordinary people.

I should tell a tangential story as anecdote here: in the 1980s, Ceaucescu, the president of Romania, decided to pay off the entire debt of his country by exporting all of the food surpluses (and even some essentials) from the country and importing as little as possible. So the Romanians were deprived of many goods and the shelves were often empty. By the late-1980s all of the debt was paid off, but he did not change policies. By that time Gorbachev's perestroika and glasnost was making its way through the whole of Eastern Europe, and the Romanian people seized the moment to get rid of Ceausescu. Now, it is hard to tell whether he would have been able to remain in power had he not done austerity on his people, but he might have persisted more amicably (he was shot in 1989 in a show trial) had he not done it.

Austerity is a fraud, and can neither serve the interests of the people of Greece nor of any other European country. If people in other countries think they can be spared this treatment they should be forewarned. The German intransigence with regard to a debt haircut is particularly bewildering for historical reasons: Germany had seen its debt partially forgiven in 1953 by the allied powers, because they were in a bad economic situation after the war. This time the allied powers were smarter than after World War I, and they allowed the haircut in order to allow the Germans to grow and develop their economy. On another note it were the Germans that led the tragic example of austerity during the 1930s between the Great Depression and Hitler's accession to power. The chancellor, Heinrich Bruning, decided to signal "credibility" to the creditors by cutting the federal budget at a time of mass unemployment, shrinking tax revenues and growing poverty. The Nazis received less than 5% of the vote before the crisis. By 1932, their voter support had grown to one-third of the total vote. The communists also become stronger, but could not capitalize as well on mass discontent as the Nazis could. Hitler reversed the disastrous Great Depression with rearmament policies in clear violation of the Versailles treaty for which he could care less (and he plundered middle class and wealthy Jews, in part, to pay for it). This is not to defend Hitler's policies in any way. I happen to believe that military spending is a very bad way to rev up an economy, but it is better to spend money than to save it during bad times. This is the logic that must not be forgotten.

In a neoliberal world, the lessons don't seem to be learned. The same nonsense policies to remain in good standing with creditors, whose foolish speculative investments have in part contributed to the crisis, are going to produce more debt, political radicalization, extremism, violence, discontent and in some cases even war. The lessons will have to be relearned, and the high priest oligarchs will have no choice but to make concessions if even they want to survive in a building, whose walls and foundations have become shaky, and threatening to engulf all of us below in a huge pile of smothering rubble. In the meantime, let us cheer on the Syriza party, and hope that they can fight the austerity mantra with better ideas. Greece should rage, rage against the dying of the light!

Defending Piketty against His Critics

Posted on February 11, 2015

There has been a critique against Piketty's Capital in the Twenty-First Century (2014), by Philip Magness and Robert Murphy (2014), and I defended Piketty's argument in a Facebook post:

There was a Kopczuk and Saez study in 2004, looking at the estate tax data claiming a falling share for the top 1%, and this data, which Magness cites, apparently undermines the claim of Piketty. But why would you want to take estate tax data, when the rich have cleverly worked to undermine the estate tax? Congress kept on passing exemptions for the estate tax, and so the estate tax can't fully capture the amount of inequality (Figure 4)

Magness points out that for the US, Piketty there are missing data points on the total tax as share of national income between 1870 and 1900 (Figure 2). Okay, Piketty should have left that part empty and not extrapolate, but I would like to read Piketty's own response if he ever cared to respond (probably not).

In Figure 5, Magness attacks Piketty for picking and choosing data from different studies, but I don't necessarily find that problematic if the methodology is the same for each.

Figure 14 shows that North America has a flatter U-shape curve of the capital-income ratio than Europe. But there is still a U-shape.

It is good that Piketty's work has been critiqued, but I still don't see the fundamental argument challenged. There has been growth in inequality, and much of it is not properly accounted for, because there is no world police to track down the wealth of the rich. The US IRS has tried to go after Swiss bank account holders that are US citizens, and there was some success there, but these are happenstance events, and haphazardly enforced.

Magness ironically makes fun of Piketty for demanding a global wealth tax just so he can measure inequality. The analogy is to Freud's disease of which it purports to be the cure. But there is some truth to Piketty's point. Most working people account their entire earnings to the IRS on an annual basis. Most middle class people do the same, because they (1) want to get some taxes back from the government (refund), and (2) their earnings derive from wages, which are deducted automatically from the payroll. For this group of people, the IRS data pretty accurately captures their earnings and possessions. For big investors and corporate bosses, the tax story is different: they are too rich to get a refund, and if they do get a refund it is by bribing Congressman to write them a loophole, not via IRS filings. Their earnings are subject to taxation after-the-fact, not before-the-fact like for workers. In other words, the transaction happens, money goes into the pocket of investors and bosses, and then at the end of the year they report their amount to the IRS. If I am a mafia boss, and can count the cash on the table before the tax man comes in, would I not want to first hide half the money elsewhere before I meet the tax man?

The Politics of Delusion: How Republican Presidential Contenders Are (Not) Fighting Against Inequality

Posted on April 7, 2015

The US presidential elections are beginning to gear up, and we hear presidential candidates from the Republican Party trying to convince us that inequality is something that they have are concerned about. Four years after the Occupy Wall Street movement had been quashed by police departments all over the country, the Republican contenders are admitting and no longer denying that income and wealth inequality is something that we should be concerned about. (99% of all new income goes to the top 1%, the top 0.1% owns nearly as much wealth as the bottom 90%, and the Walton family owns more wealth than the bottom 42% of Americans.) And these pronouncements are happening even though the political establishment has been completely bought by the Koch brothers, who have already pledged to donate nearly 1 billion dollars into the presidential elections next year.

In this post-Citizens United world, we need to ask ourselves whether any of the pronouncements of the Republican contenders about inequality can be taken seriously at all. I would claim that, of course, they cannot be taken seriously, and to believe that they have serious proposals to resolve the inequality problem means to fall victim to their politics of delusion.

In a crude sense, one can judge any of the Republican contenders (Ted Cruz, Rand Paul, Jeb Bush etc.) by the money that they generate from wealthy donors, who have become increasingly important in a world, where there are no more campaign finance restrictions for very wealthy people. It is not very likely for any of these contenders to speak out against the people, who fund them to become president.

But let us assume that the donors do not influence their views, and that they are really concerned about reducing inequality. We have to judge these presidential contenders based on their campaign promises, not on their heart-wrenching "I feel your pain" stories. Essentially, most contenders claim that the best way to reduce inequality is not to punish the "success" stories, but to encourage job creation. Okay, not bad. But how do you create jobs? Answer: by giving tax breaks to rich people, who will trickle it down to the rest of us.

Now, trickle-down theory has been thoroughly discredited, even among economists, but the belief won't die down that quickly among policymakers, receiving advice from rich people and their close associates in the right-wing think tanks and news media. We can expect that if a Republican becomes elected president, and the Republicans keep their majority in both houses of Congress (which looks increasingly likely) that the current Republican budgets, which currently receive veto threats from the Obama administration, will pass for the most part, if not in entirety.

Progressives have pinned very high hopes on the Obama administration that he would attempt an agenda left-of-center, but we know it does not happen, because the Democratic Party also has to satisfy Wall Street and the big corporations, and they don't appreciate a progressive agenda, even if that is what most of the country likes to see implemented. Tragically, Hillary Clinton is another one of those center-right, corporate Democrats, who ally with the rich rather than support a progressive agenda. She has made no statement to redress inequality, which would have required her to take shots at her wealthy donors.

For the Republicans, it is altogether a different story: they are a very strong and unified party, at least as far as the fundamental economic principles are concerned. We hear a lot about the Tea Party and the establishment wing fighting against each other, but what usually happens is that the Tea Party wing proposes to slash Medicaid, Medicare and other social programs and give tax breaks to the wealthy and big corporations, and the establishment wing usually goes along with that, though they would not necessarily want the government to shut down over those budget struggles, while the Tea Party wing is more than willing to show brinkmanship on this issue.

It is altogether, therefore, not surprising why the progressive agenda is stalled in Congress, while the right-wing agenda that cuts social programs while giving tax breaks to the rich has significant political clout. Mancur Olson (1965) had argued in "The Logic of Collective Action" that interest groups are small, but concentrated and powerful, while the general public is large and diffuse/ weak. The interest group consists of the rich and the powerful, while the general public consists of ordinary people, working people, the unemployed, seniors, children, and any other marginalized group located very far away from the halls of power. The interest groups get their way, and the general public loses out.

In any case, ordinary people should at no point in time be fooled about Republican presidential contenders' public concern for fighting to reduce inequality. They receive support from the billionaire class, promote a right-wing austerity-for-the-masses agenda, and think they can win the elections by pretending to speak out on behalf of ordinary voters. I sincerely hope that the voters won't be fooled again.

Critics of Single Payer Health Care Are Wrong

Posted on April 24, 2015

Here is an outrageous article that I read by a Forbes contributor (Goodman 2015), who speaks of himself as "promoting market-based health care solutions". He discusses the implications of a single-payer Medicare for all health care plan.

What would people be charged to enroll in Medicare? How much subsidy would they get? To make the budget balance, people would have to pay a premium that, on the average, equals the expected cost of their care. Just like Obamacare, there would have to be subsidies for lower-income families. With community rating, the healthy would be over-charged and the sick would be under-charged. None of these problems go away by shifting everything to Medicare.

The healthy would be over-charged and the sick would be under-charged. But that is precisely the point of a single-payer health care system: that the healthy buy insurance in case they need it, but in the meantime the money is used to pay for the health care of currently sick people. A functioning insurance system cannot work without cross-subsidization, and he attacks the very principle of cross-subsidization. In his utopia, people should buy their own health care out of pocket. Good luck when you have a big surgery in front of you.

For people at work, there would be enormous pressure to continue the employer contribution by requiring employers to buy their employees into Medicare. That would raise the issue of exempting small business, exempting part-time workers, etc. These are the same issues we grapple with today.

Yes, employers have to buy Medicare for their workers, but the entire risk of carrying the insurance system is transferred from the individual firm to the government, which has a much larger pool of both beneficiaries as well as contributors to the system. Why would small businesses and part-time workers be exempted? The point of Medicare is to shift the provision of insurance coverage outside the employment system. An old person does not have to work if he gets Medicare coverage, and neither should a person below 65 if we have universal Medicare coverage. This guy simply does not understand the logic of a single-payer health care system.

Medicare already has an exchange. It's how enrollees get into Medicare Advantage plans. This exchange is not going away. In fact, there would be enormous pressure to let young people participate in that exchange or a similar one. Every problem, Obamacare is currently experiencing with the exchanges will remain.

Yeah, but the Medicare Advantage approach is flawed from the beginning and poses a private insurance giveaway. It is kind of ironic that what he identifies as a problem (private insurance) is precisely the kind of solution that he would have advocated. Freud's "disease of which it purports to be the cure" is driven on steroids, and I hope that critical readers will discern this logical and self-defeating inconsistency in the argument. In a single-payer program, you don't have to worry about exchanges, because the government is simply the only buyer of health care services, so there is no choice required from consumers. Should young people participate in the health plan? Yes, of course.

Ignoring artificial prices and focusing on real resources, the United States actually looks pretty good. We have fewer doctors per person than the OECD average and we have fewer doctor visits. We also enter the hospital less often than people in the average OECD country and once admitted, we spend fewer days there. And even though we are spending less time with doctors and less time in hospitals, our health outcome measures are as good as – or better – than those of other countries.

Well, the US is very good, when it comes to providing high-end care, such as cancer, and only for people with generous insurance or deep pockets, of which there are not many in the country. How useful is a health care system that leaves so many people uninsured and many more underinsured? If people are visiting the doctor less often, because they can't bear the out-of-pocket expenses, then this is fairly devastating for overall health outcomes. In the US, there are countless people who die because they lack any access to health insurance, and somehow these figures don't show up in his analysis.

Clearly, there are countless sycophants of health care executives like this particular writer, and the goal of the left should be to be educated about the real issues in this country, and counter the narrative based on faulty premises.

What the Baltimore Riots Reveal in the US: Commonality with Occupy Wall Street

Posted on May 1, 2015

The media is now filled with images of the destruction that black youth have created in the inner-city of Baltimore. President Obama condemned the heinous actions of the protesters, who are destroying private property. Some cynics might suggest that this protest action will seal the fate of the impoverished community that sorely lacks the jobs, and now businesses will be even more deterred to come. The inflow of professionals with the purchasing power to buy various services will also soon leave the city. What are these kids protesting about anyway?

The immediate cause of the riot, which was put down by the governor's use of the National Guard, and state troopers from other cities and states last Tuesday (April 28), was the police killing of Freddie Gray. He was apparently a healthy 25-year old African-American man, who was hand-cuffed by the police and then put on the backseat of the police van. He was not buckled in with a seat-belt, which violates proper procedure, and when the car got going, his body was banging against the walls of the car, leading to the a severe injury to his spinal cord and death. The local community became very upset when they got to know about it, and went on the street.

In today's world of instant communication and cell phone videos it is very easy to capture police brutality and mistreatment and disseminate it over social networks, such that an entire town can know about it and mobilize instantly. That strategy had worked back in September 2011, when Adbusters made a call to occupy Wall Street, and within a few days, Zuccotti Park in New York City and many other spaces in hundreds of US cities were filled with anti-Wall Street protesters. The brutal crushing of the Occupy Wall Street movement, which I think would have had the momentum to go on for a longer while, had the mayors not sent in the police to remove the encampments, marked the temporary end for political activism, but the violence and the police brutality directed specifically against low-income and black communities has sparked a new opportunity for mass mobilization, but this time under more violent premises and with somewhat different goals.

In OWS there was a multi-racial coalition with the goal to attack income inequality and the bank bailouts by the government, while millions of people were losing their jobs and homes, and worked for significantly lower wages, belying any claims of an economic recovery. Some people from the middle class were also fairly sympathetic, and even agreed to attend some of the OWS events. It was principally peaceful. The black protests and some instances riots mobilize especially low-income black people, and maybe some sympathizers of other races, and much of the crowd first marches first peacefully in front of the police departments to demand justice for Freddie Gray and whoever else gets killed by (mostly white) police brutality. Justice means both to hold the police officers, who committed the killing, accountable via suspension and trial, and more broadly to reform police-community relations by reducing the level of tension between the police and the community. The goals of OWS and Baltimore protesters were different, but I would argue that they are related. But more on that below.

Unfortunately, the peaceful protests devolved into a violent confrontation, as some of the black youth then decided to attack the police, destroy the police cars, and then at the end destroy businesses and buildings. What was going through the minds of these young people, who commit these riots? Of course, it would not be wise to condone these actions, but what these riots really reveal is the despair of these youth rather than their "innate tendency" for violence, which is a crude misinterpretation of their real motives.

The principal despair is that of poverty. Black youth face an elevated rate of unemployment, 25% nationwide, and 50% where Freddie Gray and other peers resided in. Baltimore is a thoroughly deindustrialized city, and the few retail stores are not sufficient to create enough jobs. Johns Hopkins University is the largest employer in town, but they require surgeons and professors, and not nearly that many janitors and food service workers. If there are neither sufficient educational or job opportunities, it should not be surprising why there would be so many people out on the streets rioting and stirring trouble. There is no sustained daily activity that could help these kids stay away from the streets, so it is not surprising that they should find the time and energy to express their discontent in a violent fashion.

What certainly does not help is that we have police practices, which are still reminiscent of Wild Wild West days. One irony of having so many gun lovers in the US and strong 2nd amendment protections are that it is fairly easy for private people to own guns and firearms. That in turn forces police departments to also be armed with firearms to ensure that officers can protect themselves, and the stronger the weapons and the poorer the neighborhood, the more likely these guns will have to be used at some point. In Europe, for example, police in some cases do not carry any guns, but that is also because there are strict laws for private gun ownership, which ensures that only very few private individuals own guns. We need a significant restriction of firearm dissemination if we want to minimize deadly encounters.

But any kind of police reform will not deal with the question what we are going to do with the many unemployed youth that are hanging around on street corners, deal with drugs and go on rampages. To the extent that economic issues undergirded both Occupy Wall Street as well as the Baltimore protests/ riots, we have to acknowledge that only attacking the enormous amount of wealth and income inequality and creating real job and educational opportunities for young people of all races can effectively ameliorate the racial and social tensions that exist in our communities. It is sad to say that there are many more Freddie Gray's in this country, many of which receive much less attention than him. In the Oligarchic States of America, we seem to have settled the question of what we are going to do with the surplus population of unemployed people by expanding the prison-police-industrial complex. I would find it much wiser for any future government to focus on the War on Poverty and War on Inequality instead.

Why Feminist Capitalism Will Not Save Us: Structural Reforms in Japan

Posted on May 3, 2015

I was watching a panel discussion by US economists, who were trying to give advice to the Japanese government to undertake structural reforms in order to increase economic growth in the chronically stagnant country. The essence of structural reform often is very diffuse, but they all have to do with weakening regulations surrounding the basic tenets of Japan's economic institutions. The economists want the Japanese government to loosen restrictions on agricultural imports in order to reduce food prices, which will apparently boost the purchasing power of Japanese consumers. They want the government to loosen immigration restrictions to allow the most capable and skilled workers to enter Japan, which will enhance the country's productivity. Thirdly, they want a loosening of restrictions on women's economic advancement to ensure that more women participate in the paid labor force and take on managerial positions. By having more women as workers and consumers, the country can increase economic output.

How much better off the Japanese would be if they followed this advice. How smart these economists are! How short-sighted these Japanese politicians are! But let us not think too fast here. It is true that the Japanese government is trying everything that it can in order to boost economic growth, because that is what it takes to reduce the enormous debt burden facing the state. We are reminded again of James O'Connor's (1973) argument about the fiscal crisis of the state: the state has the duty to maintain a high level of economic growth (accumulation) so they can raise sufficient revenues to retire old debts and keep their civil servants fed. In addition they have to make social expenditures in order to maintain domestic social peace (legitimation).

If raising economic output is the main goal of Japanese policymakers, it is difficult to dispute these policy recommendations except that taking single-minded steps to restore capital accumulation could itself trigger a legitimation crisis. Let's look at it carefully. By deregulating food imports, the price of food will decrease, so consumers will be happy. But farmers will be very unhappy, because they won't be able to compete with the food imports. The farmers are a very important constituency in Japan, and dislocating so many farmers at the same time will create a legitimation crisis, and will force the Japanese government to increase welfare spending on an already overstretched budget.

Immigration sounds like another great avenue for deregulation, but it should not be forgotten that Japan is still a very homogeneous society, and kept the social peace by keeping it homogeneous. The largest immigrant community in Japan is the Koreans, who have lived there for many generations. These Koreans in Japan can trace their ancestors to the early colonial days of Japanese in Korea. As far as I know, these Korean immigrants have still not received full citizenship rights and are still discriminated in employment. Given that there is some cultural proximity between Korea and Japan, one can only imagine what would happen if a large number of non-East Asian immigrants were to enter the country. It would create a crisis of legitimation, which no Japanese government has been willing to accept.

What about the women? Let us integrate them completely into the workforce! It should first be noted that women are the peripheral workers in the Japanese economy, i.e. the last hired and first fired, which is especially the case during economic downturns and periods of economic uncertainty. Japanese companies try to hold onto their core sector workers (or the internal labor market, according to Doeringer and Piore [1970]), mostly elderly men, and have to pass on the cost of downsizing onto the peripheral workers, mostly women and young people. Given that the problem in Japan is an overall lack of employment opportunities it is hard to conceive of bringing more women into the labor force. The hope of the economists seems to be that as these women enter the labor market and compete for male jobs, it will lower the reservation wage for all workers, and providing labor as cheap as possible will create the kind of full employment paradise that all mainstream economists have dreamed about.

But let us now assume that these concerns are not serious enough, and that we can integrate women into the workforce, they are a new source of labor power and a new set of consumers with purchasing power (think of beauty products, make-up, lip-gloss, skirts etc.), does that mean that we can achieve more gender equality? It is certainly conceivable that as women become more economically independent they will be more able to become financially independent of their husbands, and they will assert their rights much more forcefully than they currently do. But I think we are missing another major point here: the reason why women were pulled into the labor force to begin with is to ensure the capital accumulation process. To the extent that capital accumulation remains the goal in the economy, I very much doubt that gender equality can be the ultimate end goal.

One could even argue the opposite, that as more and more women enter the labor market the old patriarchal patterns of inequality can further become reinforced. Capitalism needs more workers, including women, but it cannot succeed if workers are all equal. The equality of workers cannot be achieved within the logic and the rule of the markets, but has to be actively brought about via class struggle and solidarity among all the workers. The most ideal condition to establish a framework favorable toward capital accumulation is if workers remain divided among each other: male vs. female, black vs. white, skilled vs. unskilled etc. Any form of division among workers has to be exploited by the capitalists. Differential wages for the same task to the benefit of men are only apparently stroking the male ego, but are really the entrenchment of capitalist interest. Factory owners in developing countries specifically favor women workers, because they are more obedient. Women are considered the primary caretakers in the family, and so they are less likely to go on strike, and accept the very low wages to ensure that their family's needs are met. The nurturing woman is the ideal victim of capitalist exploitation.

Where does that leave the struggle for women's rights? Women's rights still need to be struggled for, and it is clear that it is not sufficient for women to simply join the labor force, though I will concede that economically active women have a better fighting chance to reduce sexism and discrimination than if they stayed at home.

What we also need to understand with all certainty is that no matter what economic steps are taken in order to revive a sluggish economy, there is nothing that can fundamentally be done to permanently generate elevated rates of economic growth. Any "structural" reform, no matter how profound it is perceived to be, serves as another lease of life to capitalism. If Japanese policymakers are head-on willing to still embrace measures to reduce "structural" barriers to continued capital accumulation, they should at least be worried for a moment about whether their reforms will not create a legitimation crisis of epic proportions.

Why Yanis Varoufakis Is the Best Finance Minister in Europe

Posted on May 4, 2015

If we follow the ruling mantra of the Eurozone group, then Greece is a recalcitrant negotiating partner, which is not willing to make concessions to the other Eurozone countries. The Greek government led by finance minister, Yanis Varoufakis, is not interested in credibly committing itself to an austerity plan, which will ensure that the Greeks will finally repay their debt. Just make a few more cuts in pensions, wages and social services. Raise the level of competitiveness further, increase exports, reduce imports. Greece will see the light at the end of the tunnel. Jeroen Dijsselbloem, the chair of the Eurogroup finance ministers, thinks that Greece's debt to GDP will soon be lowered to 120%, and by bringing another reassuring deal, Greece's borrowing costs will come down after they spiked significantly when the left-wing Syriza party came to power. We are going to have light at the end of the tunnel, if only those damn Greeks make enough concessions with their creditors (90% of which are not private investors, but the "institutions", i.e. EU and IMF). The Greeks have made a heavy mistake in the voting booth, and would have been much better off if they kept the previous conservative government in office. They could have completed the task of continued "structural reform". Now that Varoufakis had been sidelined by his own prime minister, real reform will become possible.

This is a very comforting narrative, just as the stereotype of the lazy Greeks, who have gotten themselves into the fiscal crisis, and then reject any help from their Eurozone partners, who only have the best of all intentions for their Greek brethren. Except this narrative is all wrong.

It should first be noted that Yanis Varoufakis (2015) is probably the only finance minister, who understands what the real problem of Greece is: cutting wages and pensions in an already depressed economy will depress the economy further and reduce the ability of the country to repay the debt. How can someone repay a debt with a decreasing income? Second, further austerity undermines social support for any future government program, and without legitimacy it is impossible to rule in a democratic country. Greece has transformed its pre-2008 Ponzi-growth strategy (based on huge government loans financing current consumption rather than investments) to a post-2008 Ponzi-austerity strategy (based on debt repaying debt resulting in more debt, while social programs and wages are savagely cut) (Varoufakis 2012). It is not surprising, therefore, that Varoufakis has tried everything that he could to block the Eurozone partners from forcing the Greek government to adopt even more austerity measures.

Because Varoufakis knew that he was the "finance minister of a bankrupt country" (Gatzke and Schieritz 2015) he did not have many tools at his disposal to oppose the crazy austerity agenda. The creditors did not want to create a precedent of unilateral debt forgiveness for Greece, while the other countries (Spain, Portugal etc.) were savagely cutting their own public budgets. Ironically, Varoufakis has also indicated that they wanted to make the loan repayments in full. On the other hand, nobody (not even Varoufakis) wanted to contemplate a Grexit, whereby the Greeks would exit from the euro, devalue the currency and write off the euro-denominated debt (which will plunge the country into a potentially deeper crisis and significantly lowered standard of living).

With the other two options forestalled, the Greek government could only hope to buy more time. Buying more time means to receive more financial aid from the EU, but the EU only wants to hand over the cash after more austerity is inflicted on the Greek people, but the Greeks have voted into power an anti-austerity party. When Syriza capitulates in front of the creditors, then they will be removed from power as quickly as they were installed to it. In that situation, Varoufakis did the only thing that was feasible to him: reject any further demands from the Eurozone partners, and hope that they will fork over the financial aid anyway. For that reason the financial and right-wing European media denounced Varoufakis for pursuing brinkmanship (see Smith 2015) without admitting that the Eurozone partners themselves were pursuing a brinkmanship strategy.

Varoufakis is doing the best that a finance minister, who really cares about the well-being of his country, can do. Since he does not control the cash flow, he needs to hope that he can win the war of arguments. And he clearly has won the war of arguments, because the European partners can only hope to undermine the Athenian position with reference to their "bad negotiating style", their "lack of manners", their "unwillingness to compromise", and other kinds of formalistic defenses, which lack any substance. The European narrative is completely bankrupt, and cannot stand up to strict scrutiny, which makes it all the more important for the Eurozone partners to shoot down the innocent messenger, Yanis Varoufakis.

Now prime minister, Alexis Tsipras, has appointed his deputy Euclid Tsakalotos to head the negotiation team confronting the

Eurozone group. The bond markets have "rewarded" the Greek government with slightly lower bond yields, which demonstrates that the financial markets still wield significant power over European governments. But sidelining Varoufakis would be a very wrong move, because if Syriza cannot deliver on a better deal for their people (they tried by raising the minimum wage and reinstating state workers), there will be further political disruption. We need cool and reasonable voices like Yanis Varoufakis in order to change the European discourse around how to tackle the Eurozone crisis.

In my view, Greek debt has to be cancelled, such that the debt-to-GDP ratio falls below 70%, and they can have some breathing room to recover. They should also be assisted with a Marshall plan (good luck pushing the reparations claims against Germany for the Nazi invasion) to strengthen their investments, which should create jobs and boost their depressed economy. Other countries of the periphery will not be happy about this, and I expect the Spanish Podemos party to become even more influential than they are currently. Germany is fearful that leniency on Greece will open up the box of Pandora for other commitments for the bigger Eurozone partners. But these are the costs, which Germany has to help bear, because they have so shamelessly benefited from the Eurozone, and their hyper competitive economic system (i.e. paying their workers less than the productivity increase).

Europe is very far away from developing a fair and social system, but listening to sane voices like Varoufakis keeps the light at the end of the tunnel alive.

The Food-Medical Industrial Complex: What is Good for the Economy Is Not Good for Society

Posted on May 17, 2015

This morning I saw a doctor on television, one of the thousands in this country, who are trying to convince the American people that with a better diet, they would be less likely to suffer from common American ailments like obesity, heart attack, high-blood pressure, diabetes and cancer. These are really wonderful doctors! And, on the other hand, we have really evil food giants, like McDonalds or Kentucky Fried Chicken, who are selling us a lot of bad unhealthful foods. We need the good to fight the bad!

Another narrative is that fat, obese and sick people have no one to blame but themselves. Don't we live in a free country? Does not everyone have the free choice to eat the kinds of food they want to eat, and buy the foods they want to buy? This libertarian narrative is the single narrative that can most easily be dismissed. There are areas in the country where we have so-called "food deserts", particularly in low-income neighborhoods. The promise of non-processed, all-natural fresh food is absolutely great, but only if you have the extra money to pay for that or grow it yourself. The truth is that the mass-based food, containing a significant amount of high-fructose corn syrup, which is government subsidized, can always undercut the healthy food of organic farmers in terms of price.

But what about the first narrative? Do we have good doctors and evil giant food corporations (yes, they are evil: consider Monsanto, who force farmers in developed countries to continuously buy their seeds, bring them into unrepayable debt, and suicide)? The answer is no. Even the doctors as part of a very complicated health care system, which is the most inefficient and expensive system in the world, while leaving 35 million people without any health insurance at all- despite Obamacare- contribute to the health crisis in this country.

The disorder of having so much cheap, processed foods which brings all kinds of health problems to the public have to be compensated by significant outlay in health care. Because we do not have a single-payer health care system, we also have a highly inefficient health care system, where doctors are incentivized to earn more income when the patients get really sick. It is certainly not the case that the doctors have the worst intentions in mind for their patients, but in a system, where the rewards in health care go toward greater quantity rather than quality, I am not surprised that the doctor benefit is greater when the patients are sicker. And, of course, we also have the doctors, who write their books and publish their audiotapes, thinking they are doing a great public service, but cashing in particularly on middle-class consumers, who tend to be more health-conscious anyway (and failing to reach out to lower-income, obese people, who really need it). But doctors are not the main culprits, but the many powerful administrators in the hospital, insurance and pharma bureaucracy, who also have the incentive to maximize their revenues by treating sicker patients. Health care capitalism is an internal contradiction if we define health care to be a human right with the interests of ordinary patients at heart.

Patients themselves are encouraged to delay their medical treatment as long as possible, because the high-deductible and high co-payment health care plans deter particularly lower income people from seeking medical treatment. By not bringing lingering chronic health problems under medical attention, more severe diseases develop, which require more intense and more expensive treatments in the emergency room.

And, finally, we should not omit the irrational food production system in this country, where there are no restrictions to GMO and to adding high-fructose corn syrup. All of our breads taste much sweeter than in Europe. Chickens are larger than elsewhere, and the tomatoes barely have any natural taste to them. The government really subsidizes unhealthful food, because we have giant corporations like Pepsi, Coca Cola, McDonalds, Wendy's and others, who make sure that the politicians only pass policies which are friendly to their interests. In a capitalist society, there is a constant need to increase output, because that is the source of all profits. But producing more food to feed the growing population is apparently not enough. What they want to do is to increase the calories consumed *per person*. The epidemiological crisis derives from the profit logic of our capitalist economic system!

The only upside to this story is that creating and then treating many obese people is really good for the economy: agricultural companies can continue to make a giant profit, because they can receive the generous government subsidies, and sell large quantities of unhealthful (and addictive) foods to US and foreign consumers. (Though, there are not many jobs behind it, so not much trickle-down either: most of all new income since 2008 goes to the richest 1%.) The health care system can remain highly profitable, because in addition to the many old patients with chronic and severe illnesses, there is also a lot of health care demand from non-elderly obese populations. And the health care system, indeed, has many jobs ranging from the hospital janitors to clerks, nurses, doctors and administrators. What is good for the economy is not necessarily good for society.

So how can we disentangle this food-medical industrial complex, which works so nefariously in tandem with each other, making us physically (food) and financially (medical) poorer? The health care system should be changed by establishing a single-payer health care system. Many layers of the profit incentive should be removed out of the health care system. Physicians should join together in cooperatives, and provide low-cost medical care to more patients with the intent to maximize health and not profits. Then we can also spare ourselves the doctor TV commercials. The agricultural system should change incentives by having the government charge much higher taxes on unhealthful foods (processed, fast food, soda etc.) and use the revenues to subsidize healthful foods (organic, fruits, vegetables etc.). The agrarian lobby will kick and scream, and so will the private health insurance, hospital and pharma lobby, but people have to ask themselves whether the greater social good is more important than the private financial interest.

Transportation Chaos and Why Doing What Everybody Else Is Doing Is Stupid

Posted on May 18, 2015

These past two days, I should be doing what other 22 or 23-year old people should be doing, which is to celebrate their achievements in receiving a college diploma and attend the graduation ceremony. I find it quite odd to formally celebrate graduation, because it has a self-congratulatory aspect to it. The other problem was that it was very hot and humid during both days of the ceremonies that I had attended, and being huddled together with other fellow graduates, certainly did not make us feel any better. It was like classroom time all over again. This time it consisted of a physical rather than merely a mental torture (which is not to say that some classes were not enjoyable).

But what was even more aggravating was to be stuck in traffic at 7am on Monday morning, and once more (though less intense) on the way back from downtown Philadelphia to the northeast suburbs around 3pm in the afternoon. We had not anticipated that there would be a significant traffic jam at 7am, but one could guess that it would have to happen, because most workers were trickling in at 9am in the downtown office. They anticipated the long delays, and decided to "beat the crowd" by heading out at 7am, while realizing that if everyone takes off at 7am, they might get to work on time, but they will surely also be stuck in the traffic for an hour or more, when it really takes only 20 minutes during smooth traffic.

Beating the crowd is a really terrific idea, but it only makes sense if you actually know what the crowd thinks, and not simply assume that you can beat the crowd. (So take off at 6am, when other people take off at 7am.) As a socialist, I am naturally skeptical to rank-ordering and elbowing out other people, but in the reality of personal life, such as in transportation where personal space is often limited, and anyplace where we find scarcity, one has to think in terms of competition and conflict.

Cars are often presented as an ideal. Since the days of mass consumerism and advertisements, the American Dream has included the car as a necessary feature of American life. Thousands of jobs from mechanics, assembly-line workers, to salespeople are reliant on the car industry. We all need to buy cars to be independent, to be individuals, to do our own thing, to not be constrained. Cars have allowed the creation of suburbs, because people can toggle into the city for jobs, and come back to live in the suburbs, where they can have their own lawn, backyard and big house.

But how much independence and individuality is there really if it becomes a national culture, and everyone thinks this way? It is stifling conformity to own a car, and not owning it makes one not be part of that culture. Also there is not much independence if you are stuck in traffic jam with all the other suckers, believing that you are "free". (It is aggravating to be in a traffic jam: the Beijing people have a good understanding of it, after being stuck in a traffic jam for a whole week.)

So what's the solution? Public transportation. Yes, I am spoiled by Philadelphia's public transportation system. I really do enjoy reading my books on the 20 or 50 bus (40 minute ride) and the Market-Frankford Line subway (25 minute ride), while being ensured that it would take me one and a half hours to commute one way, and being at ease that a professional driver and operator operate the vehicle (rather than me having to concentrate during the stop-and-go rush hour traffic). In a big city, there really is no incentive to have a car, and it is quite burdensome to purchase, maintain and fuel the car, while finding parking in expensive and crowded areas. City traffic is a genuine nightmare, because the roads are so narrow, the red traffic light phases are long, the distance between traffic lights is short, the drivers are enormously reckless, and the cars are so many.

Public transportation is only part of the story. In order to make public transportation a service that is constantly used, urban planning has to ensure that cities grow more compact. The city has to become the key place to live. Most city-dwellers agree that most of the buildings they like to access can be reached by bike, bus, train or by foot, while driving a car in the city is a nightmare, as I just described. As long as we encourage the suburban lifestyle we cannot be surprised that cars will continue to remain the national fixture.

Why the US Carries a Part of the Blame for the Creation of ISIS

Posted on June 10, 2015

The people in the US are expected to have a very short memory. We are not supposed to remember that the US and their Western allies have started the Iraq War, which destabilized the country and created the conditions favorable to ISIS. Saddam Hussein was a brutal dictator, but at least there was a little bit of political stability under his regime. When the US imposed their vision of democracy on the Iraqis, the majority Shia faction took control over the government, allowed the Kurds to occupy their own territory in the north, and left the Sunnis with nothing. So they began sympathizing with ISIS.

We are not supposed to remember that it was only after Western weapons made their way to the Syrian opposition since 2011 to get rid of Iran-friendly Assad that ISIS was able to take control over substantial portions of the country. The West thought that it would be enough to supply the rebels in order to topple Assad. But four years into the conflict, Assad still holds onto power, even though the territories and the manpower support he gets is much smaller than it was at the beginning of the conflict. In the meantime, the rebel weapons fell into the hands of those Islamist extremists, who are making headlines by beheading, kidnapping, looting, occupying and conquering.

The US now triumphantly gets up and says that they have to continue to supply their allies, Kurdistan and the Iraqi government, because we cannot allow these Islamist terrorists from taking over Iraq and Syria. But the problem is that the Iraqi government is so corrupt that supplying them with financial aid and weapons will only make the situation worse, because the ISIS fighters use the weaponry that they have stolen from the demoralized and weak troops of the Iraqi army to then use these weapons against them. I doubt that the Saudis will want to crush ISIS, because they have their hands full in crushing the Houthi insurgency in Yemen, resulting in countless of innocent lives lost. The most reliable fighters are the Kurdish Peshmerga forces, who have stood their ground in Kobani in northern Syria, but they scarcely have sufficient manpower and equipment to defeat the 20,000 or so ISIS fighters.

There is absolutely no doubt that ISIS is a major destabilizing factor in the Middle East region, but it is certainly not true that they are the root cause of the regional turmoil but only the symptom. Confused US policy in the region has significantly contributed to the rise of ISIS. The US has no consistent policy of enemies. First, Saddam is our friend. Then he is our enemy. First, Assad is our enemy, so we have to supply the rebels with weapons. Then the rebels turn into our enemies and we have to defeat them.

Ironically, at this point, it does not even matter whether the US wants to prosecute another war or not. There is no easy way out. President Obama had celebrated his move to withdraw US troops from Iraq and put an end to a shameful chapter in US history. But by withdrawing the simmering ethnic rivalries and political tensions could explode, because the Iraqi central government does not effectively share powers with minority groups and cannot provide for internal security. Now Obama has committed to send in more military advisers and more US air support for the Iraqi fighters, but the advance of the Iraqi army is fledgling, while ISIS continues to capture more cities. If Obama decided to withdraw air support, which is a position that I would advocate, then the region can still destabilize further, because the Iraqi central government is too weak by itself to hold up against ISIS pressure.

In Syria, US strategists are facing a dilemma: they hate Assad and want to get rid of him, but they fear what will happen after he is gone. The hope that at some point a moderate Islamist or secular US ally will take the reins of power, like in Egypt, is very much unlikely. The Libyan chaos scenario sounds much more realistic as I see it. ISIS dominates a large part of the country, and the US will want to do everything to thwart their victory, though a full-scale military engagement is denied by the Obama administration, who does not want to continue a full combat quagmire of the previous administration.

The victors in this protracted conflict can never be the civilian population in any of these Middle Eastern countries involved, because they always have to pay the high price of the cost of war, the countless civilian and military casualties and the devastation of the physical infrastructure. The victors can only be the military-industrial complex, which will receive contracts and revenue streams from both sides of the conflict. The victors will also be the new rulers in Iraq and Syria, whoever they may be. ISIS? A new dictator? By having an enemy in front of them, the leaders can always push for ritual solidarity and complete loyalty of their followers regardless of the outcome. What can an authoritarian leader, whether he is religious or secular, demand more than the complete obedience of his followers?

It is so obvious that the Middle East conflict will have to continue until foreign powers cease their support for oppressive regimes; those oppressive regimes relent in their oppression of the population; uncorrupt authorities are intent to provide security and social services to the impoverished public; real economic and educational opportunities are created for the millions of young people, who desire to earn a good living in peace rather than go to the Jihad. Sounds too idealistic? Any good solution has to begin with good ideas.

Even Forbes Admits that the Oligarchic-Finance Capitalism Is a Serious Social Problem

Posted on June 21, 2015

Steve Denning (2014) from the billionaire mouthpiece, Forbes magazine, has written a fairly insightful article titled "The Surprising Truth About Where Jobs Come From". The direct answer to the question is that young and relatively recent businesses tend to create many jobs, while older businesses (usually big corporations) do not really create many jobs. But the key insight is also that the Federal Reserve and the government generally ensure that these big corporations and the top shareholders and executives steering them are the ones that gobble up virtually the entire gains of the economy, in addition to the lackluster investment in plants and jobs.

The Fed's role, in the most recent years, has been to pump significant liquidity into financial institutions and the large investors standing behind them, which are the large corporations. Small borrowers, businesses and working people, can only dream about receiving so much Fed cash at virtually zero interest rate. More perfidiously, what do these big corporations do with all the cash, and all the profits? They do share buybacks. They artificially increase the value of the firm, which will guarantee that more real value cash ends up in the pockets of those CEOs, whose sole incentive is to maximize shareholder value.

Shareholder value maximization has the expected consequence that investments in the real economy are neglected, which form the basis of job creation, demand and future investments. Out of a lack of investment, there will be a lack of demand and jobs, and the national income will continue to be transferred from the global working class to the global oligarchic class. If you are really upset about the lack of job creation especially in sectors of the economy that pay high wages, then we know that you need to blame the principle of shareholder value maximization, which is really the sanctification of greed for the global oligarchy.

We have been sold the idea that the financialization of the global economy would turn out to be beneficial for most people, because we would all be part of the ownership society, owning stocks, owning 401k pensions, owning houses. But that is all a hoax. I have been trying hard to think about what is exactly meant by 'financialization' of the economy. We can tell that when the big five banks have assets equivalent to 60% of the national GDP, there has been significant financialization, but that's not it.

Financialization boils down to two problem areas: (1) shareholder value maximization, whereby firms maximize profits and dividends for shareholders rather than expand investments in the productive sector, which are the essence of job creation and a higher standard of living (consider that GDP growth in the most financialized economies of the West have been lower than in, say, China, where finance- until most recently at least- had been relatively contained). One aspect of shareholder value maximization is the rise of private equity finance, whereby private equity companies use debt to buy up companies, fire some workers, make the remaining workers produce more at less pay, and then resell those companies at a profit. A tragedy for workers, a great outcome for the equity partners.

(2) A sharpening social divide between debtors and creditors, as the nominal and real debt continues to explode. Consider that debt has been expanding significantly over the last couple of decades. It is the debt, the contractual claim of future repayment of a loan, which is the nexus that makes up the modern financial system. The more debt there is outstanding, the greater the level of financialization, and the sharper the division between debtor and creditor. Homeowners had taken on too much housing debt until 2008. Students continue to take out too much student debt to complete their college education. The government needs to borrow more money from the private sector to pay off the debt, which the private banking sector has incurred, and to ensure that the private-sector can sell enough products. Growing debt is the essence of increasing inequality, leads to a growing financialization of the economy and risks future financial catastrophe beginning with widespread debt default.

Bernie Sanders' populist presidential campaign can continue to pick up so much popular support precisely because more and more people begin to realize that the entire economy is rigged in favor of the wealthiest people. How is it possible that most working people should work longer hours for lower wages despite all the gains of technology, which make workers more productive, and the nation more wealthy? It is a complete tragedy that in the wealthiest country in the history of the world, there are so many people who are needlessly living in poverty and scrambling for ways to buy their meal and find shelter.

It is becoming increasingly obvious that the current financial system and the onerous debt obligations favoring the global oligarchy at the expense of everybody else is becoming an increasing fetter to the successful development of a good society. This is a point that Marx had made 150 years ago. Marx recognized the contradiction between the productive relations and property relations in capitalist society. The productive relation is that of workers needing to band together in huge factories to create a desirable output that can potentially be enjoyed by all. But the problem is that private property does not allow that output to be enjoyed by all people, but allows it to be concentrated in the hands of a few capitalists.

By the same token the financial system has become the impediment to the full development of a good society, where all people can live in peace, prosperity and dignity. We are usually told about the essential role that finance plays in the capitalist economy, that we need to take the idle savings of those that have much money and little use and give them to those who can do a lot of useful things with that money. That is the basic role of finance, but the reality is that current finance has gone well beyond those initial limitations to actually prevent society from advancing. Why do we throw more money after banks and other financial institutions, when all they do is promote further share buyback options and not more job creation and productive investments? In addition, debt claims that have become so huge and onerous for the debtors (see Greece) do not allow countries and people to contemplate options for a better life and more opportunities. How is that useful finance?

Finance needs to be tamed and placed under democratic control. That would mean that we need more national and state-owned banks that provide credit to the productive economy, lend at moderately low interest rates, pay their executives modest salaries instead of huge compensation and stock options, and return the surplus/ profits to the state treasury to ensure other investments like education or health care. It can be done, but people need to at least rethink their approach to finance.

At the end, I want to concede that finance from time to time will run out of control in the framework of a capitalist economy, and that has to do with the nature of private property, which privileges the few creditors over the interests of their debtors. Secondly, I think that the move toward neoliberal financialization of the 1990s is connected with the realization that a well-balanced, Keynesian class compromise of the post WW II era is no longer sustainable.

Some academics make the argument that all we need to do is to tame finance and use it to benefit the development of the real economy (which I have also suggested in the last paragraph...). But what if the real economy is not subject to the kind of economic growth trajectory that we find necessary to keep the class compromise (between workers demanding regular pay rises and job security, and employers demanding stable profits) alive? If we cannot hold the economic growth trajectory of years passed, then social forces develop that will want to challenge the class compromise, which will lead to the class warfare, social polarization and financialization that we have been able to observe over the last few decades. A few years of additional growth may be purchased with more finance (see China since 2008), but such growth is unstable and unsustainable.

Financialization, consisting of shareholder value maximization and growing debt claims, are merely a tool to dismantle the previous class compromise, and (a bad way) to cope in an era of a low-growth environment. Our history suggests that huge economic growth is only obtainable by enormous technological innovations or by a global war, which destroys enough means of production and the physical infrastructure that rebuilding the country leads to huge growth in itself. The latter option is not really desirable and the first option is highly uncertain. Besides, untrammeled economic growth will exacerbate the climate change and global warming crisis, which threatens our existence as a species.

My complex rumination has to end with a simple statement: socialism or barbarism. In other words, if we want to continue to live in a habitable planet, enjoy a good standard of living, share wealth equitably, and remove ourselves from the growth (and finance) imperative, then we need to embrace a form of socialism.

Why Bernie Sanders' Family Values Agenda Is to the Right of European Conservatives

Posted on June 30, 2015

Not too long ago I wrote a post, describing Vermont senator Bernie Sanders, and Democratic presidential candidate, as a moderate center-left, social democratic politician compared with European standards. Today, I have to correct my view, and say that while this is mostly correct, he is to the right of some European conservatives as far as his "family values" agenda is concerned.

It should first be noted that Sanders views on family values is much more accurate than US conservatives, who have appropriated the term to mean a ban on abortions, access to contraceptives and gay marriage. But what does Sanders himself stand for? He argues that family values involve a set of economic and social policies, which improve the material status of working people and allow them to spend time with their families and get paid to do so. Sanders advocates for the US to end the disgrace of being the only industrialized country that does not guarantee paid family/ medical/ maternity and sick leave and mandatory paid vacation. It is, indeed, time to end this disgrace, which is only helpful in padding the bottom line of the companies that employ and exploit these workers.

But before somebody should claim that Sanders' agenda is radically leftist, we should step back for a minute and consider the details of Sanders' family value agenda (Sanders.senate.gov, "Sanders Announces Family Value Agenda", June 11, 2015), and then compare it with the family policies of other European countries.

Sanders on Maternity Leave: 12 weeks of paid leave for mothers to spend time with their children.

Canada, Croatia, Serbia, Denmark and UK: 52 weeks or a year. Sweden: 420 days

Sanders on paid sick leave: 7 days per year

Austria: 6 weeks at full pay, additional 4 weeks at 75% pay. France: 12 months in 3-year period. Germany: 6 weeks at full pay, and 78 weeks in 3-year period. Netherlands: 2 years at 70% pay

Sanders on paid vacation: 10 days or 2 weeks per year

Austria and Portugal: 35 days. Germany and Spain: 34 days. France: 31 days.

My selection of comparison countries was, indeed, very selective, and I picked the more generous countries, but I do want to show that

Sanders' proposals are not radical, but make him to the right of even conservatives in Europe. It is certainly not realistic for Sanders to demand a Scandinavian paradise in the United States, but it would certainly be wrong to suggest that his family values agenda is a fringe proposal in the context of industrialized countries.

Given that the US is a developing country when it comes to giving workers the most basic social amenities, we certainly need a family values agenda that prioritizes more social benefits to workers and their families. As far as I know, no other presidential contender has put forward such a comparably determined family values agenda, and for that Sanders should certainly be commended.

The Bailout Referendum in Greece Does Not Mean an End to Austerity

Posted on July 8, 2015

The Greek people have spoken, and they have quite unequivocally rejected the terms of the bailout offered by the EU partners. The EU wants to impose even harsher austerity measures than previously on the Greek people. But the Greeks were wise enough to reject further pleas for those failed policies. Many European policymakers have given the hint to the Greek government that a no vote on the referendum would be tantamount to leaving the eurozone and the EU altogether, which is a rumor as it was blackmailing.

It was firstly very wise of the beleaguered Greek government to call for a referendum, because the creditors' demands were too overwhelming and could not be accepted by a newly elected government that came to power on the promise to end austerity. By letting the Greek people have the referendum, the creditors were in the unfortunate position to have to accept a democratic decision, though some EU leaders like Sigmar Gabriel, the SPD German vice chancellor, have attacked this democratic decision as undermining the trust of the creditors.

A Social Democratic vice chancellor is saying that Democratic decisions cannot be taken seriously given the dire financial straits in which Greece finds itself in. How dare the voters speak out about serious economic issues of which they have little understanding? First, it is questionable whether someone can consider himself a Social Democrat if he so seriously questions the most basic method of democratic legitimation: the referendum. But second, Gabriel is wrong in suggesting that the electorate has no understanding of economic policies. In fact, they are living through it on a daily basis, which a German government minister living on over 14,000 euros a month cannot understand well. The Greeks are experiencing with their own senses that austerity, what Yanis Varoufakis, the exiting Greek finance minister, referred to as 'fiscal waterboarding', is a complete failure, and that if the EU creditors continue to demand more of it, they will (1) make Greek lives more miserable with more pension, wage and social benefit cuts and indefinite periods of high unemployment, and (2) reduce the likelihood of EU taxpayers, who generously bailed out the German and French banks, to ever get their bailout money back, because it is impossible to repay debt with a shrinking income.

The Germans evidently want to have their cake and eat it too. As Piketty correctly remarked, the Germans have never repaid their debt in full and had it forgiven after World War I and World War II, which contrasts to their current pressure on Greeks to pay up their debts. Second, the Germans have benefited from an export boom thanks to the weak euro currency from the standpoint of the Germans, and now do not want to pay the costs for loaning their southern neighbors all this money.

There is no doubt, therefore, that a reasonable way forward would involve significant debt restructuring. Prime minister Tsipras should use his opportunity- with the strong mandate of his no referendum- to push for debt restructuring with the EU partners, whereby half of the nominal value of the debt are cancelled, while the other half are stretched out into long-term and low-interest loans, say 2% interest at 50 years. For people who claim that these proposals are outlandish and radical, they should consult the fact that the Germans have benefited from a similar debt restructuring in 1953.

The not unjustifiable fear, however, is that the EU creditors will pass over the decision of the referendum, and prolong what the former finance minister Yanis Varoufakis referred to as "extend and pretend", i.e. the ineffectual policy of letting the Greeks suffer with more unreasonable austerity, while they get more EU bailouts. One could consider these bailouts as a blackmailing strategy to further the stranglehold on the weak economy of Greece.

In none of the discussions were the creditors ever made responsible for exacerbating the debt crisis. As George Monbiot (2015) recently pointed out, Greece is merely the latest victim of the IMF strategy to "dismantle public spending, destroying health, education and all the means by which the wretched of the earth might improve their lives". John Perkins (2014), a former economic hitman, has quite plainly revealed the strategy of the global oligarchy:

Essentially, my job was to identify countries that had resources that our corporations want, and that could be things like oil – or it could be markets – it could be transportation systems. There're so many different things. Once we identified these countries, we arranged huge loans to them, but the money would never actually go to the countries; instead it would go to our own corporations to build infrastructure projects in those countries, things like power plants and highways that benefited a few wealthy people as well as our own corporations, but not the majority of people who couldn't afford to buy into these things, and yet they were left holding a huge debt, very much like what Greece has today, a phenomenal debt.

And once [they were] bound by that debt, we would go back, usually in the form of the IMF – and in the case of Greece today, it's the IMF and the EU [European Union] – and make tremendous demands on the country: increase taxes, cut back on spending, sell public sector utilities to private companies, things like power companies and water systems, transportation systems, privatize those, and basically become a slave to us, to the corporations, to the IMF, in your case to the EU, and basically, organizations like the World Bank, the IMF, the EU, are tools of the big corporations, what I call the "corporatocracy."

There is absolutely no democratic accountability for the IMF, nor is there for the EU, which has become a cruel neoliberal "straightjacket" as Wolfgang Streeck (2014) states. The unfortunate thing for Greece is that their vocal finance minister, Yanis Varoufakis, who irked all of the other EU finance ministers for his refusal to follow the self-defeating austerity and "structural reform" mantra of his European colleagues, stepped back from office. After six months of intense scrutiny and pressure against him, he was certainly all too relieved when his boss, premier Tsipras, wanted that he resign. Varoufakis is a natural academic, not a politician. He brings to the table clear ideas about how to overcome the Greek impasse, but he certainly lacked the power and the money to realize any of his goals (like having the debt restructured in the form of growth-linked bonds, or getting infrastructure investment bonds issued by the ECB). If Varoufakis is no longer at the table, while his successor, Euclid Tsakalotos, be equally as insistent? If not, it would be a big blow for the Greeks.

Some people claim that the Greek government has to relent so the ECB and EU will stop the blackmailing and send the needed cash to Greek banks, which will allow it to open up and normalize business relations in Greece. But this logic is flawed, because the Greeks, by resisting austerity, are defending themselves against further inhumane cruelty. Yes, it looks like heads, they lose, tails, they lose again. But if their negotiating person remains hard, then it is the EU partners that will be forced to relent.

The Greek tragedy is complete: those who have the vision lack the power, and those who have the power lack the vision. The banks and the oligarchs standing behind them can continue to celebrate their spectacular investment success, while the population continues to be tormented by senseless austerity measures. But as more and more people wake up to the lies of the EU creditors, and realize that they could be the next Greece, there is going to be continuing electoral upheaval favoring the forces challenging the status quo. If leftist governments have the opportunity to take power in more countries than one, then the days of undivided corporate and oligarchic rule could be over. However, without significant mass mobilization, such a democratic outcome remains unfeasible.

Why Donald Trump is a Hot Celebrity and Leads the Republican Polls

Posted on <u>July 29, 2015</u>

Donald Trump, the real estate mogul and multibillionaire (estimate of 10 billion dollar net worth), had announced his presidency only a few weeks ago and has immediately catapulted himself to become one of the most popular candidates in the Republican Party. Trump has made many antagonizing comments to Mexican immigrants, who were allegedly bringing the crime and drug problem over the border, and so he would be the president that will keep Americans safe and secure by sealing the borders. It is now easy for the liberals and those on the left in this country to, therefore, denounce not only Trump, but the entire Republican Party for being a party of clowns that cannot be taken seriously by the vast majority of the American people.

But I would argue that we can probably not maintain such a dismissive attitude against Trump. Of course, Trump's immigration position is outrageous, and so is his proposition to massively lower taxes on everybody (especially on the rich, with a 15% marginal income tax, lower capital gains taxes, and abolition of corporate, inheritance tax, Phillips 2015), thereby reducing government spending and the associated social programs into rubles, though he apparently also supports the maintenance of Medicare and Social Security (Kirell 2015), which will endear him to old people. His economic and fiscal policies do not add up arithmetically, and something will have to give.

On the other hand, Trump speaks to the need of the Republican base for somebody to talk about the genuinely bubbling resentment that is building up against the political structure. If we want to claim that Trump is just another clown, then we have to say that this clown cannot be much worse than the host of Republican governors and senators that are running for the presidency, all of them yelling louder in their quest to earn the trust of their billionaire donors. Trump will have the strange advantage of not having to worry about raising money from his fellow plutocrats, and so he can have the greater freedom to express ideas that the poll-tested other candidates would not dare to formulate.

I do not endorse Donald Trump's quest for presidency in any sense, but want to emphasize that his bid is the expression of right-wing populism in the American political system, while his left-wing antidote is Bernie Sanders. The political system in most western democracies is bound to become more extreme as time passes. This polarization has nothing to do with formal political phenomena (like gerrymandering, because here it is about the presidency, not congressional districts; or even Citizens United, which is just an icing on the cake). Polarization is the direct result of growing wealth and income inequality, where millionaires and billionaires rig the entire political process, thus forcing a political gridlock favoring specialized lobby interests of the already wealthy, while stymieing and obstructing general interest causes like education, health care or infrastructure programs. It is precisely those general interest causes, which ordinary working and middle class people care about the most. So they feel disenfranchisement in the political system, as our politician-prostitutes are focused on milking more cash from their billionaire donor-johns, in order to hand them even more taxpayer-funded bailouts, subsidies, grants and tax breaks in return. The only people, who can fight back are independent billionaires (Trump), and lone-wolf democratic socialists outside the original two-party system (Sanders- though he now runs as a Democrat).

As far as the right-wing populists are concerned, they never offer real and viable solutions to their followers. In Trump's case, he is, of course, pushing the agenda of his own class, but wants to distract the masses with outrageous statements against illegal immigrants, who lack the political rights to defend themselves, and punish him electorally. The divide-and-conquer strategy of Trump's "silent majority" (borrowed from Nixon's presidential campaign) is meant to energize a right-wing political base that will secure him the votes to potentially win the bid for presidency, and then use that victory to carry out a really regressive right-wing agenda.

At this point, Trump's chances of electoral victory are understandably limited, but in a crazily oligarchic country such as ours, I question why we should continue to accept the mainstream narrative that so-called "fringe" candidates are not worthy of our attention because they can't win the general elections. A retired Congressman told me that the 2016 lineup would be Clinton vs. Bush, the same last names that appeared in a presidential contest in 1992. But why? Both candidates represent the worst kind of establishment politics, which fundamentally accept the premise of the Oligarchic States of America, and would, at most, tinker at the margins and cross both fingers that the whole political system does not blow up (which it has to sooner or later).

I would be eager to see a Sanders-Trump lineup, so that the American people have the choice between real alternatives. One candidate will demonize immigrants and exploit social divisions for political capital, while the other candidate will put forward a credible plan to restore the middle class and challenge the oligarchy. (It is very evident that I am a staunch supporter of Bernie Sanders' campaign.) No other lineup would so clearly show how radicalized the US political process has become, but only because our economic and social relations have become so radicalized. Every socio-economic tension will affect the body politic eventually. My hope is that the symptoms of the disease will hit heavy enough to trigger an appropriate political response before every cure comes too late.

Response to Critics of Socialism

Posted on August 4, 2015

In the following blog post, I respond directly to a comment, which was written in response to my post on democratic socialism (Liu 2012):

I would think the main reason self-proclaimed liberals don't go as far as they dream, is because they deep down know it doesn't work. Take the very first settlers of our country. They did try the socialist/commune idea of everyone gets an equal share, shares the rewards and labor of everyone else. At first it did work. But just as then as it is today, you forget the human element of "why do the work when someone else can do it for me?" Soon, groups of people didn't do as much, or any at all work as the others yet still got the same benefits. Only after people were given their own parcels of land to reap what the sowed, did the colony flourish. The same can be seen today. The less regulations and red tape a business, individual, or group of people have, the more productive they are.

Unions for example were there for a need in a certain time and place. But they are not needed anymore today. Do you really think if certain regulations, the minimum wage taken away for example, that people would be forced to work for $!/hr again? I don't think so. In this age of information and the power of the media bias, no company would ever dare to do such a thing again. Plus, if you don't want the job, don't work there. If anything, it would just be funny to watch these types of businesses pretty much commit suicide.

Is capitalism bad in some ways? Of course. When in anything the human element is injected to the equation, things like self-satisfaction and greed to come to be, but not rampantly. Compared to the other alternatives, it is the best option we have. As long as you have people with a sense of entitlement, resentment, and demand for equality by robbing others that are willing to put the work forth, you are never going to achieve the utopia of socialism that is desired. Jealousy: the mane fuel for leftist ideals.

In the first paragraph, the commentator states that only when people own the land or the means of production that they will begin to work hard and produce wealth. It is certainly true that the Soviet Union and the other forms of really existing socialism, where the government owned all of the means of production, were less than ideal circumstances to develop the enthusiasm of the workers to contribute to the wealth of the society. But it is equally wrong to presume that our current capitalist society allows ordinary workers to own the means of production. They are owned by holders of private property- the very wealthy- who constantly have to look for ways to force other people- working people- to contribute their labor, maximize productivity and reap as much private profits as possible.

The capitalist utopia is always predicated on the assumption that everyone, whether a worker or a capitalist, have the same degree of freedom. The capitalist has the freedom to make investments and dispose of his machinery and labor as he sees fit, while the workers have the choice to find the kind of employment that fits their needs and interests. But behind this apparent freedom lurks a great power imbalance between the workers and the capitalists. Adam Smith correctly pointed out that while workers barely have enough savings to subsist even for a week, many capitalists have enough wealth to survive for more than a year. In a capitalist system, alienation of the workers is a design of the system, and is no greater than under state-dominated, authoritarian socialism. If we want to create a better society, we need to acknowledge the weaknesses and problems with both and discuss better solutions.

The mantra of "less regulation and red tape" becomes then not a means to achieve greater freedom for everybody, but merely greater freedom for the capitalist class to advance the exploitation of the working people. Regulation and red tape, as expressed in environmental and labor regulation as well as social welfare benefits for the public, are designed to protect workers from the worst kinds of abuses from their employers, who want to hold the reservation wage (the wage at which workers begin to sell their labor services) as low as possible, such that workers are desperate enough to look for low-income jobs.

This description is a good segway into the point that the commentator made in the second paragraph, where he is skeptical that workers can be living in dire poverty if regulations like the minimum wage are lifted. I would like to share the optimism of the commentator, but I think that he/she fundamentally underestimates the power of the capitalist to lower workers' reservation wages. Why is that? Let us think about it this way: there are about 4.7% of workers who earned the minimum wage of $7.25 or less per hour (Bureau of Labor Statistics) in 2012. This sounds like a small percentage, and the percentages naturally increase as we go up the income ladder. The median hourly wage is $17.09 as of May 2014 (Bureau of Labor Statistics).

But what is revealing here is that there are quite a substantial number of people, who are not really far away from the minimum wage, and if we took that minimum wage away, employers would exploit the situation by reducing their base wages, which could have a ripple effect on higher paid employees, whose employers now know that they will not have to fear losing workers to other industries, when the base level wages are substantially lowered.

The capitalists and the right-wing media try to convince the public that we all can only be paid as much as we are worth, but the reality is that workers can, and in many cases, are paid less than they are worth, otherwise we should not really have anybody who earns at, below or slightly above the minimum wage.

The commentator's remark that the worker has the freedom to not work with an exploitative employer is emblematic of the false sense of freedom that he ascribes to the workers. My question hereby is, if workers had so much freedom to choose another job, then why is this not happening? Workers don't have all the available information, and the job search is made complicated not only by the fact that workers are not educated enough to search for it, but by the lack of availability of good jobs. The evidence are the many very well educated people, who are still unable to find good jobs.

To make my point even clearer, we should now imagine an economy, where most jobs are paying very highly, where there is a significant labor shortage. In such an economy, it is then easier for people to reject current job offers, and take on another job, where they can earn more income. The fact that this does not happen is a reflection of the inner workings of a capitalist economy, which relies on a continuous labor surplus to function.

Under communism, there was a permanent shortage of goods, because the administrators set the prices below marginal cost, which made the production of goods uneconomic. But at the same time, the economy suffered from a constant labor shortage as well, because plan targets kept on increasing, while the level of technology remained obsolete because of low levels of innovation. So hire as many workers as possible to fulfill the plan target. On the other hand, capitalism is an economy of surpluses, which is good for consumers, who can often find ten different types of chips and twenty different types of cereals on the supermarket shelves, but it is potentially bad for workers too, because the phases of greatest capital accumulation and profit are those where wages are low, unions are weak, and unemployment is high (all three correlated, of course).

Paying attention to the aggregate employment picture requires quite some leap of thinking, and is not as straightforward as the belief that everyone is free to make his/her choices of investments or job search, but for workers, who know that they tend to be on the weaker side of the bargaining table, it is absolutely essential to grasp the aggregate employment situation.

The commentator's final point is that communism is all about stealing money from the real producers, but we know that is precisely the essence of capitalism, not communism. The essence of capitalism is the generation of surplus value from the workforce, and paying off the capitalist class, which puts some of the money in their own pocket, and the rest is reinvested to create more profits in the next cycle. To the extent, that the commentator does not want one person to exploit the next person, I absolutely agree with his/her sentiment, and would welcome a struggle for a non-exploitative world, where workers can produce what they need to produce, and then find ways to share the fruits of their labor.

Do I believe in perfect equality? Yes, in the ideal world, but I will concede on one point, where I appreciate the reality of human psychology. Of course, if all workers are paid the same amount of money, then all workers want to crowd in the least strenuous and socially useless jobs, while nobody will do the strenuous and socially useful jobs. So, we would have many janitors (easy) and few doctors (difficult). That would be a social disaster. What would we do with all the sick people?

I, therefore, do not advocate for the equal payment of wages for all people, but agree that we need to increase incentives for more difficult jobs that require extensive training and expertise. But the regulation of payment for different workers is different compared to the regulation of payment for investors, landlords and capitalists, who gobble up the society's wealth via rents. The commentator confuses the (unearned) rents with (earned) wages, and by fatally lumping both together, he/she can claim that perfect equality must be bad, so we should allow inequality in both the spheres of wages and rents, while moderate socialists might agree with inequality in the former, but certainly not in the latter.

Why We Should Avoid a War with Iran

Posted on August 10, 2015

The Republicans have just finished their first debate, and all of the presidential candidates are trying to beat each other with respect to who is most convincing in tearing apart president Obama's nuclear deal with Iran. Scott Walker, Wisconsin governor, would terminate the Iran deal on day one of his presidency, and he would push Congress to impose "even more crippling sanctions" on Iran. Senator Ted Cruz from Texas says that he would "cancel the Iran deal". Senator Rand Paul from Kentucky rejected the deal, though he favors negotiations from a "position of strength" (whatever that means). Trump claimed that "What's happened [with] Iran is a disgrace." (Quoted from Wong 2015)

The right-wing punditry, AIPAC, the right-wing Jewish lobby and the defense contractors were jumping up in celebration in response to these announcements. For right-wing, Israeli prime minister, Benjamin Netanyahu, the Iran agreement was a "historic mistake for the world". Netanyahu and his other right-wing allies believe that if the West made significant concessions to Tehran, it would allow them to build nuclear weapons within a few weeks (Mitnick 2015).

But what does it mean to leave the negotiating table, and applying more sanctions on Iran? Of course, it means war. Before one can argue that it would be a good idea to increase pressure against Iran, it is relevant to lay out the details of the agreement: the nuclear agreement with Iran would curb Iran's nuclear program, whereby it has to give up most of its centrifuges, convert a weapons facility into a research facility. The agreement obliges Iran to let foreign inspectors into the country at any moment. In return, Iran will continue to be allowed to enrich uranium, which it will use for peaceful, civilian purposes. The economic sanctions against the country are also lifted, which allows foreign corporations to sell their wares in Iran again (Peralta 2015).

This is precisely what companies like Mercedes-Benz, Total and Hewlett Packard have done. Iran provides a significant market for foreign corporations. It has an educated population, containing 81 million people, and has high demand for Western products. Iran has the second highest natural gas and fourth highest oil reserves in the world. There is a lot of potential to tap into the energy, mining and manufacturing sector, which have not been fully developed yet

(Dorell 2015). From an economic viewpoint, there is no reason to continue sanctions, and business leaders are right in applying pressures against their governments to repeal the sanctions as quickly as possible.

Back to the deal: is the outcome really so bad for the West, and especially for Israel? Will Israel be nuked because the Iran agreement went into effect? No and no. One might argue to the contrary that it is when the US provokes a war with Iran over imaginary nuclear weapons, it will lead to a further destabilization of the Middle East, which will also result in a destabilization of Israel's security outlook (remember the Scud rockets fired by Iraq's Saddam Hussein against Israel during the Second Gulf War?).

There is an unholy alliance between right-wing factions in the US and in Israel that want to start a war against Iran, and have absolutely no interest in re-establishing economic relations with Iran. President Obama now has to send the agreement through Congress, but he will likely apply a veto against Congress rejection of the deal. Obama does not mind to take any further political heat, because he is approaching the last year of his presidency. Facing the ire of the right-wing lobby, he didn't push strongly for the agreement early on in his administration. The Iranian hardliner regime of Ahmadinejad, which was not deposed until 2013, also made an agreement quite complicated.

Now is the opportunity to complete an agreement with Iran, and put the discord behind us. The US is certainly not doing it for purely altruistic reasons, though it helps that we don't have neocons running the administration. The US has massively lost the political capital, that George W. Bush thought that we could spend. The Iraq and Afghanistan wars have economically and politically bankrupted the country, and the conquest and expansion of ISIS on formerly US-controlled areas of Iraq serve as painful reminders of the misguided and criminal foreign policy initiated under the Bush administration.

The rise of ISIS shifted the power balance in favor of Iran, which is the Shi'a bulwark against the toppling of the thoroughly corrupt and ineffective (yet pro-US) regime in Baghdad. The Ukraine feud with Russia has triggered realignment in international relations, whereby the Russians forge closer links with Beijing and Tehran, which by definition weakens the hand of the US. The US has also involved itself in the regional "rebalancing" effort or "pivot to Asia", which is a sophisticated way of stating that military resources should be concentrated in Asia to contain the growing Chinese military strength (and foolishly risk provocation and war). It would be too much asked to focus again all economic and military resources in the Middle East region, which had received enough US-induced turmoil.

Finally, despite all claims to the contrary, I think that unrivaled US economic power in the form of the dollar as a reserve currency is waning. Yes, every crisis in Europe or elsewhere results in another run on the dollar, which drives up the dollar value, and cheapens the cost of importing foreign goods into the US without ever having to repay the full value of the US debt claims owed to foreigners. But the global Minotaur (Varoufakis 2011) is weakening, and can no longer pull up the global economy to the same extent as was possible before.

On a more humiliating note, among all the powerful US allies, only Japan had so far refused to sign up to the China-led development bank, while Britain, France and Germany, along with Russia, India, Brazil and South Africa have no problem in signing up as founding members of the development bank, as all of these countries realize where the international winds of commerce are blowing. The US and Japan ridiculously hold out against joining the bank for "lack of transparency" (Obe and Taylor 2015). Washington is really displeased about the challenge to the World Bank led-regime.

Declining empires can either allow their air to deflate, pull out of all forms of international conflicts, invite other actors to participate in the world police game, and hope that the transition to a more genuine multilateral system happens without much strife and conflict, or they can double down with promoting war, exacting more tribute from others, and thereby gaining temporary advantages against others, though at great cost to all of us. It should surprise nobody that the neocons believe in the latter strategy.

I do not predict that the dollar will be toppled as a reserve currency in the immediate future, but I do think that Obama's relatively soft approach in the final years of his presidency is linked with a weakening global minotaur, and the realization that driving more military conflicts across the world cannot address the real economic and social challenges that plague the world today. The successful completion of a nuclear agreement with Iran paves the way forward for future US foreign policy actions (as did the normalization of relations with Cuba).

Is Money Equivalent to Free Speech?
Posted on <u>August 10, 2015</u>

I am representing a Facebook debate on the Citizens United Supreme Court case (2010) which ruled that money is equivalent to freedom of speech, allowing any person or entity to donate as much money as they want toward political campaigns. The quote is the statement of my fellow debater, and the response below is mine.

If money should be kept out of elections, because it "distorts democracy" shouldn't speech be kept out of election as well? The volume of one's voice in the public sphere can distort public understanding and participation in elections; just like money... it seems rather arbitrary/naïve to think critically of one and not the other. And aren't there other factors that distort democracy, including education background, other currencies of social interaction, and now social media power? The ability to protest/commit civil disobedience/create public outcry is also disproportionately allocated, right? Single parents can't afford necessarily to spend all day protesting in favor of Bernie sanders, but 20 something college students can? Many social currencies, including money, are disproportionately allocated.

I don't think this objection is valid here. Your argument is that just like free donation rights create inequality (rich vs. poor), so does free speech (good vs. bad orators, or smart vs. dumb or something like that), and if we oppose some kind of inequality we need to oppose all kinds of inequality to be consistent with our values. But the difference is that under the latter condition, democracy is difficult to realize, while it is impossible under the latter. Of course, we can now revert to the question whether democracy is desirable or feasible, but I don't want to venture that far, and presume that most people agree at least that it is desirable.

Our risk with freedom of speech is that some people will speak out because they are educated, have the leisure and are good speakers or writers, while others will not, but we can still maintain democratic principles, because we have enough of a critical mass to make sure that elected representatives are held accountable. Let us imagine the alternative system, where freedom of speech is restricted. Have we served the interests of equality and democracy better? I doubt it, because the rulers will exploit the situation and impose authoritarian policies that no sane person on the street will want to endorse. In the case of freedom of donation, we know that it will be inimical to democracy, because most democracies have capitalist economies where the rewards are stacked in favor of the owning class, and they will have the greatest amount of political influence. Here we cannot have these educated, leisurely and oratory skills of a few wise people intervene and hold their leaders accountable, because now it is the moneyed interests who speak while everyone else is silent.

I conclude by admitting a weakness in my argument: people who don't believe in democracy will dismiss my argument, and if they actually believe in oligarchy, then they should come out and say that that is what they believe in and not disguise their political beliefs behind a cloak of "freedom of speech=freedom of donation".

I think your response does not get at my point, at all. My argument was not that there was a disparity in speech equality like there is a lack of economic equality (though that's true). My argument was just as those with more money can spread a message farther, so can those with a louder voice. My argument is that there isn't a free market place of ideas with traditional speech, as some voices so largely over power the smaller ones that we don't even get a critical mass. At that point, distinguishing between spreading a particular political message through investing a lot of money or socially investing in one very powerful speaker seems silly. Especially since those actions are rarely so separate. If I can spend money on a particular message or convince Fox News to disseminate it, is there a really a difference in those two processes. In the first, I needed to find someone to take my money, in the second, I needed to sway one person/organization. Neither process rings particularly democratic to me

The question that your point raises is whether or not we should permit freedom of speech as well as freedom of donation, and treat them as having the same principle of the strong dominating over the weak, which we apparently agree is undemocratic and undesirable. Your argument seems to be that if freedom of donation is bad, then freedom of speech is bad too, and we should prohibit both or allow both, but I don't see why any of these two choices are desirable. Under freedom of donation, democracy is defeated, period. Under freedom of speech, democracy is not perfectly attainable, but it is more attainable than if there were no freedom of speech. So yes to speech, no to donation.

I think you misrepresent how donations are used. Donations to campaigns are used to further speech, gain voters, etc... they're not "donating to the government" So at that point, freedom of donation allows for the same person to donate money, to maximize speech...giving money to campaigns ultimately is used as speech, sending a message, etc. so at that point money and speech might become the same thing

Let us go back to the premise of democracy. We can only equate money and speech and democracy if the distribution of wealth and income is roughly the same, but it is not. If only freedom of speech is in effect, then I would stand next to the Koch brothers and do a shouting match with them, and hopefully the sane opinion will prevail. However, if you add freedom of donation to that, then I can scream like a monster, and the Koch brothers and their friends will win regardless. Therefore, to argue that donation is an extension of speech is extremely undermining to democratic principles, and the only honest argument that I think people can make in this regard (i.e. money=speech) is if they actually believe in oligarchy, which I and many other non-billionaires in this country do not believe in.

Why It Can be Frustrating to be on the Left

Posted on <u>August 11, 2015</u>

A group of black women stormed the stage, where Sen. Bernie Sanders, Democratic presidential contender, was supposed to give a speech defending Medicare and Social Security against cutbacks. They grabbed the microphone, and claimed to represent the Black Lives Matter movement, which had been gaining traction since the murder of Michael Brown (gunned down by police), and the ensuing race riots in Ferguson, Missouri. It was possible to attack Sanders' speech, because most other presidential contenders had much tighter security precautions, such that it would be harder to disrupt their speeches and embarrass them. The protesters believed that by interrupting the speech of a presidential contender, they would be able to receive significant publicity for their cause and speak truth to power.

Yes, Sanders is a sitting US senator, the more powerful body of Congress. Yes, he is running for the Democratic presidential primaries and is second in the polls behind Hillary Clinton. Yes, he needs to listen more to the needs and interests of black people that make up only a very small constituency in his home state of Vermont, where 94% of the electorate is white.

But that is about it. Sanders is the best ally that the black community can have. He has marched with the civil rights movement, opposed housing and school segregation in the 1960s, was arrested for that action, and endorsed every piece of legislation advancing civil and voting rights for African Americans. But that is not what went through the minds of the two women, who interrupted his campaign rally. That was also not in the minds of my very left-wing friends in various social media groups, who are venting their anger against the political system, such that they become cynical even of Bernie Sanders presidential run. Their reasoning is that because he is running within the mainstream party, the Democratic Party, which had sold out the American worker for the very longest time, that Sanders himself must also be a sell-out to the big corporations, despite all his flowery speeches in favor of the little guy.

But the reality is that Sanders has consistently advocated the same political positions, going back as far as the 1960s when he was arrested for his protest against housing segregation, and the 1970s, when he was a political gadfly in his home state of Vermont where he ran for governor and senator multiple times. Even back then, he was attacking the growing gap between the rich and the poor, the military-industrial complex and advocated other kinds of left-wing issues. So who is helped by undermining Sanders' campaign if not the right-wingers, who are always united in their pernicious cause?

I had long ago pointed out (Liu 2013) that it is frustrating to be on the left even though it remains an inherent necessity. The left has the moral and philosophical strength to be advocating the cause of democracy, justice and equality, but when it comes to political action, they tend to stymie each other, because they can never agree with each other. Whereas right-wing reactionaries have been indoctrinated in the inherent goodness of a hierarchical society, left-wingers reject any kind of authority, and the same critical reasoning which they have applied against the injustice of our current economic and political system, are also used to attack other left-wing groups and opinions. Some members in the left set purity standards that are so high that only the proverbial savior (God?), who will let milk and honey flow across the whole world, can convince them of good leadership.

I have run into socialist groups, who either don't know much about other left-wing groups, or have suspicions about their intentions. The lack of coalition building is excellent for the ego of those individuals involved, but it is devastating for the prospect of generating genuine social change that benefit the masses. Thinking about problems and criticizing political leaders is the strength of left intellectuals, but creating and supporting an organization which is bringing about real change is a much more difficult task. But if we are interested in abolishing poverty, reducing inequality, fighting climate change and supporting democracy, we have no other choice but to get into the struggle, support the best candidate, hold him/her accountable and make the best of the situation.

Should We Support a Universal Basic Income?
Posted on <u>August 27, 2015</u>

If there is a policy that would violate the political sensibilities of the status quo, it is the proposal for a universal basic income (henceforth UBI), which is a guaranteed amount of income paid to every citizen of a country regardless of his/her other sources of income. People on the intellectual left have long ago begun to propose this policy idea (Andre Gorz (1999) being the one most foremost in my memory, and Guy Standing (n.d.) more recently). But in more recent years, it is less and less likely even for more moderate and mainstream thinkers to ignore UBI as an important policy to reduce poverty and create a stable livelihood for the vast majority of lower class and working class people.

The reason why we can no longer avoid a discussion of UBI is quite plainly because the Biblical model of "you work or you should starve" is becoming increasingly anachronistic given the current conditions of technological development and the labor market. Plainly speaking, technologies are destroying jobs at a rampant pace. And jobs are the major way to survive in our contemporary economy. How can people survive if there are not enough jobs?

In a poor society it made absolutely a lot of sense for most people to work on the field, and the reason why most families had so many children was not only because infant mortality was so high, but also because every child meant another labor hand on the field. The more workers you had on the field, the more food you could produce, and the more stable your economic livelihood was (the family being better fed and capable to sell the surplus on the farmers' market).

Even before farming, hunting and gathering, the natural activity of all our ancestors, was also a very labor-intensive activity requiring the labor input of all tribal members. As societies gradually became more complex thanks to technology and the production of grain surpluses that could also be stored, a whole layer of government bureaucrats, kings, tribal leaders, military officers and priests were created to run this more complex society. For the first time in human history, it was possible to have a small group of people, who were not primarily responsible for doing the most basic tasks of survival for humans (excellent depiction in Diamond 1997).

Fast forward to 200 years ago, the production of the steam engine implied that factories could produce manufacturing goods in vast quantities and shorter periods of time, allowing a new and more complex form of division of labor to be created. Farmers were moving out of the farms, from which they were either forced out or lured out because of the greater economic opportunities connected with city wage work. In the most recent industrial transformation that is going back at least to the mid-20th century, most factory workers lost their jobs in the factories due to increasing automation in the factories, and gained jobs in the service industry. But what about today? Technological progress has resulted in an increase in material wealth, but labor market data shows that not all workers that lost their jobs were reabsorbed into the growing service sector, and part of the reason is that the service sector itself is facing growing automation. (See the falling rate of US labor force participation, Gandel 2015).

The result of all of this has been a growth of the precarious low-wage labor force that is too scared to put up demands against their employers, because of the insecurity of labor market access and career advancement, and the growth in technological rents, which are benefiting the Jeff Bezos' and the Bill Gates' of the world rather than the working class as a whole, which has become a shrinking political force. It is quite obvious under these circumstances that wealth has to concentrate further and further into the hands of the few, and it certainly does not help that globalization allows the very rich to play off one country's lax tax regulations against another countries' strict regulations, and that the very rich in all countries are ensuring tighter control over the political process, resulting in ever more favorable policies for the very rich, like the abolition of the inheritance tax.

In the short term, the turn toward regressive politics and economics implies that any chances for discussing UBI, which would pose a redistribution of resources to the popular masses, are very slim. The only sustainable progressive hope for introducing the UBI, as it was tried in some localities, is if a political shift can stimulate those discussions. The powerful don't tend to implement progressive reforms, unless they feel the popular pressure. Left-wing parties and their platforms should increasingly adopt UBI into their agenda, and argue that such policy is one of the few effective mechanisms that we have to reduce poverty and distribute the fruits of the national wealth more equitably. For those, who care about freedom, it stands to reason that a person can only be free if he does not have to worry about his survival.

But what are the critics saying about UBI? Why would it be such a bad idea? The most coherent response is that UBI would result in disincentives for work, because why would anybody want to work if he/she gets paid to do nothing. Some of my economist friends have put forward such argument, even though there is not much empirical truth to it. Firstly, it should be noted that traditional welfare schemes are the real disincentive for work, because earnings that are very small result in huge cuts in public benefits, which might even result in a lower standard of living when welfare recipients begin to join the labor force. UBI would counter this disincentive effect, because benefits can never be reduced. UBI wherever it has been tested usually results in higher worker productivity and willingness to work, not less (Standing 2015).

Secondly, even if UBI results in work disincentives, why should this be a terrible trend? It might very well be possible that people's morale will sap as they no longer feel the compulsion for work, but it is easily conceivable that they instead develop independent interests that they could only pursue because the immediate survival problem was solved. Joanne K. Rowling, the famous writer of the widely popular Harry Potter series, wrote her novels in the subway and on restaurant tables, while collecting welfare. One should imagine that Rowling had lived in a poor society without welfare services. We would not have received the pleasure of reading the Harry Potter series, because it probably would not have been written at all. It is very much conceivable that we would have more Rowlings if UBI is in place. And even if not, people would spend more time with their families and do other productive things for others.

Third, we must not forget the original motivation for putting the UBI scheme in place: growing automation makes human labor increasingly redundant, so UBI is necessary to stabilize consumption for all people. The work disincentive argument as it is proposed by economists is related to the presumption of labor scarcity and not moral imperatives (i.e. biblical principles for work being good for worker morale). Labor is considered scarce because if all workers stopped working at the same time (presumably because the utility of leisure by far exceeds the utility of work in an UBI environment), our society would collapse. I agree with the mainstream economists that labor scarcity has not been completely removed from contemporary society. Just walk out and take a bus driven by a bus driver, order a latte at Starbucks served by a barista etc.

But, on the other hand, the original reason why the UBI proposal became palatable is because the *degree* of labor scarcity is less today than it was even 20 years ago. It does not make sense to propose UBI in a poor society that is labor-intensive (where are the surpluses to pay for UBI to come from?), but it does make sense to have UBI in a capital-intensive society. UBI should be used specifically to allow people to purchase products from the capital-intensive industries (manufacturing and agriculture), which have hitherto produced enormous amounts of rents for their owners, but not sufficient benefits for the lower and working class.

It is, of course, conceivable to solve the labor scarcity problem in a different way, namely to reduce the working hours by redefining the full-time work week to less than 40 hours. I would certainly endorse the proposal if it came up for debate, but it currently does not. Restricting per labor work hours will lead to a fairer distribution of work, but will not fundamentally address the issues of automation and optimal distribution of labor. We know that automation of work is continuing apace, and we would constantly have to recalibrate the number of work hours per person, and such a policy cannot be implemented without some heavy class and social struggle. It is possible but not straightforward or automatic. The second problem is that by reducing the work week we would allocate less amount of work hours to people, who like to work more, so the allocation of labor hours will not be optimal relative to the preferences of the workers. Under UBI, workers would work as long or little as they saw fit.

The second major objection is that UBI cannot be considered realistic, because all countries are in direct competition with each other for greater market share, which forces every country to implement a labor regime that keeps workers disciplined enough to produce products at great quantity and moderate price (i.e. low wages). The reality is that UBI would dramatically revolutionize the labor regime by reducing the degree of discipline. What do I mean by discipline? Under the current labor regime, people work in order to get paid, and if they don't work they collect 6 months of unemployment insurance, and then they have to spend down their savings before they can apply for welfare, which has a five-year lifetime limit. This is a fairly strict labor regime, and forces workers to accept any job regardless of how little it pays. Labor discipline is maintained. One can easily imagine that labor discipline disappears or is substantially weakened when UBI is introduced. Workers will apply for jobs, work a couple of months, realize that their boss is a jerk, quit, enjoy a few months of holiday while collecting UBI, then go back to work whenever they like. What a nightmare for the capitalists.

What will likely happen is that the cost of production has to increase, as labor wages face runaway increases. In order to remain profitable, capitalists will raise product prices, but consumers are not fooled and import the same products at lower cost from other countries that are keeping a tighter lid on labor costs. This is a real problem now. If we stuck within the capitalist-competitive-global economy framework, we would have to support faster technological development to boost labor productivity and square high labor wages with moderate and internationally competitive prices. But suppose this fails to happen. Now businesses will go bankrupt or are bought by foreign companies that refuse to support the lax labor regime.

There is a genuine possibility that UBI could decrease the competitive position of a country, which destroys the original premise of UBI, i.e. that it could only succeed in an already rich country. If UBI results in lower standard of living because businesses fail, then the amount of UBI payments has to be reduced, and that would hurl workers back to the labor market as the price of necessaries continues to increase while purchasing power decreases. The preceding discussion quite clearly shows that UBI seems to only make sense if all countries sign up for UBI as well. Therefore, transcending capitalism is the ultimate goal. But there is another way to look at it: UBI lowers the reservation wage at which employers can attract labor. If a worker knows that he can survive with UBI, and considers the work wage as a supplement, then the wages do not have to be so high relative to the competitors to attract him to work. The state uses the general revenues to subsidize capitalists with low-wage workers, which it has been doing all along. For the UBI to function, the rate is set low enough that the state can maintain the program, but high enough that work compulsion disappears. (Some people argue that UBI has to be set below a minimally acceptable threshold to ensure work compulsion, but I think that would go contrary to the intentions of the UBI.)

There is one more problem that UBI has not yet addressed: What about the survival of capitalism given the lack of disciplining the labor force? We should not forget that the history of capitalism is about commoditizing labor and making it exploitable for the capitalist class, such that labor can produce surplus value. Without the discipline of the labor force, wages are high enough for profits to disappear. If there are no profits, then the capitalist system has to collapse, because where would there be further incentives for continued investments? Some Marxist scholars have noted that the 1970s was a period, where labor was unusually strong, resulting in a profit squeeze amid rising wages and inflation (Moseley 1997). Part of the neoliberal counter-offensive was to crush labor unions, or at least their political clout by enforcing a permanent austerity regime, weakening the welfare state, and exposing labor to more market forces to drive down wages and restore the rate of profit.

Scholars on the left now need to ask themselves which route they want to pick. The left Keynesian response would be to deny the inherent contradictions in capitalism, and insist that UBI would increase market efficiency, economic growth and private-sector profit. After all, we are currently concerned about a crisis of underconsumption, resulting from the many robots that consume nothing but electricity and the many unemployed and underemployed human workers, who cannot afford to buy all the products that exist in the economy. The crisis of underconsumption is a major reason why the neoliberal agenda is bound to fail, and we can see that prediction realized in the ever-worsening cycle of debt-based boom and bust in the global markets (currently manifested in Chinese stock volatility). With a UBI, we can hope to smooth the consumption patterns of most households, which in turn provide a reliable source of demand, which is the basis of private-sector profits.

Left Marxists and other types of socialists always suspect that every barrier and contradiction in capitalism justifies the terminal demise of the capitalist system. In this case, we could either argue that the profit squeeze theory following UBI is accurate, and we should quickly work on devising an alternative economic system, where profits and economic growth are no longer priorities but only the byproduct of rational economic planning. We could also argue that the Keynesian solution to the underconsumption problem is only temporary. Maybe capitalist animal spirits will die down if every person gets a UBI, and there will no longer be incentives for investment and innovation. A lack of innovation results in economic stagnation. (Keynesians could counter that constant and guaranteed demand will raise animal spirits because of the secure basis of the market.)

Luckily, this discussion is still based on heavy theory, and to test whether the predicted outcomes are true or not we actually have to introduce UBI to see what happens. Maybe we can square UBI with labor discipline, international competition and capitalism, maybe we can't. The uncertainty of what the outcome of UBI is going to be is a sufficient justification in itself why we should experiment with the UBI. Andre Gorz writes, "Let us make no mistake about this: wage labor has to disappear, and with it capitalism." (Gorz 1999: 77)

The European Refugee Crisis Reveals the Blunders of US Imperialist Foreign Policy and Other Crises

Posted on <u>August 31, 2015</u>

When the United States and other allies defeated Nazi Germany, there was grave uncertainty hanging over Europe. After years of war devastation, Europe was divided in two parts. The western half was capitalist, while the eastern half was communist. The capitalist half of Europe was protected politically, economically and militarily by the US. The first question they had to deal with was what to do with Germany, which now had become only West Germany. Unlike in the Treaty of Versailles, the western victors were now no longer interested in pursuing vindictive reparations against the war perpetrators and losers, but were intent to rebuild West Germany to provide a solid bulwark against communism.

The price for German and West European reconciliation, recovery and economic prosperity was the acceptance of the US as the hegemonic power. The US dollar was pegged to gold for the first 26 years after the war, while the other European currencies were tied to the US dollar. After the end of the Bretton Woods system, the world (and especially Europe and Japan) continued to price many of their purchases in US dollars (especially oil) to ensure the stability of the US currency. US hegemony has weakened somewhat after the introduction of the euro. But we know that the euro is no longer the bulwark against US hegemony as it once was, because the eurozone monetary system was poorly designed, see the Greek crisis. But as far as US foreign policy in the Middle East is concerned, the Europeans provide the willing cannon fodder and cheerleaders for US imperialist endeavors.

Now your question after reading the first two paragraphs will be what my discussion of US hegemony in Europe has to do with the title of my post, which is the current refugee crisis in Europe. And let us not be mistaken: this is a serious refugee crisis. 70 migrants died in a truck in Austria. Thousands died crossing the Mediterranean, and 300,000 refugees have taken the Atlantic route. Hungary is trying to seal their borders to Serbia, as tens of thousands of refugees make their way to Budapest and other parts of Europe (Sweden, Austria and Germany tend to have rather permissive asylum laws). Most of the refugees come from Syria, Afghanistan, Kosovo, Eritrea,

Serbia, Pakistan, Iraq, Nigeria, in that order (see Eurostat, "File:Countries of origin of (non-EU) asylum seekers in the EU-28 Member States, 2013 and 2014 YB15 III.png").

Why are all these people coming to Europe? Why now? What is the link to US imperialism? Well, I have said that Europe supports the US in most foreign policy endeavors, which includes wars. The most fatal ones in recent years were the wars in Iraq and Afghanistan that were fought with significant European backing, the no-fly zone over Libya and the air strikes in Syria. The latter operation has not yet stopped and is an ongoing campaign. Should we be surprised that most refugees are Syrians? All these wars lead to displacement, and people, usually young men, who are deemed to most likely survive the arduous and uncertain trip to foreign lands, leave and run to other safer (and often richer) countries, which include European countries. Notice that in all these wars, the US is dropping the most bombs, and the Europeans (and Turkey, Lebanon, Jordan etc. even more so) pay the highest price with the refugees they have to handle.

The Europeans are still thanking their American partners for their liberation from Nazi rule by supporting the aggressive and militarist US foreign policy, which backfires terribly for them because of the huge refugee influx. The no-fly zone in Libya is another case in point. One of the important facts that have so easily escaped public discourse is that while Muammar Qaddafi was still in power there was a silent arrangements between European governments and Qaddafi, that Qaddafi would secure the borders for the Europeans, i.e. do not allow the African-based refugees to escape by boats via the Mediterranean to Europe. In return, the EU accepted Qaddafi and also paid financial aid to the Qaddafi regime.

But the US, of course, demanded to get rid of Qaddafi, who refused to affiliate himself (i.e. make himself subservient to) with the United States. The US financed the rebel uprising- fortunately enough for the US there were enough rebels in the country's eastern province around Benghazi, who belonged to a different tribe than Qaddafi. When the rebels were about to be crushed by Qaddafi's forces, the US, supported by UK and France, declared a no-fly zone in Libya, which is a euphemism for a NATO air war to smash Qaddafi's easily overwhelmed forces. Fast forward four years and Libya has been transformed from a politically stable country to a virtually anarchic country without functioning institutions, civil war, looting, destruction and no internal order. Now all the refugees that were previously held back in Libya could hop on boats and try their luck in crossing the Mediterranean into Europe (Delapaine 2015).

Why are the European political leaders so helpless? Why are they supporting US military interventions and invasions, when they so clearly backfire given the refugee crisis? There is an apparent schizophrenia in the minds of politicians who have no problem supporting wars of military aggression and domination, while at the same time accepting the high political costs of the fallout of these policies.

It should be noted that not all refugees come just to escape war, as there are also many who seek to escape simply poverty. We also know that all of the factors are intertwined with each other, including struggle over scarce resources, inequality, poverty, war and environmental degradation. Let us take say the environment: as we are gradually destroying the earth with climate change, many parts of Africa become uninhabitable (e.g. not enough water), so the ability to grow food crops decrease. This produces a scarcity of vital food resources, so groups of people get together, import weapons from the developed world (primarily US and Russia, but also France, UK and Germany among others), put up roadblocks and blackmail farmers with guns to their throat asking for food "donations". Too many high testosterone males that are armed to the teeth inevitably leads to violent conflict and civil war, and that produces refugees.

We also know that inequality, resulting from inherently corrupt political structures benefiting the elite exclusively, who send their cash to the global money laundering agency, called Switzerland, and their kids to elite private schools of the west, also triggers political and military conflicts, because the vast majority of the poor population can simply not benefit from these unfair political and economic arrangements, and have, therefore, every reason to go to Europe.

Naysayers will, therefore, tell me that my critique of US imperialism is too one-sided, and that there are multiple causes for the European refugee crisis. I won't deny for a minute that there are other important causes of the refugee crisis as well. But I still think that US imperialism remains a major factor, because it is a proximate trigger for the immediate crisis. In other words, climate change, inequality and institutional failure are gradual and long-term processes, which create the pressure for migration over the long term. But political destabilization, as is the case in Libya, Syria, Afghanistan and Iraq, are the immediate triggers which explain why the refugee wave is accelerating since 2013.

The sad thing about historical depiction is that it does not help us to mitigate the refugee crisis. What should Europe do given this huge refugee influx? How are they going to physically cope with so many strangers in their country? What is the political reaction to this influx? The last question can hastily be answered: the rise of right-wing populism will accelerate. I would argue that they are already strong because of austerity policies and a poor macroeconomic environment, but that the refugee crisis tops their electoral performance even further (Liu 2015).

Racism is a latent force in Europe, which can quickly turn manifest. The current economic era is no longer so buoyant such that all factions, native and immigrant, can be satisfied simultaneously. Native voters will resent the meager public benefits that are paid to the refugees at a time when their governments convince them of the fiscal necessity of welfare state retrenchment affecting domestic citizens. Local and provincial governments that are not used to huge refugee waves will be overwhelmed by the continuing increase in people. We will read more horrendous news stories about dead refugees that were badly treated by their smugglers, drowned, suffocated or beaten. It certainly does not help that so many refugees are young men, full of energy and testosterone, who are without families, property and jobs (i.e. without things to ground them). They have to clash with the local population, where many native youths of the male gender also lack jobs and a good perspective.

Some politicians are pinning their hope on restricting the inflow of refugees by sealing their borders, but that would be a logistically difficult task, as there are always ways to circumvent border fences. If there is a will there is a way, and the smuggler effort will simply increase, and the human danger that it poses to their helpless clients is also incalculable. How many more dead bodies will we then find on the barbed wire fences of "fortress" Europe? What kind of humanitarian commitment is that in a continent that had at least made the commitment to outlaw the death penalty?

My hope is that it is merely a matter of time that the refugee wave subsides. Europe can then integrate some of these refugees (only very few will actually return), allow them to bring their families, get jobs, and halt the demographic decline in Europe. More people means more economic growth over the long term. Is this a happy end or a just a straw of hope to cling onto?

Book Review of Claus Offe, "Contradictions of the Welfare State" (1984; *Cambridge, MA: MIT Press*)

Posted on <u>September 6, 2015</u>

One of the things I absolutely enjoy when reading a certain group of German social scientists is that they are (1) interested in studying contemporary issues affecting global economy, society and polity, (2) strong in formally setting up theories, and (3) are often straightforward to follow. Claus Offe's book "Contradiction of the Welfare State", which is really an assembly of 11 of his essays plus an interview with the editors, is just one such example. So what is he saying that is of such great relevance to most of us, studying social policy, income inequality, welfare states, the crisis of capitalism, labor markets and class power?

To explain his thesis it would make sense to reveal the usual portrayal of welfare states as we understand it in public and occasionally scholarly discourse. Traditionally, neoliberals think that welfare states are too big, that they have served their function a long while ago, and that they have become unsustainable. The welfare state was originally seen as a social insurance policy against life risks associated with modern capitalist societies. All of the industrialized countries have accepted some modicum of welfare state to insure their workers against disability, unemployment, old age, sickness, child-bearing and other related issues.

But the issue with the welfare state is that they also reduce the attachment of the workers to the labor market. By allowing people to opt out of the labor market, and collect welfare payments, the disciplining mechanisms of the welfare state are weakened, such that it becomes possible for the remaining workers to endlessly bid up wages in an unnecessarily tight labor market, such that profits are squeezed, and price-wage inflation erodes investor confidence and economic growth.

Growth is, of course, the essential lubricant in our capitalist economy, and how dare the workers have such a great life and endanger wholesale the capital accumulation model on which all of our livelihoods depend on? Down with organized labor; down with labor market "rigidities" (i.e. make it easier to fire workers and cut benefits); down with the welfare state, and capital accumulation will return. And even if those on the left want to hold on to their cherished welfare state, without capital accumulation out of which state taxes are paid, the welfare state can no longer be financed. Let us not forget how the US presidential candidate Jeb Bush wants to restore 4% economic growth to the US economy, *and* cut Medicare benefits. He is certainly using the neoliberal paradigm to justify his policy ideas!

Leftists are, of course, instinctively uncomfortable with the neoliberal take on the welfare state, but surprisingly the neo-Marxist theoretician, Claus Offe, agrees partly with the neoliberal critique of the welfare state (consider especially chapter 6, pp.147-61). Yes, the welfare state will result in disincentives for labor market attachment. Yes, higher wages will diminish profits. Yes, investors have the power to withhold their investment, resulting in the self-fulfilling prophecy that if investors think the welfare state leads to an undue burden on capital accumulation justifying their lack of confidence in further sustaining necessary investments, it will yield in less capital accumulation. Yes, the continuing existence of the welfare state is premised on economic growth, which results in inevitable welfare state retrenchment resulting from lower growth.

So, how is Offe's biting critique of the welfare state any different than those of the neoliberals? Offe states that the "basic fault I see in this [neoliberal] analysis has less to do with what it explicitly states than with what it leaves out of consideration" (p.152). Offe says that it is politically not possible to get rid of the welfare state, and that advanced capitalist countries without the welfare states would *not* work. This results in his crucial insight that the welfare state poses a contradiction in the contemporary political economy because "while capitalism cannot exist *with*, neither can it exist *without*, the welfare state" (p.153).

The neoliberal response to such depiction would simply be, why should they believe him? How does he know that capitalism would collapse if there is no welfare state? Let us think about this question carefully and deconstruct the origin of the welfare state. The reason why welfare states arose was because the old forms of social support systems (family and church) could no longer provide for the needs of an urbanizing and proletarianizing population. (Churches become weaker as the urban population is becoming more secular, and families become weaker as wage labor reduces common family activity and slightly greater wealth lead to a proliferation of nuclear families to the detriment of extended families.)

Wise leaders like Otto von Bismarck realized these monumental social changes, and gave workers social protection against unemployment, old age, disability and sickness. The proletariat rewarded Bismarck and his successive leaders with electoral support and political docility. Karl Polanyi, recognizing the social tensions that arise from the proletarianization and the development of insecurity for the working class, theorized that for every liberalizing, market-friendly move, there would have to be a 'double movement', or a socially protective counter-movement, which is the state-provided welfare state. If today the welfare state would disappear, how are people going to survive if no employer hires them and pays them a wage? There would be social chaos.

For the capitalists this situation is not necessarily the same thing as paradise. Yes, in the absence of the welfare state, wages would collapse, but it is questionable whether the workforce will be available as desired. Every capitalist needs workers, who are reasonably healthy, so not investing in workers' health means a sicker and less productive workforce. Every capitalist needs to have the maximum amount of labor available, which requires some state-funded child care facilities to allow women to work. Every capitalist needs to have a literate, educated and trained workforce, and without these state investments, which are included in the welfare state, he would not have those skilled workers.

Every capitalist needs to have social peace and stable industrial relations, which a society where workers are facing the brink of starvation (without the welfare state) cannot supply, as these workers are more than ready to disrupt their work and protest for their rights, while putting the factory on fire and occupying the capitalists' home. Industrial relations, on the other hand, can remain stable if during times of economic and employment crisis, older and sicker workers can be sent into early retirement or disability, which is what happened in many of the richer European countries. The welfare state is thus not only a hindrance toward capital accumulation but also the foundation of it.

The reproductive and regenerative function of the welfare state is a classic responsibility of the state, because of the collective action problem. Every capitalist would surely benefit from having a strong welfare state, but no single capitalist will voluntarily make that investment, because it would bring them a competitive disadvantage against other firms, who are more than eager to freeload on the capitalists' workers, who were so generously provided for. The state can cut through the collective action problem by imposing taxes on all businesses to help pay for the welfare provisions. To make it palatable to the capitalists, governments usually promise the capitalists that only taxes on wages (i.e. payroll tax) will be used to finance the welfare state, while taxes on capital remain low to allow for a smaller burden on capital accumulation.

We know that the tax structure has become increasingly less progressive, as the payroll tax burden increased, while the corporate and capital tax burden decreased. Capital accumulation works splendidly, but only for a limited amount of time. As these strategies are by necessity time-limited, neoliberals want to dismantle the welfare state and free greater amounts of money to re-direct it toward capital accumulation. But, as we said, by destroying the welfare state, the social framework conditions would not exist, which allows labor to be exploited in the first place. And labor, as per Marx, is what creates value and is the basis for future capital accumulation.

The most fascinating part about Offe's work is his unmistakably clear depiction of the contradictions of the contemporary political economy. The conclusion on the welfare state is *damned-if-you-do-damned-if-you-don't*. And there are several contradictions, which I have listed on the inside flap of the book, where I usually make running notes on what I read. I have reproduced them below:

1. Welfare state produces commodification and de-commodification of the workers (p.14; p.140, 142)
2. Welfare state reproduces exploitative employment relations and increases the ability of workers to resist such exploitation via withdrawal from the labor market (p.152)
3. Welfare state strengthens and weakens capitalism (p.16)
4. Capitalism needs the welfare state and can't coexist with it (p.153)
5. State socializes infrastructure costs to the benefit of capitalists and creates greater taxing and borrowing costs for the private sector to the detriment of capitalists (p.19
6. State budgets maintain conditions for capital accumulation and are an "unproductive" waste crowding out the private sector accumulation (p.57)
7. Capitalism is about the privatization of production and the socialization of costs (welfare state, infrastructure spending etc.) (p.83)
8. State helps capital capital accumulation but is not in control of capital itself (p.120)
9. The state in its institutional form is a democracy, while in its material form privileges private capital accumulation (p.121)

10. To create effective administration bureaucracies are created, which in turn reduce effectiveness because of goal displacement (p.184)
11. By solving the demand/realization problem, one exacerbates the production/exploitation problem and vice versa (p.196)- i.e. higher effective demand (and realization of profits) are only possible if workers have high incomes, but high incomes weakens the exploitative power of capitalists; exploitative power can be restored with lower wages, which results in lower effective demand.

Contradiction over contradiction is what makes Offe's work so theoretically powerful, and so popular among Marxist theoreticians, who recognize the complexities and contradictions of social life, and ironically enough, see the contradictions as the basis for the desirable utopian society which they seek to create. Offe is no exception to this line of thinkers, and noted in the interview (chapter 12) that he is a democratic socialist, who wants to exploit any opening to transform the society away from capital accumulation and toward an ecologically and socially more sustainable order (p.296-9). But as so often with Marxist theorists, the theory of capitalism is strong, but the theory of revolution is weak. How is the utopian and idealized order to emerge out of the current ruins?

Offe blocks the Keynesian solution, which is essentially the restoration of amicable capital-labor relations with high profits, high wages and strong unions. That only works if there is huge economic growth, which is becoming increasingly unrealistic because of demand saturation in developed countries and the undesirable climate and environmental effects of the growth machine.

In the absence of good solutions we are left satisfied and unsatisfied, which seems to be one final contradiction. We are satisfied as social theorists having done our duty to 'demystify' (p.260) the neoliberal lies that pervert present discourse and shedding light on what has long been ignored by mainstream analysts, and we are dissatisfied because we feel more hopeless than ever about our prospects for changing society. At least, neoliberals think that if they could dismantle the welfare state, increase labor market competition, drive down wages and reward private-sector capitalists more, they can restore high economic growth, peace, prosperity and a good society. On the left-wing end of the spectrum, the human-rights activists, labor organizers and women's rights activists are dreaming up their social change with their petition drives, demonstrations, and picket lines- doing *something*!

The message of hope is what explains their credibility, mobilization for mass support and eventually political action, not the message of despair, falling in the realms of social theorists and philosophers.

Contradiction in Population Choices: India and China

Posted on <u>September 11, 2015</u>

In a recent post, I had argued that welfare states are prone to contradictions, because it has to be subject to the rules of capitalism which require labor commodification and social protection simultaneously, which per Claus Offe, is inherently contradictory (<u>Liu 2015</u>, "Book Review of Claus Offe, "Contradictions of the Welfare State" (1984)"). But one does not need to restrict such analysis to the welfare state, but can extend the contradiction to population policy as well. The two biggest populations in the world are India and China, and they are both now complaining about the male surplus. The male surplus is the disproportionate ratio between men and women at any given birth cohort (usually 120 boys for 100 girls, while global average is closer to 105 boys for 100 girls). Some research has suggested that Chinese men are becoming more violent as the gender ratio becomes more skewed toward males (Winkler 2014), and Indian girls living in strongly skewed regions are more likely to experience early marriage and forced sex (Trent et al. 2012).

The social effects of a skewed gender ratio are of particular interests for sociologists and gender studies scholars, and should be further researched. However, in this post I am very much interested in the relationship between demographic development and capitalist development. The essence of capitalism is economic growth, and this has mostly been correlated with a continuously growing population. Western capitalists and scholars have promoted the accession of China and India into the global community because these two countries had a very young and vast labor force that was eager to out-compete their western counterparts on price. Especially China has transformed from a largely rural to a largely urban society based on manufacturing development. India has relied more heavily on services to grow, and their urbanization and global trade growth has been slower than in China, but development figures point in a similar direction as China.

It is not surprising that western corporations and investors were eager to exploit this demographic bounty over the last few decades. But the large cohort of young workers has been the essence of this inflow of investment capital. But while all of this development was happening, women were pulled into the labor force in very great numbers (declining infant mortality rates certainly helped in that), which is more acutely the case in China where women had long ago been engaged in formal employment, as befits a communist system.

Women in the labor force results in more barriers to child-bearing resulting in a declining birth rate, which is of course more acute in societies where public child care provision is poor. Right when the Opening Reforms were implemented, the government imposed the one-child policy, fearing at that time overpopulation rather than a lack of population. India imposed no such policy, but the secular decline of birth rates in India indicates that women are becoming more educated and contraceptives are more available than previously.

Urbanization is a third contributing factor to a declining birth rate. As people have more income as they work city jobs, they also tend to spend more money on their children's education and other forms of expensive entertainment. Children are now primarily an economic liability to parents for much longer than previously (and the author of this post can confirm this out of personal experience). This is a dramatic reversal from the old days, when most people were farmers and regarded their children as an asset. The more hands worked the field the more likely they were to survive. Farmers were not buying their children toys, but made sure to exploit their labor for family survival. A more expensive lifestyle with more expensive children also favors people's choice toward fewer children.

So there we have multiple factors (female education/work, government one-child policy and urbanization) that explain the declining birth rate, and that produces a very peculiar choice model for couples contemplating what gender their children should have. This decision has been strangely made possible by medical innovations, which allow parents to see the gender of the fetuses, and then make a decision on abortion or not. Traditional culture in both country favors boys, because they are expected to take care of their parents, so girls get aborted in significant numbers. One look at the Chinese and Indian population pyramid reveals that the male surplus is continuing to grow and getting worse.

The economic calculation is quite similar in both societies, but confusingly differs on one point: the bride price and the groom price. In Chinese society, there is a bride price, meaning that the husband and his family need to have saved up sufficient income to purchase a house or give some starting capital to the bride, and the couple uses that to, for example, start a business. In Indian society, there is a groom price, the so-called dowry, and it is the wife's family which pays money to the groom's family. Ironically, whether a bride price or a groom price is paid makes no difference to the parental preference for sons. The reason is that in both cases the traditions are patrilocal, which means that the wife has to vacate her parents' house and move to the husband's parents' house, and later take care of them, when they are old, which automatically results in the "loss" of the daughter. The incentives for female infanticide are perhaps even stronger in Indian society, because dowry and the loss of the daughter are both negative factors for raising a daughter.

As I have said, the preference for boys and female infanticide is becoming more acute as the birth rate is declining. The resultant male surplus results in a further reduction in the birth rate, because women, not men, are the limiting factor for population growth. This is the fourth factor explaining a declining birth rate. It is no coincidence that the fertility rate is measured by the number of children for women. To illustrate this principle one should imagine a society consisting of one man and ten women, and another society with one woman and ten men, and calculate which society will grow faster. The fact that an Arabian prince with hundreds of concubines had fathered more than 800 children illustrates that women are the limiting factor for the birth rate. The many men in China and India, who see little prospect of finding a mate, clearly illustrates the possibility for a shrinking population.

So far neither Indian nor Chinese society are on a declining trajectory and that is because even faster than the fall of the birth rate is the aging of society resulting from an increase in the life expectancy. As people are getting older and living longer, the society won't shrink as fast as would be the case if most people died at a young age. Technological, agricultural and medical progress is certainly tremendously helpful for many societies. But on the other hand, the growth in the old-age population does not resolve the crisis in capitalism, because any growth-oriented society relies on millions of young workers and consumers, who keep the system going. With the exception of the health care and retirement community industry, I cannot imagine many other sectors of the economy which can expect huge growth rates amid an aging population.

A few decades onward, population aging itself can no longer halt the demographic decline, and societies will shrink quite quickly. In Japan, the population peaked in 2004 (127.8 million), then stagnated for a few years at that level, and then began to decline (127.3 million as of 2013). Many countries in Europe are facing a similar development, though they cushion their population decline with the intake of immigrants and refugees. Ironically, the growth of refugees from Syria and other war-torn countries of the world (mostly young people of primary working age) could turn out to be a demographic and economic boon for Europe.

For China and India, the population dividend is gradually exhausting itself, as they have to handle a growing old-age population with rising social security needs (families have become smaller and a less reliable source of old-age insurance). China has already seen the peak in the labor force, and has been declining in the last few years. Amid talks of an overheating economy, rising wage claims of restive workers, who no longer accept the oppressive low-wage model, and thereby put downward pressure on profits, Chinese leaders have to fend off allegations of corruption and mismanagement in the inevitably slower growing economy. Managing less growth is unavoidable, which lies partly in the aging and eventually shrinking population and declining fertility rate. In addition, investors will no longer be as patient with China, and seek to find other areas to sink their investments. For the Communist Party, however, less growth could mean an even more dissatisfied population, which may force them to increase their crackdowns on the population, as we have seen with the many prosecutions against human rights activists in the recent past.

India, on the other hand, still has room to grow. Its total labor force grew from 466 to 481 million between 2010 and 2013 (World Bank). Given that the population expanded by 46 million people in that same time period, labor force participation has barely budged and, in fact, even declined from 55 to 54% (World Bank). There are certainly more barriers to complete capitalist development in India than in China, but both countries will converge at some point in their development.

We have to go back to the original problem formulation and ask ourselves what the ultimate cause of the declining birth rate was in the first place: capitalist development. This cause is different than the other proximate causes that I have outlined earlier (women's empowerment, one-child policy, urbanization and male surplus), because capitalist development is related to each of these policy solutions in some way, except the one child policy, which is a unique administrative fiat of the Chinese government. Rising affluence creates different choices for people, which prioritizes work and consumption over child-rearing. Outdated male-centric traditions themselves work to undermine the foundation for further population and economic growth.

Capitalism is such a contradictory system, because it produces unforeseen social results, which undermine the basis of its own continued existence. Population surplus favors capitalist investments in cheap labor, which drives up wages, which favors technological investments and labor-saving technology. Development and growing wealth, however, result in different social choices favoring fewer children, which undermines the basis of further development. Countries like Canada and the US, which have long invited more immigrants on a vast territorial space, can gloss over demographic problems given their popularity among immigrants all over the world. It is altogether a different story for India and China, which have only allowed few immigrants to enter, and if so under tight conditions. It is questionable whether even an open-border policy can reverse a demographic decline in China and India given that their combined population is already one-third of the total in the world, and a few million immigrants won't tip the scales in terms of growth.

The concluding thought, however, takes the opposite tack: we know that a growing world population is quite harmful to the world given our resource scarcity and the negative effects of environmental degradation and climate change. The worship of population growth can only be justified under a framework of capitalist economic growth, which I think should rightly be questioned. My brother has argued that a growing world population is positive, because if there is more of us, then there will be more ideas that are circulated, and that has to drive innovation and progress. I certainly have access to a larger variety of people than even my parents and grandparents, whose social life were much more restricted to their personal friendship network. But I shall still ask: when is enough enough? When can we divorce population developments from the economic growth engine, which is bringing our planet ever closer to disaster?

Jeremy Corbyn's Victory Is a Reinvigoration of Left-Wing Politics and Economics in Europe

Posted on September 13, 2015

Recently, the UK Labour Party has announced that the left-wing Jeremy Corbyn became Labour leader with 59.5% of the vote (Mason 2015). This is a candidate, who had very low odds of winning. He only came on the ballot because 15 MPs submitted his name for the Labour leadership ballot at the very last minute, seeking to expand the debate, and push the party somewhat further to the left. They never expected that Corbyn's anti-austerity message would resonate so quickly and widely in the Labour electorate, resulting in his victory. Corbyn's election was certainly favored by his predecessor Ed Miliband's decision to allow not just Labour Party members, but also supporters, who paid a nominal 3 pound fee, to participate in the electoral contest. This decision encouraged many, especially younger and progressive voters, to cast their ballot in favor of Corbyn.

The reaction of the party establishment is predictably quite negative. Tony Blair (2015) has denounced Corbyn as living in Alice in Wonderland, who wants all these things that sound nice, but will never get the Labour Party elected to power. He claims that Labour lost the last elections, not because voters were critical of Ed Miliband's right-ward austerity-lite campaign, but because he was too left. The electoral mandate was much more in favor of the "realistic" economic policies of David Cameron and the Conservatives, who have implemented enormous austerity in the name of "responsible" governing. Blair sees himself vindicated because he was Labour leader and prime minister for 10 years, so this guy must know what he is talking about.

Except he is wrong this time around. The rise of Corbyn does not reflect the rise of left-wing dreamers, who always wanted to seize opportunities for radical social change and revolution. No, the rise of Corbyn comes amid the brutal austerity policies of the Tory government, and the lack of alternative by the Labour Party. Blair's war in Iraq and Afghanistan, proliferation of private- finance initiatives, including the health services and public infrastructure projects, favoritism toward the financial sector, decline of secure economic opportunities for the working class indicate that Blair's Labour Party was too far to the right.

For someone like Corbyn to stand up, oppose brutal austerity policies, oppose cuts to the welfare state, favor public investments in the infrastructure, oppose the growth of inequality, protect health and school services from cuts, and oppose wars means that the people in Britain finally have an alternative to the self-defeating policies of the neoliberals.

British dissatisfaction with the status quo is not unique to the country, but is also reflected in rising voter disgust across all advanced capitalist countries, who are struggling from the same issues of low economic growth and the rise of economic insecurity among the 'precariat' (Standing 2011). At the beginning of this year, Greece was in the front line of the neoliberal assault on the living standards of the working class. Electing a left-wing government (Syriza) was too much "risk" for the elites of other European countries, who thought that forcing a dying patient to pay the full bill of the debt and soothing creditors is more important than establishing a more humane and rational economic strategy toward recovery and debt repayment.

The Greek Left was defeated. The most charismatic spokesperson, Alexis Tsipras, bowed down to the external economic and political pressure building up against him and his government. He declared snap elections, and his legacy is in shambles, while his party is now internally divided. The "responsible" (read: centrist, neoliberal, pro-finance) leaders in Europe breathed a sigh of relief, but they were mistaken to believe that that was the end of the line for radical left politics.

The strategic chessboard is merely shifting into other locations. In Spain, Podemos still has some voter support, though the defeat in Greece set them back in the polls. In France, Marine Le Pen's right-wing populist party carries more and more voter support, and she advocates an expansionist welfare state (at least for citizens), and the same drift to the right (with populist left economic policy) can be observed in Austria too. A genuine left has now come to power in the UK, at least in the opposition, again reflecting the desire among the EU electorate for an end to austerity. The next target is the US, where Bernie Sanders needs to win the Democratic primaries and the general elections to become president.

The naysayers are in the media and the political establishment, but ironically these forms of public discourse are no longer the only way for ordinary people to receive their political information. The wide dissemination of internet blogs and social media websites has allowed people to receive a somewhat greater variety of viewpoints, though it is true that social media tends to restrict the posts to the political opinions that one favors (I get lots of news on Corbyn and Sanders, for example, on my newsfeed).

I do not wish to answer the question whether or not left-wing forces can reach power, because the results will obviously have to speak for themselves. The populist sentiment is certainly stronger than ever, because of the failure of austerity to result in restored investor confidence, economic growth and sustainable job creation, while the establishment voices offer no escape to their misery.

The more important question will be whether a left-wing government can lead to a restoration of economic growth, which is the only outcome permissible in a capitalist economic system in order to satisfy all factions- from investors to workers- in a society. The answer in the case of Greece is obviously 'no'. But Greece was laboring under constraints which the bigger and more powerful countries did not face. Real test cases would be the core powers, especially in Germany, France and the UK.

Those on the Keynesian left have long argued that if we stopped with the bloodletting austerity policies, and would promote pro-poor redistribution and public investments, we could recreate the old economic growth model, which would be correct if we establish the fact that much of the economy is currently paid as rents toward the oligarchy, while not enough income is trickling down to the masses, who want to consume and stimulate the economy, but can't because of their low incomes.

I am, of course, more of a pessimist, and have argued repeatedly that any hope to restore high rates of economic growth in the very developed countries need to be buried, because of demand saturation and the undesirability of more growth amid resource scarcity and climate change. The political left has to offer a very different vision from the ones that we have seen so far. They have to show that low rates of economic growth can be squared with greater economic egalitarianism (a similar point made in Galbraith 2014). But to articulate such targets, we will require a greater and not a smaller public sector. One of the crucial insights in Claus Offe's analysis of the welfare states is that state activity is trapped in a contradictory situation of simultaneously enhancing and undermining the social basis of capitalism, because the state has to operate within the confines of a capitalist economy driven by private property and private accumulation of capital (argument developed in Liu 2015, "Book Review of Claus Offe, "Contradictions of the Welfare State" (1984)").

By expanding public investments, public employment and spheres of activity of the state, the sphere of the private sector will thus become more restricted, and allow the decommodified sphere of human life expand. (By decommodification, I mean the lack of reliance on the market to survive, e.g. a worker not having to sell his labor to survive because he collects unemployment insurance, see definition in Esping-Andersen 1990: 21-22.) So far, the state has made itself a subservient force to the private-sector, and cannot transcend the capital accumulation model. Libertarian socialists believe that private actors should work on achieving socialism if that is what they desire. It would be much better than state-directed socialism, because if an arrangement is produced voluntarily and with the consent of all actors, it will lead to more legitimacy, durability and system stability. The latter point is certainly true, but it does not make libertarian socialism any more feasible, because private-sector actors face a collective action problem, which intrinsically benefits those interests that place self-interest ahead of common interest. That is why the state socialists have preferred the "commanding heights" approach, where the state takes over the most important industries, while leaving a few residual sectors like agriculture or retail to the private-sector.

Interestingly enough, Jeremy Corbyn is an advocate of the state-centric approach of regulating the economy. However, whether he will push the renationalization agenda really far is still quite questionable, because he faces significant opposition from other Labour leaders and more centric backbenchers, who have grown very accustomed to the the centrist strategy of Blair and Brown, which have gotten them quite cushy government jobs around Westminster. But if he could convince the party to embrace a platform of stopping further privatization of the health services or tuition increases in the universities (which works just like privatization because rising tuition privatizes costs and strengthens the hand of the private university administrators), he would have significantly changed the course of debate. Ironically, it is the austerity-mania of the Tory government, which makes Corbyn's positions more palatable to the more centrist middle class voters, who have thus far backed the Tories.

In the US, Bernie Sanders does not advocate nationalization, and it would currently be quite foolish to demand that to be part of his agenda. The US has a much deeper history of anti-state activity than in the UK, where Labour governments since Clement Attlee have demanded more welfare state intervention to protect the most vulnerable people from misery (and cover the electoral basis for the Labour Party). What Sanders needs to do is to effect a more limited goal of expanding the welfare state and bringing it up to the level of the European countries. Given that the aggregate US tax take is between 5-10 percentage points of GDP lower than other developed countries, and the rich are able to dodge many taxes, there is still significant room for welfare state expansion. It is a very gradual approach known to theoreticians like Eduard Bernstein (1899), who believed in evolutionary socialism- the gradual achievement of socialism with bourgeois-democratic means. But strategically, this road is the most viable one to take in the US.

The other European countries naturally have a greater understanding of socialist history, but it would be wrong to assume that they are travelling quickly in that direction at the moment. We know that the neoliberal EU elites are offering no alternative vision to austerity, and push it as a permanent policy to discipline the workforce in this more globalizing economy. Ironically, now that globalization is so important, it is more important than ever to have functioning European institutions to handle the challenges that the continent faces on a European level. But whether it is the refugee crisis, where the Europeans can't agree on a common refugee intake policy, or whether it is the Eurozone crisis, which resulted from a flaw in the design of the Eurozone itself and shows no signs of resolution, there is less political unity than ever.

This unfortunate political dynamic implies that the national left-wing movements and parties need to first consolidate their own base via strong electoral performances in national elections afforded by an anti-austerity, pro-poor agenda, and secondly, to use their stronger voting base to coordinate more activities across borders. Currently, the problem is that most European left social-democratic parties are not really on the left, because they are helpless in front of the neoliberal assault. Yes, inequality is growing, the middle class is collapsing, the good jobs are disappearing, austerity is pushing more people into poverty, but the social-democratic leaders think these measures are "responsible" and "necessary". The Blairs, Jospins and Schroders have had their day, and the rise of Corbyn points to real-world alternatives that challenge neoliberal dogma.

As Polanyi (1944) noted a long time ago, any move toward commodification of labor results in the counter-movement toward decommodification. Likewise, any political swing in one extreme direction triggers a political response going in the other direction. For our humanizing mission of the world and making it a better place, we can afford no other outcome.

Fighting Another Cold War in Syria Makes No Sense

Posted on October 12, 2015

The New York Times reports the increase of Russian airplane attacks on Syrian territory to bolster the position of their ally, President Bashar al-Assad, while the US continue their bombing campaign to defeat ISIS and their support for the Free Syrian Army. Russia also wants to fight ISIS, but simultaneously targets the Free Syrian Army and other rebel factions that were doing their best to get rid of Assad, also one of the US enemies. What is developing on the ground can best be referred to as a proxy war between the US and Russia, as they are struggling to hold greater influence over the troubled region (Barnard and Shoumali 2015).

There is a golden window of opportunity for the two former Cold War powers to get together on a common negotiating table and broker a peaceful solution. Unfortunately, what is more likely to happen is that each side will continue to support their own favored faction and in the meantime each superpower hopes to defeat their opponents and, of course, ISIS. Russia's side has greater prospect of winning the battle, because Russia supports Assad, which is a much weakened, but still quite influential central government. The US side is weaker, because after pouring in 500 million dollars of funding for anti-Assad and anti-ISIS rebels, many of these rebels took the US weapons and funding and defected from this Free Syrian Army to develop their independent forces to attack Assad.

I am no supporter of Russian foreign policy, and would find it better if they did not actively engage in a battle that could turn into another Afghanistan for them, where the Soviets were worn down and beaten, which significantly lowered national morale, and eased the collapse of the Soviet regime. But I have to say that the current Russian position is much more feasible and morally defensible than the American position. Russia supports Assad and opposes ISIS and other pro-US and anti-Assad rebels. The US supports the Free Syrian Army (fledgling and small), opposes anti-US rebels, Assad and ISIS.

The simple realpolitik question is which policy position is more feasible? Of course, the Russian position makes more sense. Assad, as brutal and ruthless of a ruler he may be, is still the president of the country, and he commands a significant military force, otherwise he would have been ousted by now. Four years of active western support for the anti-Assad rebels have not yet led to his downfall, so why should they be more successful this time around? The US genuinely hopes that they can install an el-Sisi type, pro-American dictator, but that goal conflicts with defeating ISIS. If ISIS is such a big threat to US national security, then why would the Obama administration not focus its effort on defeating ISIS rather than wanting to defeat both ISIS and Assad? To an extent, Pentagon experts are quite confused at this point, because they are quite uncomfortable about Assad, while they know they have to commit military resources to beat back ISIS. I think their plan is to keep both enemies engaged, but I doubt that this will be efficacious, because the US lacks solid partners in the region.

This confused US position reminds me of the former Chinese commander, Chiang Kai-shek, who argued that "communism was a cancer while the Japanese presented a superficial wound" (quote from Wikipedia, "Zhang Xueliang"). The Nationalist government was facing two enemies at the same time, the Communists and the Japanese, and even though the Japanese began invading China in 1931 (1937 beyond Manchuria), Chiang still prioritized the capture and destruction of the Communists. This diversion of resources clearly resulted in the loss of Nationalist territory to the Communists, and their eventual defeat after the defeat of the Japanese. The moral lesson is that you can't fight two powerful enemies at the same time.

So what is the way forward? In an open-ended war, it will be difficult to make really accurate predictions, but let me try my best. In a realistic scenario, the Russian military strikes will defeat ISIS and bolster the Assad regime, which will get another 10 years of guaranteed power. The rebels will still be there, but their force will subside as US officials recognize the futility of supporting unreliable rebels to get rid of Assad. That could conceivably create peace, even though there will be continuing resentment against the Assad regime, which results in more civil war. In the second scenario, Russia is merely buying time for Assad, and he will have to step down (or be assassinated). The country enters anarchy until the Islamic State takes over Damascus, as they are the most powerful faction after Assad. Russian and American policymakers are incensed, and will now fight together to beat back ISIS.

The third scenario is that the Free Syrian Army receives US military personnel support (boots on the ground) given that a Republican president (Donald Trump? Ben Carson? Jeb Bush?) wins the elections, and they smash Assad and beat back ISIS. The Russians will be quite incensed, but what can they do against the world's most powerful military? However, the US-enforced peace will remain very unhappy and fragile, and civil war will break out any time. Mounting costs of a US military occupation characterized by high financial and human cost will drain US public support for the war, which will result in US retreat, and the nightmare scenario that we witness in Iraq, Afghanistan and Libya today.

The most likely scenario is the first one, but I hate all of these scenarios. So let us dreamers propose a fourth scenario: stop supplying your side, pro-US or pro-Russian, with guns and weapons. There is no net benefit for bringing in more weapons, which will encourage the fighters to continue their warfare. Give peace a chance by having multilateral forces, especially US and Russia get together on a bargaining table to bring about a non-violent solution. As cruel as Assad, ISIS or other rebels may be, it is important that they are all brought to the bargaining table to hammer out a peaceful solution to the crisis.

It may very well mean that negotiations could result in the legitimation of ISIS, and this is a huge price that needs to be paid to secure a peace treaty. I do not support ISIS, but there have to be non-violent ways to undercut the support for ISIS. After years of mismanagement their public support will fall away. People will realize that guns, fear and terror don't feed people. A fire can only continue to burn as long as we add oxygen and oil into it. If we stopped doing that, the flame has to die down. I wish we had more committed fire-fighters in the halls of power today.

The Irreversible Trend of Growing Inequality?
Posted on October 13, 2015

For those on the political left, there are plenty of reasons to complain about current social trends. Principally, there are certain structural and institutional forces which are in place, which increase the level of income and wealth inequality within countries. A new Credit Suisse report makes it clear that inequality of wealth is bigger than in the past, and there is little hope that these trends will reverse themselves in the immediate future. The richest one per cent of the society owns 50.4% of all household net worth, and the bottom 71% of the world population owns less than $10,000 (Credit Suisse 2015).

Economists like Thomas Piketty have argued that given the current trend of low economic growth and high rental income growth, it is inevitable that the few rental owners (Wall Street executives, hedge fund managers, real estate moguls etc.) have to move far ahead from their less well-endowed brethren, who are not capital owners and rely on labor market income (subject to economic growth constraints and investment decisions of the capitalist class) to make a living.

We know that Piketty's explanation is somewhat static, as he is only interested in the long-term structural forces of growing inequality, thus neglecting similar other important factors like the strength of political lobbies of the rich to create government policies to benefit them even more. But he is putting his fingers on a highly important topic, which has not much been reflected upon in contemporary discourse.

Is this outcome of growing inequality such a big tragedy? For people like Joseph Stiglitz, growing inequality is harmful for social cohesion, sense of fairness in the economy, and further economic growth. There is absolutely no doubt that if we are interested to maintain social stability, we need to change the system such that more people can feel that they are part of the society rather than being marginalized.

I have the strong suspicion that growing inequality creates a political environment, where the needs of regular people get neglected. One major area of application for that is labor. As the tremendous wealth of the very few at the top suggests, it should be very simply possible to take care of the needs of all our people, whether it is housing, health care, education or food. It should also be possible to provide everyone with the employment that they see fit, and live in dignity with good incomes. But for some reason (deindustrialization, more inequality) the good-paying jobs are simply disappearing, and the few high-paid jobs are in the consulting and finance industry, which involves plenty of busywork and crazy hours. For most of the rest of the workforce, work is associated not only with drudgery but with toil, low pay and no job security.

By transforming economies into winner-take-all systems, where only the rich can gain the upper hand with their successful wealth accumulation, working people have very few avenues to take advantage of the immense wealth that would otherwise be available if we found a better way to manage our resources.

Is there going to be an endpoint for growing inequality? There has to be. Human history tends to tell us that inequality is a very old problem, and has never been completely reduced. Governments can merely take steps to mitigate this problem, but can never solve it. On the other hand, if inequality becomes too huge, regular folks become aware of their exploitation, get active and realize that their activism can change the dynamic in the political process. There is no natural endpoint to inequality, but it is possible for people to manipulate seemingly inevitable social trends even if it takes a war or a great depression to produce action.

For those on the political left, which are skeptical of my predictions, I should remind them that hope is sometimes the only positive force that we possess. As Antonio Gramsci said, "Pessimism of the mind, optimism of the will."

What is the Importance of Freedom?

Posted on <u>October 23, 2015</u>

My libertarian friends have a very strong attachment to the notion of freedom. So do I. Yet we always disagree on the policies, because we have different value attachments as far as freedom is concerned. What is freedom? What the libertarians mean by freedom is that the government does not interfere in the lives of private citizens. If we were freed from government coercion, people would have a good life, because the free market would regulate our lives, and we need no bureaucrat to tell us how to live wisely.

On the face of it, this reasoning is very poor, because the state has to set the rules of the game, and the only relevant practical question is how the government should regulate private activity, and specifically in whose interest. If the rules are set such that only 1% of the people can gain all the wealth, then it would be very disturbing and no sane person can support such a position. This is how our current economy is structured, however. Even philosophically, I question how much freedom there is in a political economy, where private property wealth appropriation means that a few people can become phenomenally wealthy, while so many other people are trapped in low-wage jobs despite hard labor. Marxists and socialists actually agree with a classic libertarian assumption that freedom means to own one's own source of labor. But the difference is that right-wing libertarians think that the current oligarchs are the rightful owners of the labor, while socialists believe that workers themselves are the rightful owners.

But that is the socio-economic discussion of libertarianism and freedom, and I think I have engaged on this question on multiple occasions in the past, such that I doubt that I have much valuable input to offer. The other type of freedom is that which we encounter in personal life. Let us take say education. One of the main accomplishments of the human mind is the creation of art, music, literature, philosophy and the like. There is a very strong value in studying the liberal arts and humanities, because it makes people much more reflective about themselves and society. Naturally, in a highly insecure neoliberal world, it is not really appreciated to nurture independent thinkers, who only want to be paid to philosophize and reflect on the human condition. Having too much free-thinking carries the risk of disturbing the ruling mantra of individual work, merit, competition and strife, which we are told is a natural condition of life. We are going to school, such that we can learn the skills, which train us for careers. We receive the instruction from the teachers, and we need to be obedient to their orders, just as we are obedient to our bosses at work.

This instrumental approach to education, which is backed up by powerful forces intent on eviscerating the humanities and replace them with vocationally-based systems, is naturally inimical to the pursuit of knowledge for its own sake. Once we accepted the framework of individuals striving for their own success, and leaving everyone else behind, and then blaming the inevitable losers from such a cutthroat economic environment, it is very difficult to establish alternative values to neoliberal dogma, such as learning for its own sake, and solidarity with other people that are facing political struggles, such as those faced by homeless people or people of color. It makes a lot of sense to defend the humanities, which will be structurally weakened by powerful social forces, but will hopefully continue to exist as long as there are people, who can spare a little bit of leisure time to carry out their interests.

But let us return to the question: what is freedom in a personal sense? I have made the observation that it is better to pursue personal research projects rather than things that are dictated on the class curriculum. I would be able to tell you a summary of the two dozen or so papers, which I have written up to this point, but I would not be able to tell you what I have done in 12th grade mathematics. I have total respect for math wizards, yet I lack the passion and energy to pursue a very mathematically oriented direction of research. I have gone through the government-mandated school system, and have continued on with college-based course work. Every time, when I read something that was required of me, such that I could write a paper about it or complete an exam, I retained much less information over the long term than if I read something based on my own interests.

Reading, writing and thinking are very individual processes. While I am typing up this blogpost, I am sitting in the library by myself, only staring at the screen to produce the next words on the screen. If there is an interest in a certain topic, I tend to write these blogposts rather quickly and almost effortlessly, while class assignments vary, and can take a long time, especially with respect to subject material with which I lack familiarity and/or interest. The freedom to discover things on your own is one of the greatest freedoms to have, yet within the confines of our society it is hard to attain such freedoms.

There are other education examples of freedom that also come to mind. I can recall more things in random public lectures that I chose to attend than class lectures in my assigned courses, even class lectures that somewhat interest me. While there is no clear extrinsic reward for attending public lectures (it won't boost my GPA, and might even reduce it, because it takes time away from my formal studies), they are more meaningful, because we have actively chosen to attend it; we have the freedom to choose how much we want to get out of this experience (or how much we want to forget because there is no examiner to test and grade us); and we don't have extrinsic tools to control our behavior and thinking. Full self-control implies complete freedom.

But education is not the only realm where freedom is possible. Most people experience their work as drudgery. We have this proverbial proliferation of "bullshit" jobs (Graeber 2013), i.e. jobs like accountants, managers, lawyers, consultants and financiers, which are paid a lot of money, but lack intrinsic value for the society. We could argue that we need lawyers to be able to cope with the complications of modern society, but we could not explain why countries outside the US would not have so many lawyers and unnecessary litigation. Of course, what is necessary is defined in the context of every society, but I very much doubt that people would miss out if the society would be able to solve social problems more peacefully and with different means. The better example are the financiers and bankers, which have made the economy more risky with their casino-speculative operations with downside insurance for them if things don't work out for them. They get government bailouts, which is not available to working class people. These bankers are neither creating value, nor is their exorbitant pay justified from the standpoint of fairness and social justice.

In the low-wage jobs, there is also plenty of drudgery, such as in the retail sector and among some low-level administrative positions. The capitalist economy apparently feeds off from these many low-income workers, who should never experience the notion of freedom within their lifetime. Currently, there are many governments which are using the guise of an unaffordable welfare state and an aging population to justify deep cuts in pension programs, which will force more senior citizens to return back to the workforce and keep the wages low for everyone. Seniority won't help with pay, because nowadays companies can dismiss older workers and rehire them at lower wages.

No one can claim that either the high or the low-wage workers-experiencing so much drudgery- are experiencing any degree of freedom. I don't doubt that there are a few workaholics, who relish the prospect of spending their lifetime at work, and dread prolonged phases of downtime. But these are the exceptions to the rule. People cannot experience any freedom if they are not given any. Even to the workaholics, I have to say, have you ever thought about which environment you enjoyed more? Meeting clients at work, and trying to sell them a worthless product, which you have to sell anyway, because that is what your boss wants you to do? Or meeting co-workers and friends after work in a dinner party, where there is plenty of good food and wine, and the opportunity to recapitulate a day of work and talk about sports?

It is so obvious that the latter situation has significantly more allure than the first one. In the first example, which is tied to economic activity and work, there is the bondage of work, business and capital accumulation/ profit-making. Some people feel in their natural element while doing so, because they feel happy about making money. Though I have to say that this is contrived and reveals the pitfall of modern market societies. But the fact of the matter is that making money takes primacy over any other interaction, and that tends to reduce the meaningfulness of work-related conversations.

I have noticed it myself after having worked in the retail industry for over four years. I was just an employee, and hated selling shoes, though I enjoyed the fact that it was a rather leisurely job. But what I really enjoyed was when there were only very few customers in the store, and I could meet and have very meaningful discussions with customers, who in turn were very happy about not just buying shoes but also sharing their wisdom and insight with a shoe clerk. There was a mutual benefit that was created in a work environment, but the primacy was nonetheless the economic transaction (selling shoes). So when the store got really busy, I could not have these kinds of conversations, and needed to process the customers like on a conveyor belt. Nonetheless, I am sure that I was able to generate a higher level of job satisfaction than someone without that social experience at work.

The second situation (the dinner party) I described earlier is very different from the first one. Because the interaction is not tied to achieving any tangible outcomes (making money etc.), there is a much greater potential of having simply very relaxing and rewarding conversations with other people. That situation constitutes freedom, and so we as social human beings seek to repeat these rewarding encounters by organizing many parties and get-togethers. However, it is possible for some people to not enjoy such dinner parties, either because they are very introverted people, and don't enjoy mingling with so many other strange people, or because they are too extroverted, and want to make as many friends as possible, while lacking the time to do so. In the former case, there is a degree of social awkwardness (to which my advice is: go out and don't be afraid) , but in the latter case, there is a strong resemblance to the profit-making motive. Immanuel Kant argued that we should not regard other people as means to an end, but as an end in itself. That was his categorical imperative.

If I care about how popular I am and how many friends I have (and Facebook oddly quantifies that, and makes available the number of friends that people have, even though the number of real friends, i.e. people that we meet regularly and have strong sympathies for, is much smaller), then I am no longer concentrating on the moment in the dinner party with the individual that I am talking to. The human being turns into a number or an instrument rather than an end in itself. This is part of the competitive nature, which is nurtured in our current society, and which I have forcefully attacked earlier.

When describing freedom, there can be no doubt that freedom has to mean that there is a freedom from externally induced coercion; a freedom to self-control and self-direct time and effort. Homework and exams are a bad way of learning, but self-instruction and reading are good ways of learning. Spending time at work is a bad way of gaining satisfaction, but spending time at leisure is a good way for that. The former activities reduce freedom, and the latter activities increase it. That was known to most thinkers in history, who were privileged enough to live the life of the mind, because they were either born into aristocratic families or were financed by one to do things which they enjoyed anyway (though, it is one notch less of freedom).

But even if we now assumed that I have now convinced you that attaining the greatest amount of freedom is a desirable thing to have, you might argue that I am a dreamer, who wants to accomplish things, which are simply not feasible in current society. We have to create a standardized system in education, where students are told precisely what they should know, or else the discipline in society would disappear, and we would have chaos. The even worse chaos would be in the sphere of work. If people wanted to maximize their freedom and leisure time, that would mean we would not have enough workers to fill important jobs and the society would collapse.

To be honest: I am not concerned about either outcome. Let us not forget why discipline in education is so important: because we need workers, who are disciplined at work. So let us focus on work first. There currently is quite an active discussion about the guaranteed universal basic income, where every person is paid a certain amount of money just by being citizens of a country. Why has that discussion arisen? The way I see it, the reason why we want to discuss the basic income scheme is because the world of work has changed sufficiently to undermine the laborist political economy, which relies on wage labor to function (see my discussion in Liu 2015, "Should We Support a Universal Basic Income?").

We are currently concerned about the creation of an army of unemployed people, because technology encroaches on so many jobs. Of course, it does not have to end so dramatically, because we could just expand one of these bullshit jobs like finance or consulting, and feed more people with jobs that are only about swapping empty paper promises and giving nonsense advice to managers. But for the sake of creating a good society, we should be mindful of what this is all about: bullshit jobs. Unnecessary jobs. The original attack against the leisure-maximization scheme is that there would not be sufficient production to keep the society going, but what if there is plenty of production, and we merely have a proliferation of bullshit jobs without which the employment picture would be even worse than it currently is? Let us just stop producing these bullshit jobs, pay out the UBI, and allow people to decide themselves whether they feel free at work or at leisure.

The discussion of work naturally affects the way how we look at education as well. If we don't need to have a disciplined workforce in a very automated society, we also don't need to have disciplined students, which would eliminate the intrinsic requirement for threatening assessments, and open up the opportunity for most students to study what they like to study. Not everyone will pick the route of more education, and we certainly require a minimum amount of schooling, so that people can function in society (e.g. read and understand cooking instructions in the supermarket). But we should not have to force people to take it. I find it even more likely that in a society where the obligation for work disappears, the prospect of undergoing lifelong education becomes more and not less likely.

The basic income scheme is not really an outlandish proposal, though it is certainly considered as such because we lack the political imagination, which is itself the outcome of a world, where going according to formula, i.e. GPA-maximization, income-maximization and profit-maximization lie at the heart of our political economy. The mark of true education and the pursuit of freedom would be at least to acknowledge that there could be desirable alternatives to the status quo.

Disputing the Scarcity Principle
Posted on October 30, 2015

One of the basic tenets of economics is that there is a principle of scarcity, which gives rise to economic theorizing and observations about economic life. The evidence of it can be taken from two simple examples: the air and a house. We evidently need both things in order to live, but the one thing exists in abundance and is for free, while the other one is scarce and quite expensive. Why would housing be scarce? Well, housing is created mostly from human labor. We, therefore, need construction workers to build the house for us. We need the raw material such as brick and cement, which requires more workers. We need an architect to plan the design of the building for us. We need city officials to give us the approval for the project, because the new house cannot conflict with zoning regulations. We need realtors to tell us about the availability of houses in the neighborhood, and so forth.

All of these people that are connected to the process of getting a house need to be paid off, such that I can enjoy the comfort of a home. It is not surprising that housing is one of the most expensive items for our daily budget, while we scarcely worry about enough air to breathe. (It is a somewhat different picture in countries where the water and air are so polluted that it is hard to breathe or drink the water there. What a great externality!)

The factor of labor that is embedded in the final product has a great influence on the final price. This is an old insight in classical political economy, and was theorized as such from Smith, to Ricardo and Marx. Labor is the decisive scarce factor in our political economy, and if we want to cut down on our personal expenses we need to expend as little labor from another human being as possible. If I want to save money on food, I would go to the supermarket and buy raw meat and vegetables, and cook it at home. It costs more time to cook it myself than go to a restaurant, but I am not paying another cook, so I get to save money when I do the cooking.

If we look all around us, therefore, the scarcity principle must be the most important factor that is ruling our material lives, and we are constantly facing a trade-off between consuming different items, because we are facing a budget constraint resulting from our limited wage income (or other income, usually for more affluent people, such as rents and dividends). Richer people face a smaller budget constraint than poorer people.

But I would argue that the textbook scarcity model is increasingly becoming obsolete. We are facing quite the opposite situation: a society of surplus production, which does not really trickle down to the masses because of growing wealth and income inequality resulting from private property laws favoring the owning class. US presidential candidate Bernie Sanders is correct in pointing out that the US "is the richest country in the history of the world. But most Americans don't know that because almost all of the wealth rests in the hands of the few. America now has more wealth and income inequality than any major country on earth, and it is worse today than at any time since 1928." (C-Span, Sen. Bernie Sanders Speech at Iowa Democratic Party Dinner, July 18, 2015)

So why do I think that the scarcity model is wrong? Let me explain. During the time of the industrial revolution, most people shifted from farming to manufacturing, which has been such a labor-intensive activity. This is merely a labor-shifting activity, as human needs have grown with the increased scale of production. In other words, in addition to just eating food, and having a regular food supply, people began to purchase cotton clothing and later household gadgets like refrigerators and so forth. The displaced workers in the farming sector, which has increasingly grown more productive have found a safe haven in manufacturing production.

One essential insight provided by Schumpeter (1942) is that the capitalist economy is a very dynamic socio-economic system, which is marked by growing innovation and increases in labor productivity. Machinery, technology and R&D are important aspects for capitalist dynamism and growth. Increasing labor productivity could be translated into more jobs, because more people consume the stuff that gets produced, but that is a short-term effect. The long-term effect is usually a saturation of demand, such that consumers use their savings to buy other commodities, and create jobs in other sectors. In an ideal economy, we could endlessly produce new and good jobs, and the economic circulation functions pretty well.

However, we know that is not what has happened. As labor productivity continues to increase, we are certainly moving up the frontier of development and production, but we are pushing most workers out of the nice high-paying and high-productivity jobs, which today encompass agriculture, manufacturing, oil, gas, utilities and transportation among a few other industries. These are all sectors, which explain why our standard of living is so high today, yet it is not in those sectors that most of us work in. Why is the link between the standard of living and work so important? Because our political economy is still based on wage labor and the principle of scarcity. Workers need to be able to justify their existence by selling their labor power to any employer willing to hire them at a given wage.

But the problem is that most of the new jobs are low-income service-sector jobs, where the ability to unionize and get better wages and working conditions are simply terrible. Attempts to unionize Walmart hit the barrier that it is difficult to coordinate a united strike in over more than 4,000 stores nationwide, which was not the case for auto workers, who needed to shut down two plants to shut down the entire car industry, and could press their demands more effectively against recalcitrant management.

The other problem is that of stagnant productivity in the service industry, which is associated with Baumol's cost disease, as it is applied to education or medicine, two of the most labor-intensive industries of the present. Labor productivity remains constant, but wages need to increase to attract sufficient talent into these areas, which has a crowding out effect, according to this economic theory. But let us slow down for a minute and take away the economist-speak. It is true that doctors and teachers don't tend to increase their productivity, but would you say that seeing your doctor for five minutes is better than seeing him for half an hour? Would the quality of his service be really much better for you if he processed you faster? I very much doubt that. Would you say that a teacher, who can process a larger amount of students in shorter periods of time can fulfill his pedagogical duties to his students? I very much doubt that.

Overcoming Baumol's cost disease in many service industries, therefore, makes no sense, even though the automation geeks want to innovate these sectors too, e.g. expanding Web MD and online education courses. The doctors and teachers are still quite lucky, because they are professionals with scarce skills, but the high-demand, low-skill, low-productivity jobs are now associated with low wages too, and there is great hesitancy to raise their wages for the market-distorting effects it will have (I doubt that claim, because I think current minimum wage laws are way too low to have adverse employment effects.) Now neoclassical economists will insist that workers that, therefore, work in low-productivity industries will have to toil in poverty forever, because that is all the economic contribution that they are making.

But let me go back to a point made earlier: the conundrum is that we have a few capital-intensive sectors with very few jobs that tend to pay high wages (though that is also a function of organized labor power) and dish out high profits, while we have many service sector jobs that pay low wages, especially in lower end health services, hospitality and retail, where the bulk of the jobs are. Education, medicine, business and professional services tend to be rather well-paid, but given the increasing level of job competition and education credentials that many young people are racking up, I cannot imagine that their wages will stay so high indefinitely (unless they purposefully limit entry, like the doctors).

But there is no law of reason or economics which says that the profits which remain in the capital-intensive sector should stay within that sector. Yet in a private-enterprise and private property based economy, we are stating precisely such. Exxon Mobile is a massive oil corporation with $40 billion in annual profits. This is plenty of cash to help out communities that are struggling to keep their libraries and schools open, but the latter will continue to be starved, while the oil giants continue to collect huge subsidies and tax breaks from the government, which simply enriches the few shareholders while hurting almost everyone else. Growing wealth and income inequality has negative consequences for the spiritual well-being of society, and also diminishes future growth prospects, because the rich only spend a small fraction of their total income (see Dabla-Norris et al. 2015).

For leftists to demand a universal basic income, flowing to the beleaguered low-income workers and unemployed people, financed either via the taxation of the highly profitable capital-intensive industries or direct public ownership over these industries is precisely right and reasonable. To finally reclaim to the communities what are now royalties and rent payments to the global oligarchs would be a huge win for most ordinary people, and a blow to the principle of scarcity, which has controlled the livelihoods of so many workers around the world.

I am mindful that scarcity will continue to exist, because we won't be able to continue our growth, waste and consumption model and live in a habitable planet, but we should go away from the idea that poverty and misery are in any way essential to a 21st century modern society. Resources will need to be rationally allocated under any new system with strong consideration for environmental impacts, but rational certainly does not mean that a few people own almost everything while everyone else owns almost nothing.

Historic Meeting among Two Chinese Leaders
Posted on November 8, 2015

There is a very delicate relationship between the two Chinas, which still proclaim that there is only one China. Taiwan says (somewhat quietly) that it is the Republic of China, and China says triumphantly that it is the People's Republic of China. My word choice, of course, is heavily tilted toward Beijing (henceforth also just 'China'), and that has to do with the greater political and economic power of the People's Republic, while Taiwan has kept itself afloat with US promises of protection and the deployment of air craft carriers to guard the Taiwan strait. The China-Taiwan conflict in diplomatic terms has been frozen in time. In other words, when Chiang Kai-shek took his army and fled to Taiwan, and the Communists under Mao Zedong seized power in the mainland, there has been no change in that peculiar political configuration.

It is all the more surprising, therefore, that the two Chinese leaders, Ma Ying-jeou from Taiwan and Xi Jinping from China have decided to meet up in Singapore, a neutral host country, to informally discuss their political positions and differences. There must be some political calculations involved on both sides. Xi tries to gain more amicable relations with neighboring countries, and hopes that the talks could be the beginning of a unification policy. 一国两制, one country and two systems, is what the current Chinese government strongly prefers, while Taipei, as the weaker partner, will want to delay this question of reunification as long as possible. The fate of Hong Kong, which is increasingly feeling the authoritarian pressures from Beijing, reveals that there could be clear disadvantages to promoting a one country policy from the perspective of Taiwan.

Opposition leader, Tsai Ing-wen, in the meantime, is criticizing her president, Ma, for meeting with the Chinese leader, because it "does not increase the safety of the people in Taiwan". There is evidently a fear that Ma will make concessions about the political status of Taiwan, even though there is no formal statement that the two leaders will issue, so there will be no face-losing. What is also quite unusual for Chinese traditions is that when the two leaders met for lunch, they were splitting the bill evenly, which is not unusual in the west, but quite so in China. It is also ironic that Ma has waited until the very last minute of his term, which expires in January 2016, to initiate direct talks with the Chinese leadership.

What is Ma trying to accomplish at the very last minute? Does he want to force his own opposition that is poised to win the presidential elections next year to make serious concessions about their pro-independence stance? When Chen Shui-bian from the Democratic Progressive Party (DPP) was in power (2000-8), there were no strong official exchanges across the straits, reflecting China's suspicion against Taiwan's pro-independence leadership. It is all the more ironic that Beijing only feels comfortable to work together with their former enemies, the Nationalist party. Whenever the Nationalists were in power, there were signals toward rapprochement between the two Chinas. It could possibly be that the Nationalist stance of one China allows sufficient ambiguity to suppress China's ire against Taiwan.

Whoever will become the next leader in the presidential elections in Taiwan will have to confront the fact that an ever more powerful and wealthy China will want to press the reunification issue even harder, and not weaker. I find it very unlikely that a DPP president will make any pro-independence statements. I also don't find it likely that the current or future US president wants to press for a war against China just so they can make a point about protecting Taiwan's freedom. The real policy outcomes will tend to be muddy and unclear, which can benefit either Taiwan or China more, depending on their negotiating skills.

Over the long term, I don't see many alternatives to the one country, two system model, as it is envisioned by China. There will be some discontent among the Taiwanese people that have worked so hard to entrench their democratic system over the last 25 years. Will all of that be for naught once the Beijing rulers claim full sovereignty over the island? The US will likely add a veto to any such resolution, but as day passes by, the US imperial power is not what it once was, and it cannot afford to antagonize China too much.

Another possible outcome is that China and Taiwan maintain the status quo into the indefinite future, where Taiwan simply refuses to respond to China's overtures toward reunification. It is unlikely that China will implement a stiff sanction regime against Taiwan, because we are talking still about a very rich island, whose investment resources are still sorely needed to develop China. So brutally antagonizing the Taipei leadership will also not help in bringing the outcast sheep back to the herd, and may make armed conflict more rather than less likely, and China is more than reluctant to play the bad cop when it needs peace to prosper.

Whatever outcome either side is contemplating on, what needs to certainly happen is that the personal contacts increase (which is evidenced with cross-strait family and relationship ties, and business connections), and also the high-level contacts. The presidents of each country should regularize meetings perhaps once a year to ensure that any differences in policy approaches can be figured out beforehand so as to avoid an intensification of conflict. For that reason, I strongly welcome this great historic meeting between the two Chinese leaders.

Why the Paris Terrorist Attacks Should Concern Us All

Posted on November 14, 2015

According to various different news reports, over 120 Parisians have been killed by a string of terrorist attacks. The terrorists traveled throughout Europe, came to France, detonated a few bombs, and used AK-47s to produce mayhem in night clubs, a stadium and the streets of Paris. Leaders all over the western world are issuing statements of solidarity with France. ISIS has indicated their responsibility for these attacks, and the various western governments have vowed to step up their attacks against terrorists, who "oppose our way of life".

Very understandably, besides the mourning among the families of those killed, and the shock of a whole nation, there are already political preparations to respond to these heinous attacks. What can be done? What should be done?

The immediate knee-jerk reaction would be to desire to send ground troops into Iraq and Syria. The US already has 50 Special Forces stationed in Syria. France has stepped up aerial raids in Syria since the end of September. Should there be even more involvement? One thing that is clear is that if president Hollande stepped forward with a plan to destroy ISIS with boots on the ground, he would get the overwhelming public support, which is reminiscent to Bush's war on terrorism campaign following 9/11. We know that both invasions in Iraq and Afghanistan were quagmires, which hurt US international reputation, and have not made the security situation in the Middle East much better. In fact, the US certainly made it worse by creating more political instability than existed before their intervention.

One difference, though, is that France is not the US, and does not have the same military capacity to wage long-winded wars. When the French tried to keep their beloved Indochina colony after the end of World War II, they were badly defeated by the Vietcong, despite heavy US military and financial support. When the Algerians declared independence from France, they were again routed out despite their brutal massacre. Lastly, when the French and the British were carrying out their no-fly zone in Libya, they would have accomplished nothing without US logistical support to sustain these air raids.

If we read the statements of the British and US governments closely, there are indications that if the French were to pursue a boots on the ground strategy in Syria, that they would back up their French allies. The US would be pulled into another long-winded and bloody conflict, which comes at tremendous cost to them. This is precisely the calculation that I am very afraid will be played out.

I have no doubt that ISIS is a major security threat to western countries, which needs to be contained. But it is not practicable to support another ground invasion with insecure political and military outcomes. The reason for terrorist support is the lack of functioning political institutions in the Middle East, which produce significant support for terrorist activity. The other problem is the so-called homegrown terrorists, which carry western passports, but have been sufficiently brainwashed by terrorists, who tell them that their life is meaningful if they enter the jihad.

But the solution cannot be to increase bombing campaigns in the Middle East, which thwart further advances in building political institutions that are stable, and provide the people in the Middle East with a more hopeful perspective. The answer can also not be to increase police surveillance and re-establish the borders, so that ordinary and innocent people are eventually victimized by an over-eager police state. Unfortunately, in an atmosphere, where financial and economic austerity is the only acceptable political decision, we are also not doing anything to give the marginalized populations any hope, such that they can't be so easily convinced to join terrorist organizations. Loic Wacquant (2001) had pointed out that the penal state, where many people are put in jail and criminalized, is intimately connected with the state's desire to manage social insecurity in a neoliberal political economy.

It is the logic of despair, and the politics of despair, which dominate our current discourse surrounding security and terrorism, and allow our leaders to make potentially stupid choices. Ironically, of all organizations that seek to profit from insecurity, it is Facebook, which just rolled out the "mark-safe" feature, where people can mark themselves and others safe if they happen to be in Paris or wherever terrorist attacks happen. We are showing our gratefulness to the multibillion dollar corporation, which is absorbing (and controlling) so much of our waking time- and surely increase our loyalty to it because of these nice extra features; and yet, at the same time, we are reminded that conflicts are business opportunities for some that cannot be wasted.

So what should we do? In the absence of an international agreement of the major powers, there is a real likelihood that this conflict will not be settled in the immediate future. Russia and the US cannot be working at crossroads here, but need to work together to make it difficult for ISIS to gain more ground. The Arab states

(Saudi Arabia, Qatar and UAE) need to be more involved in fighting ISIS. Let us hope that these heinous terrorist attacks remain the exception in western countries. They are, unfortunately, quite a regular sight in the Middle East.

Are Men and Women Different?

Posted on <u>November 29, 2015</u>

The simple answer to the above question is 'yes'. Pro-feminist discourse usually emphasizes the full equality between the two sexes. And it is fair for women to demand a greater degree of equality when it comes to pay, sharing of housework, sharing of child care and family care, and other activities in social life. But, on the other hand, to say that men and women are the same in all respects would neither be at the service of increasing women's social and economic advancement, nor will it help us to explore the very real biological, psychological and sociological differences in gender.

In politically correct speech today, it is apparently not possible to discuss very real gender differences without adding a long-winded preface that one supports most if not all of the practical political objectives of gender equality advanced by feminist groups. But I will venture the risk and devote this post to uncovering and stating the precise distinctions between the genders drawing from my personal experiences and some research that has been done on it.

Let me start with a personal observation. I have recently attended a seminar group, which had an about equal number of men and women, and we were supposed to debate for and against a proposition. I was naturally looking forward to debates like these, as it placed me mentally back into high school, where I had participated in the school debate team, and eagerly looked forward to engage other hormone-driven teenagers of my caliber. I never won any competition, but I relished the experience of defending my argument against others using evidence. To some extent, I was very much used to this environment, because I grew up constantly debating my brother on political and social issues, and he would sure be my devil's advocate. I would make a proposition, and he would often attack it, even if he agreed with me. That would usually enrage me, but it taught me quite useful debating skills. What was even more disheartening when I was younger, was that my brother was three years older than me, and so he was much ahead of me, and I had to struggle even harder than him just to keep on par with his arguments.

So, there I was, a naturally groomed and passionate debater. I took careful notes of what the other side said, and then drew arrows underneath on the sheet of paper. Beside the arrow I would craft the counter-argument that came to my mind as quickly as I could, and use these notes in the rebuttal phase, where I made quick counter-arguments to weaken my opponent's position. I sparred with the other guys, felt the increased heart beat and adrenaline, and savored every moment of it.

There was a teacher, who monitored the whole debate, and toward the end she noted that the women did not talk at all. So here I was cued in to pay attention to the gender dimension. When she finished the comment, there was one woman, who then raised her hand, and made her point of rebuttal after the debate was virtually over. Now that the teacher had pointed out what had appeared to be a problem to her, the one woman broke her silence. So what is the explanation for female silence?

I briefly discussed this issue with a few women and men in the seminar group, and was simply curious to know what the answer was. There is a great deal of subtlety, which I had received from one of the women. One of them said that they thought a little bit too slow, and their arguments had been made by the men, who were more forceful in raising their hands. Another reaction was that of cultural backgrounds (we have Asian and Middle Eastern female students), and women from foreign backgrounds were less willing to speak up, because they lacked linguistic competence (which can only partly account for the silence, because I thought their English language level was quite high). The other woman made a much more subtle comment and claimed that it was the action of the female teacher, which influenced their silence. She claimed that while the teacher was approving of the male comments, she was quite disapproving of the female students' comments.

Now that is quite powerful, and let us consider the implications if her statement is correct. What does it mean if a female teacher behaves in such a way? This would all go back to biology. A woman admires what the man says, no matter how stupid and illogical his statement may be, because men have a certain ego, which needs to be stroked, and women know that, so that they are purposefully deferential, because that is what makes them a more attractive sexual partner for the man. On the other hand, women treat other women as sexual adversaries, and to the extent that that is the case, women will subconsciously want to put down other women. There are observational studies of how women behave in one way if they are with women only and if they are with men, when their body language becomes more flirty (see the documentary- https://www.youtube.com/watch?v=SBOtj1RmaUE - about 3min into the video).

Women will not always be other women's adversary, and we can certainly see that when women sit down together to analyze their male dates or gossip about other women (which is the pattern that I have observed) over a drink, having much fun and bonding in that way. But there are certain biological patterns, which favor my interpretation of events.

Now, I hear your objection. Why would a middle-aged female teacher be interested in stroking the male ego of students half her age, and belittle other women equally half her age (i.e. both outside her league)? Why would crude biology help in explaining a purely academic setting, where other important highly abstract issues are discussed? My counterargument here is simply that people behave like people, wherever they are, whether hunting for animals in the wild or discussing philosophy in cozy seminar rooms. We cannot escape the way how we are wired and behave simply because we rationally state that we don't behave like that in certain settings. Things like body language are pre-conscious. In other words, we do a revealing body movement, reflecting our innermost thoughts and feelings, even though our mouth says other things, which are socially more acceptable. By the time we realize that our body language is giving our true selves away, it is already too late, and we can't do too much to alter it.

In this seminar and debate setting, the female students were apparently discouraged simply because they felt put down by their elder rival, who had the institutional power as a teacher, while the younger women, who were dutifully taught how social hierarchy works, practiced silence and mental retreat. Would these women have spoken out more if the teacher was male? Or would they practice submissiveness even more to impress the male teacher, while the male teacher does all the intellectual impression work and compete with his younger male students?

It is noteworthy to watch documentaries of female textile workers in the developing world, where there are only very few male workers. Female workers are more family conscious and more concerned about how work disruptions can completely stop the money flow to the family, thus harming the family, so they are less likely to go on strike than their more self-confident and self-centered men. Capitalist bosses, therefore, appreciate their obedient female labor force. So much for the male breadwinner model.

I am sure the example can be replicated in the educational system of developed countries, where girls are more well-adjusted, i.e. stir less trouble, than their male counterparts. That helps girls to be the teacher's pet, and get better grades than boys, and get ahead in the school system until they hit the university, where their well-adjustment no longer helps them as much as creativity and unconventional thinking, which we also associate with the more rambunctious boys. So, yes, girls do tend to have much better educational performances than boys, but that is as much a function of social capital as it is of intellectual capital.

Are there definite things we can say about intellectual capital among genders? Yes, the bell curve distribution for male intelligence is flatter than for females (Schrager 2015). In other words, there are more women of average intelligence than men, and there are more men that are very stupid or very intelligent than women. Is there some biologically useful explanation at work here? The one I found convincing was that women are the nurturers in the family, so they have to make sure that things get done in the domestic sphere. If you are too stupid, then it is not possible to raise children, and if you are too smart, then you are too distracted with abstract thoughts to care for your offspring. It would be biologically stupid, therefore, to have too many extreme cases of women. On the other hand, it is okay if a man does not focus on the domestic sphere. The intelligent people are required to carry the human race forward (the Albert Einstein's of the world). But what can we say of the usefulness of the less intelligent men? To that I would ask in response, why should we assume that every person is useful for the human race?

What about sociology? Sociological gender analysis simply states that women are more silent than men in public settings, because society enforces the norm of men belonging to the public sphere and women belonging to the private sphere (Habermas 1962). Men and women speak about an equal number of words during the day, but men speak more in public (e.g. in public lectures or court rooms), while women speak more in private (e.g. with close friends and family members). In this account, one cannot say for sure that women know less or want to impress their male colleagues, but that social norms inhibit female speech. If we change social norms, we will change female speech behavior.

Hillary Clinton (2004), not afraid to play the power politics game in the front row, had noted in her autobiography (the first one as first lady, not as secretary of state) that when she testified in front of the male-dominated Congress in the 1990s to defend her health care overhaul proposal, she felt like a speaking dog. One would not expect a dog to speak, and be surprised that she would utter intelligent and coherent statements. Clinton was apparently clearly violating the social norm of women not belonging to the public sphere. I can think of other examples where women are judged differently than men. Let us think of two managers: a man and a woman, and both react to their subordinate's failures by screaming at them. The man will be perceived as authoritative, the woman as bitchy and unseemly.

This is the exciting area for feminists, because sociological analysis can show that women can break the glass ceiling, can push the boundaries of what is possible for women in the public sphere. That is perhaps one reason why my field is dominated by women. The women that I spoke to used excuses and rationalizations so as not to speak up during the debate. They mentally pre-empted their utterances, filtered it, calmed themselves down, belittled their own ideas, and refused to break their silence. I very much doubt that the women would be as silent with their close friends and family members. On the other hand, I can say as a man that this self-castigation seldom crosses my mind. If I get an idea, I find it important enough to raise it, because it is more important for me to get more knowledge and test my ideas than to keep them in secret and never find out. Once women gain enough self-confidence they can be quite powerful speakers and advocates of their own right, and be role models to other women.

But let us go back to the other famous public women, who are not afraid to raise their voice and defend their arguments. I have watched these Republican and Democratic debates, and as a reinforcement of the stereotype, there is a glaring lack of women among the contenders. There is Carly Fiorina and Hillary Clinton. Donald Trump never hides his sexism, and bashes any woman he encounters and he just can't help it, whether it is a female moderator (who apparently menstruates visibly in front of his eyes) or his fellow presidential candidate. Fiorina shot back at Trump, calling him out for his sexism, which should make any woman wary of supporting him for president. Maybe some women buy this argument from her, but Trump is strangely leading the polls and by a wide margin. He surely has less female support than male support, but Republican women are certainly not supporting Fiorina in overwhelming numbers or else she would not be trailing so far behind in the polls. I remember watching Fiorina's comments during the debate, and her response simply was not very convincing. Her voice lacked the firmness, and the nonchalant self-confidence that her male counterparts had. Yeah, public appearance certainly matters.

On the Democratic side, Hillary Clinton is the clear leader in the polls. Her main challenger, Bernie Sanders, from the populist left is trailing her campaign by 25 points, and there is not much time left for him to catch up. The entire political establishment supports Clinton's campaign, so if we were simply to judge the numbers, we could argue that my attacks on Fiorina miss the point. Maybe Democrats are just more civilized and progressive on gender issues than the bigoted, anti-women GOP (look at their cheap shot attacks on Planned Parenthood). The debates are, indeed, much more civilized in the Democratic Party, and Bernie Sanders and Martin O'Malley are clearly also supporters of women's causes. I would say Sanders even more so than Clinton, because he proposes a higher minimum wage than her, which certainly benefits more women than men, as women tend to earn less.

But let us not get bogged down by the policy content, which is interesting in its own right. Let us look at the Democratic debates as observers of intellect, body language, facial expressions, and speech intonation. Clinton presented herself as an establishment figure, who wants to preserve the status quo. Her voice and appearance are rather calm and firm, and she rarely went off script. This may be said irrespective of gender, but women certainly have an added credibility when they are good girls intent on not rocking the boat. Sanders is her clear opponent to the left, his intonation is much more vocal and vociferous, and his male gender gives him added credibility as such a challenger to mainstream politics. When Sanders attacked Clinton's Super PAC and her closeness to her Wall Street donors, Clinton could just gush in an embarrassed manner, and defend her nebulous (i.e. inexistent) plan to rein in Wall Street speculation.

Without pushing further with the details of the debate, I just want to ask you the following question: can you imagine the roles being reversed? In other words, imagine that Sanders is the establishment candidate, and Clinton is his left-wing challenger. It is like Segolene Royal (socialist) against Nicolas Sarkozy in the 2007 presidential elections in France. But she lost. Sarkozy lost five years later against her former partner, Francois Hollande. Remember the social norms: we expect women in public to be the good girls, the well-behaved students and workers- to draw from my earlier examples. The society does not appreciate Iron Ladies like Margaret Thatcher, whose determination to defend a small British island in the Atlantic scared the shit out of Argentina's dictator. On the other hand, the society does appreciate an Angela Merkel, whose dull speeches are as exciting as those of boring lecturers. People crave the steady hand, and calm averageness of a reliable grandmother (though Merkel does not have children).

For whatever reason, women are more silent in public than men, and I have made my attempt here to explain why.

The Problem with Guns

Posted on December 6, 2015

In San Bernadino, California, one couple with links to terrorists (but operating largely independently) have killed 14 civilians and injured 21 more. But terrorism itself is not the major problem in the contemporary US, but the fact that so many people (88 guns for every 100 people) own guns, resulting in over 400,000 gun deaths between 2001 and 2013 (Simon and Sanchez 2015).

The defenders of the second amendment usually claim that we should not increase restrictions on gun access and gun control, because (1) taking weapons away from people would indiscriminately target law-abiding citizens, and (2) law-abiding gun owners can stop criminal gun owners during emergency situations. And less seriously, there is a paranoid fringe in the country, which claims that (3) they need guns to protect themselves against an evil big government.

We can very easily dismiss each of these points.

(1) America is a country, which prides itself with the freedom to do many things, but the question is whether these additional rights (which some would deny, because the second amendment only grants militias free gun access, not private individuals) create more harm than good. Is it not better to deny gun access to law-abiding individuals than have criminals have access to guns?

Some would claim that preventing law-abiding people from acquiring guns will do nothing to stop criminals from acquiring guns. But the point is that if we have such an active gun culture where it is so easy for anyone, whether law-abiding or criminal, to access guns, then it will automatically be easier for the criminals to also acquire guns. Some people just want to add a background check to rule out that criminals can access guns, but I think even that measure does not go really far enough, because many gunmen do not have active criminal backgrounds, so they acquire the gun legally, and then create the mayhem.

In other countries, it is true that law-abiding citizens have a hard time acquiring gun rights and access to guns, but it is also harder for criminals to access them too. They might still get it via the black market, but the risks for that are higher, and the lack of gun culture resulting in the lack of much gun violence is reflected in the gun violence statistics in other developed countries of the world.

(2) It is a plain myth that law-abiding gun owners will stop active shooters. In most situations, even normal gun owners mostly keep their weapon safely stored at home (or not, because many kids in the US get killed by unsafely stored guns at home), which implies that during emergency situations, there won't be anybody with the gun ready. Even if they had the gun with them, I have never heard of a story of a heroic John Wayne stopping a killer with his own gun. I have heard some stories of courageous individuals, who are stopping petty thieves robbing the handbag of a woman, but I don't remember the robbers having any guns with them. The heroic savior with the gun is an altogether unlikely situation. All of the gunmen were stopped by an overwhelming show of force of the police. They come in large units with their helmet, Kevlar vests, shields and rifles. Not even policemen have been told to go in there alone, and pull a Rambo.

(3) There is this ridiculous paranoia in the country that the government will come to take away the guns of individuals, so there will be nothing for the citizen to protect himself against the evil government. All state provisions are apparently bad, except when it comes to the second amendment, which the forefathers had placed into the constitution to ensure the liberty and private property of individuals. But one should note that the second amendment was designed to erect a state militia against the British colonial rulers, because in the early days there wasn't any strong federal army, so the exigencies of the moment required the founding fathers of this country to add this amendment to the constitution.

And let us consider the substance of the argument. I am all for civil liberties and protecting people against an overpowerful surveillance state, but that does not mean that guns can make people safer against the government. Martin Luther King and others have shown the example that it is possible to challenge government policies via peaceful means, and it is not necessary to use guns to achieve political aims. In addition, if the government wanted to target individuals, they could do so easily. They could blow out our brains with a drone strike in a moment in the middle of the night, even as we are clutching our AK-47 in our sleep. It is entirely ridiculous to defend ourselves physically against a state, whose primary prerogative is the monopolization of the use of violence, or else we have anarchy and warlords ruling the neighborhoods.

The political ramifications of this discussion are all too clear. We don't need more vigil marches, prayers, sermons and other war on terrorism campaigns. What we need is commonsense legislation to significantly restrict gun rights, by making it at least difficult for most people to acquire new weapons. It would be a blow to the NRA and the weapons industry, but it is a small cost relative to the immeasurable human cost that the society currently has to pay for its foolishly liberal gun laws.

Why are Right-Wing Populists on the Rise?

Posted on December 9, 2015

Donald Trump is the clear leader in the Republican polls, and many people of the "correct" establishment claim that he is a genuine threat to US democracy, because of his fascist positions. He wants to build a border wall against Mexico, slap tariffs on China-imported consumer goods, and equip every Muslim American with some kind of criminal file. The latest statement in his rally was to limit internet access for young people (how paternalist!), so they are less likely to be exposed to terrorist material.

Only four years ago, such a radical right-wing discourse seemed very much impossible. But increasingly, we are witnessing that democratic politics in the US is undermined, but not only by their right-wing demagogues. What demagogues like Trump are doing is to channel the furious anger of the lesser educated classes against a political and economic system that is clearly rigged against them.

We cannot only observe right-wing forces in the US, but see them also in France, where the Front National is expected to win three of the regional elections, and some speculate that Marine Le Pen might accomplish what her father had not, which is to win the presidential elections in 2017. Conservative and socialist parties attempt their cordon sanitaire by fielding only one candidate, either conservative or socialist, to ensure that FN candidates don't win.

In Poland, the national conservative Law and Justice Party won the elections decisively this past October, putting Beata Szydlo in charge as prime minister, though some would suggest that it is really Jaroslaw Kaczynski, who wields the real power in the party. As a sign of their Euroskepticism, the government had removed the EU flag from their cabinet room. The new government is rather vigorous in opposing an EU quota for taking in new refugees.

In my hometown in Vienna, the right-wing FPO received 31% of the vote, coming behind the SPO with 39%. The people are voicing their anger and disgust about the refugee crisis, as many refugees end up in Vienna. The Social Democrats are in power, and are blamed for the perceived out-of-control growth of the refugee population. FPO has never been this successful, and I think they are one or two elections away from winning the mayoralty.

There is substantial evidence, therefore, that most western democracies are encountering a political challenge that it has not seen in its 70 years of existence. Why is democracy so fragile? To answer this question, I should first reject some possible answers.

It is highly unlikely that we can get some answers via essentialist bland statements, like people tend to be too stupid to discern the low-quality leadership of right-wing parties, or right-wing leaders are too charismatic and speak to the primal fears of the public. My problem with essentialist explanations is that they are not really historical. If any of these essentialist problems are so serious and so threatening to western democracy, one might expect that democracy is an experiment that should have long ago failed, and not only after more than 70 years.

If we want to explain the destruction of the democratic polity via right-wing ascendancy, we have to establish the historical developments that led to such destruction. I argue that immigration and neoliberalism are two valid explanations. In Europe, we can clearly point to the refugee crisis as a proximate trigger for the right-wing surge, but here we need to be cautious again, because the rise of the right-wing long preceded the most recent refugee wave.

Europe and the US have long become more diverse. The economic requirement of filling labor shortages, and demands from employers for more immigration, have resulted in rather liberal immigration laws for a certain period of time. Even as economic conditions changed, and immigration laws were toughened, it was rather difficult to convince the immigrants to return to ancestral homelands. Increasing diversity can occasionally be well managed, as is the case in Canada, where immigrants come according to a point-system, so that the immigrants turn out to speak better English and have better qualifications than the long-term native people.

In most cases, immigration tends to be highly contentious and rather bungled. Political leaders often have no clear idea how to integrate immigrants, even though that is what their Sunday speeches suggest. One usually hopes that over time, there is some adjustment process that is happening, and it usually does happen. But we know that integration is, in many cases, not so successful, which is partly due to native hostility, discrimination in school and the workplace, and immigrant frustration.

The frustration is particularly strong in the second rather than in the first generation. The first generation of immigrants never completely adjust to the local surrounding, they speak in a strong foreign accent, and they don't have many native friends, but they are very grateful to their host country, because they might have escaped war, conflict or poverty at home. The psychological circumstances for the second generation are altogether different. They grow up along with the other kids in the neighborhood, and want the same kind of treatment and respect as those other native kids. The fact that this is inevitably not happening leads to enormous frustration, and we have by now witnessed several cases of terrorism by second-generation Muslims in Europe. These are the home-grown terrorists, which no amount of security controls can undermine.

The consequence of terrorism is that it gives right-wing politicians a justification to increase crackdowns on Muslim groups, and the people will become even more paranoid about the insecure situation that Muslim immigrants have apparently created. There is then a negative feedback effect of more suspicion, and more social withdrawal, occasionally resulting in violence. Right-wing populist parties gain more support, because they are articulating radical policies that seem to make sense, but are not doing anything to resolve the crisis.

The second major factor for the growth of right-wing political forces is the fact that there is a neoliberal consensus in the western developed world, which is marked by growing poor work conditions, economic insecurity, unemployment, underemployment, poverty and inequality. There is a strong tendency of a secular stagnation of the macroeconomy, where little economic growth is happening, and there are few incentives for companies to make substantial investments in job-creating production.

What is more likely to happen is that wealth is siphoned off into speculative bubbles, which is fed by the low-interest and quantitative easing policies of the central banks, which are doing all they can to flood the banks with liquidity but not help out the real economy. There is some evidence showing that QE tends to benefit mostly the rich assetholders, as they are best suited to use the loan capital to acquire assets cheaply. Most of the regular people, who barely own any assets can't benefit from these asset bubbles. In fact, we struggle even more with finding affordable housing in the popular cities across the world.

We have also seen a shift from manufacturing toward service-sector employment. This trend should theoretically be rather unremarkable, because a shift in the employment structure is normal to the working of modernization and a capitalist economy. But the shift is remarkable insofar as most service sector jobs are of low-quality, whereas the jobs that are lost in the manufacturing sector tend to be rather well-paid. Now, you could say that someone, who screws auto parts together is not intrinsically more productive than someone who wipes the backs of old people in nursing homes, but the former is still getting paid more than the latter. So what is happening here is that low-paid workers in the service sector have less organizational clout (trade union power) than workers in the declining manufacturing industry.

But even workers in the manufacturing industry are giving away many concessions. The pressures tend to be twofold: first, manufacturing jobs can be lost with the threat of outsourcing to cheaper countries. In many cases, managers do not outsource, but they are sure to put pressures against the workers to give concessions in collective bargaining. Opening up new non-union plants and closing down union plants are classic capitalist strategies to generate the cheaper labor force. This is a rather ruthless strategy, which is commonly known in the US, but it has application elsewhere too.

The second threat is more serious and involves the power of automation. As time goes on, robots are taking over more and more activities that used to be done by the workers. The value-added of many routine-type jobs, which do not require human input, is much diminished. The few workers that remain, ironically, see increased labor productivity, because if the same or higher quantity is produced with fewer labor inputs, then this means there is higher labor productivity. Some companies work out automation agreements to guarantee that some of the increased company profits flow back to the workers in the form of retraining schemes and higher wages and pensions for the workers, but such outcome is highly dependent on the overall strength of unions.

Automation rather than outsourcing could be a factor that increasingly encroaches on service-sector employment itself, and some examples are the automated check-outs in supermarkets and the self-driving cars. If the service sector is lost to humans, then the competitive labor market pressure in the few remaining jobs will simply become fiercer, and that keeps a check on the overall wage level, which makes a higher minimum wage more important than ever.

What is even worse in the labor market is that the millennial generation (those born after 1980) belong to the most precariously employed generation while being the most educated generation in the entire history of the world, not only based on the facts that we know (welcome to Wikipedia), but also based on the amount of credentials that we have, which increasingly includes higher education.

It violates the sensitivity of some people that more education should result in more poverty. After all, does more education not result in better-paid employment? The aggregate statistics in the US still show that workers are better off if they have a higher education than if they drop out of high school, but aggregate data hides the fact that college-level wages have been stagnant for about 20 years, and that the fall of high school dropout wages explains much of the rising college wage premium. In terms of practical advice that means: you cannot afford not to go to college, even though a college diploma might give you nothing else but a fifty-fifty chance to get a cushy middle class job, but also an equal chance to have the entry-level qualification to flip burgers at McDonalds.

The one genuine hope that does exist is that the well-educated poor will at least not vote right-wing populist, though this option is not completely precluded. Right-wing leaders usually have suspicion against people, who are too well-educated, because they think too independently and authoritarian right-wing rulers don't like that. As Paul Mason (2013: 283) writes,

You can have political and economic setups that disappoint the poor for generations, but if lawyers, teachers and doctors are sitting in their garrets freezing and starving, you get revolution. Now, in their garrets, they have a laptop and broadband connection.

But one never knows. The fact that this economic system is increasingly producing losers, who have no other venue to vent their economic frustration but at the voting booth, does not bode well for regular democratic policymaking. People on the streets, who lack job security and are one car breakdown away from financial ruin, are rightfully asking themselves why the regular democratic process still makes sense for them if the mainstream parties continue to do the bidding of the bankers and the big corporations.

The people may not understand that to properly deal with the problem it requires more taxation of the rich and the corporations, and creative solutions like infrastructure investments for job creation and a universal basic income to ensure that everyone can enjoy a reasonable life. In fact, if people were to understand it, they would not support right-wing leaders, but left-wing parties. As Charles Binderup (1937) says paraphrasing Henry Ford,

It is well enough that people of the nation do not understand our banking and monetary system, for if they did, I believe there would be a revolution before tomorrow morning.

But people do understand very well that the system is not working well for them, and the only parties which talk a different game seem to be those on the right-wing. In times of economic and social crisis, there is also the possibility for the left-wing parties to make their case, and we see that in the US with Bernie Sanders, in the UK with Jeremy Corbyn, in Greece with the Syriza party (which was brutally crushed, and now carries out austerity with even greater vigor), and in Portugal with the new Socialist-Communist government.

But it is not altogether clear whether the left has a strong and unified response on how to deal with the crisis of capitalism and neoliberalism. As I like to say, the objective of the left is usually quite noble, but because they are interested in more fundamental transformation of the political economy, encountering more uncertainty and veto points (Lenin did not know what proper Bolshevik economic policy was), it is harder for the left to have a simple and appealing program.

My experience with left-wing groups is that, of course, they are more intellectual than most of the technocratic leaders and right-wing demagogues, but they also tend to quarrel more among each other. The bigger the requested change from the status quo, the better the potential outcome might be, but the less likely it will be for all people even within the same party to agree on a program. One might consider Jeremy Corbyn and John McDonald to be moderately left, but they are already splitting the Labour Party in two, as there are still some Blairites within the Labour Party.

It is certainly true that right-wing parties, which purport to solve all problems by shutting down the borders, hunting down real and imagined terrorists, and crowning an almighty dictator have no real solutions to offer on their own, but their vision contains a certain simplicity, which is well appreciated among the masses. The masses hunger for a solution, and I am not sure that those on the left are currently well-prepared to offer it to them. For those of us, who believe that a better world is possible, there is no choice but to resist right-wing forces and propose better alternatives.

Democracy's Best Days Have Passed

Posted on December 26, 2015

If one were to take seriously, Francis Fukuyama's prediction that we have reached the end of history, it would be a rather positive world. Communism has been defeated, market liberalism and capitalism pervade every aspect of modern life, and with the modern information technology, people from all over the world are much more connected than they ever were in the past. Steve Jobs once told us in his commercials that we should think different, and it is certainly easier to do so in a Wikileaks world, where the powerful have a harder time in controlling relevant political information.

Politically, the most important accomplishment seems to be the spread of democratic regimes which is a rather marked development since the 1990s.

Global GDP has been massively expanding these last 200 years, which means that even the regular person in the developed world can afford tourism in different corners of the world. In the western world, we are also seeing much more Chinese tourists, which is an indication of the success of the economic opening reforms in what was once a thoroughly communist and backward country.

Who can, therefore, deny that politically and economically we are accomplishing the goals of human civilization of which our forebears could only dream of but never realize? However, I would like to caution my readers about inferring the future from past trends.

All of these advances can easily be challenged and undermined if the following trends are succeeding:

(1) climate change and resource constraint fuel political conflicts

(2) automation of work, immiserization of the population, rise of finance, rising inequality, permanent austerity and economic crisis

(3) war and conflicts resulting in unprecedented refugee waves to the developed world, xenophobia, right-wing extremism and surveillance state

Let us analyze briefly each of these factors. Based on my claim that these are serious problems that humanity has to face, I argue that democratic regimes are inherently challenged, that the democratic heyday belongs to the past, and that we are on a downward trajectory in democratic development unless we can counter these crises effectively.

(1) No one can deny that climate change is among the most serious problems facing humanity. One could argue that slavery may always exist. That one man can exploit another fellow man into eternity, and that there will not be any salvation or dramatic change. We might not expect that the working class will ever realize its historic responsibility to overthrow the capitalist economy, seize the means of production, and establish an economy based on social and individual needs rather than private property and profit.

But with the environment, the logic is somewhat different. If the environment is no longer habitable for us, we are screwed and will no longer exist. Period. We have maximally exploited the environment, and the Guardian (https://www.theguardian.com/global-development-professionals-network/gallery/2015/apr/01/over-population-over-consumption-in-pictures) is showing some interesting images on how much overpopulation and overconsumption contribute to the environmental and ecological crisis today. We all need our cars, our houses, our exotic food that is transported from thousands of miles away, using fossil fuels.

The more mouths there are to feed, the more food, clothing, housing, transport and so on we need to develop. That is no problem if we all still lived like the cavemen, just foraging, hunting and gathering, and using our bare hands rather than sophisticated machines to do much of the work for us. But we are producing more and more stuff with more sophisticated technology, and are burning fossil fuels, which are polluting the environment and trapping the greenhouse gases in the atmosphere, so it gets warmer.

The social consequences of a gradually warming planet have been understudied, and part of the reason is that what we are witnessing here is a rather dynamic process, whose outcome even we social scientists are too slow to observe and predict. But let us state some contours of what might happen. The physical effect of more children, old and disabled people dying from heatstrokes should be all too obvious, especially if they cannot afford air conditioning.

As the planet is getting warmer, agriculture will be heavily affected. Summer fruits like oranges need warmer climates to grow, so we might find it nice that we can now grow oranges in Alabama as well as in Florida. On the other hand, some basic staples like wheat only grow in temperate regions. So there will be great fear that some regions close to the equator will no longer be able to handle agriculture, thus robbing the people of one of the basic mainstays of survival.

The next step will be to flee the area from which they come from, and go to more moderate climates. Somalia comes to mind. This category of people are called the environmental refugees, and they don't get the same attention that the war refugees are getting. But notice also that these two factors are linked together. The Pentagon admits that climate change aggravates political conflicts (Drajam and Chediak 2014). If people don't have access to food and water, they can easily forget being civilized, grab weapons, point it to the head of the few people who still own something, and blackmail them to surrender it. There is a rise of warlords, and a collapse of formal democratic decisionmaking.

Then there is the problem of resource constraints, which is intimately connected with population growth. We can reasonably argue that population growth is now less than it used to be thanks to urbanization, women's rights and rising economic wealth. But even at a slowed down trajectory, I have not seen any demographic forecast, which does not say that the world population will reach 10 billion at some point during our century.

Don't forget that it is not only the number of people that counts, but also the level of consumption per capita. In a world, where 15% of the world population belonged to the developed world (mostly white countries plus Japan) one could argue that it is not such a big problem if these people have a huge ecological footprint. Of course, there is environmental injustice when a few people pollute, and the people in the developing countries suffer the most, because they live in more exposed regions and lack the funds to protect themselves against environmental changes. But the overall human footprint is still smaller when a small fraction uses up a lot of resources.

The impact will be much greater as India and China, and now Africa and Latin America rightfully demand their fair share of global economic growth. We have already seen the rising importance of China, and its insatiable appetite for raw material from all over the world. By sucking in these resources, putting out manufacturing products and selling them all over the world, the Chinese are creating wealth in gigantic proportions, and no international company can any longer ignore the significance of the middle class consumer market in China (though there are, of course, issues with distribution of wealth).

Will the much deserved greater claim of China on world resources on top of what the already developed world claims impact the total availability of resources in the world? Absolutely. It is fascinating to look at one of the most popular consumer products in use today, which is the smartphone. In order to put together one smartphone it takes a countless amount of metals, which mostly come from China, though some of it still needs to be imported.

Zinc, silver and gold for instance are supposed to run out in roughly 15 years (prognosis from Desjardins 2014). Ironically, in the same prognosis, coal has the longest life expectancy (until 2136), but it also has among the worst environmental impacts, as the smog-filled residents of Chinese cities can tell all too well.

Some people might claim that we don't need to worry about rare metals or other resources running out. We have been, for instance, hearing about peak oil the last forty years or so. Every time someone said that we are going to run out of oil soon, there has been a new discovery. Forty years ago, we did not have technology like fracking, where we drill down very deeply to get oil.

But we should be very careful about this strategy, because of the unintended effects like polluting the ground water, causing earthquakes and also the diminishing returns over time. We are enjoying a strange phase of low oil prices, because of peak supply. Yes, there are some oil reserves, which the Saudis are rather willing to share with the world, while it lasts. It is blowing a huge fiscal hole into their budget, but they are doing it to beat out market share with other countries like the US. This is a lot of politics, while we should not forget the underlying logistics of oil.

Resource constraint is a very serious issue, and we have long not seen the last of it. We should expect that there will be wars fought over rather basic inputs. That has been the case in the Middle East with reference to oil. This is a chronically unstable region, where the average human life counts for little, but the securing of oil counts for much. Oil is the key input to much of modern life, whether it is driving a car or using plastic. We cannot live without oil. The fact that all of the countries are not capable to realize a serious climate agreement and reduce CO_2 emissions just reveals that our collective addiction for oil has not ended, and that we need to fight even more wars over it. War is a natural enemy to democracy.

I anticipate that we shall see more wars waged over water. The water scarce regions are in the Central America, sub-Saharan Africa, the Middle East, South Asia and China. That is where a lot of people live, and it is the most important input, whether it is the daily water that we drink, the shower that we take, the cooling facilities in the factories, or the agricultural input.

(2) The second set of problems is related to the permanent economic crisis and technological boom. We are usually being told the Schumpeterian story of economic innovation, that the more new stuff is created using more efficient methods, the better our life is. That is reflected in the overall rising labor productivity trend.

Every time, when we developed new technology, people can consume more stuff with less labor, and the workers shift from one industry to another industry. It is certainly true that we no longer have to work in coal mines, factories or rice fields to the same extent that our ancestors used to. We have seen a shift from manufacturing to service sector employment, though the level of job protection and quality is much less than it used to be.

Even the service sector is threatened, because in Japan we see experiments with robotized nurses in old people's homes, open online courses attempt to scale the university experience, and Google experiments with self-driving cars. What this means is that the few jobs, which still require human labor, will simply face more competition, which tends to lower wages and keeps unions weak. This might even result in slower innovation, because human labor is cheaply offered to employers. A bleak future with low productivity growth, low economic growth and a dearth of jobs awaits us in this scenario.

As the innovation, however, is moving apace, we should note that today we are a much richer society than we used to be in the past, yet for some reason the qualitative experience of the millennial generation (those born after 1980) is rather poor. There is first the trend that the millennial generation is less likely to purchase cars than their parents (Cortright 2015). The second trend is that millennials are more likely to live with their parents than their own parents did (Alter 2015).

Companies are crying alarm, and rightfully so. It was the pinnacle of consumerist capitalism that young people should be convinced to buy cars and houses, because that is an indicator of the economic advancement of society. What is the point of businesses to make investments and to hire people if the consumers of the future are unwilling to loosen their wallets?

Except that the millennial generation does not have much money left in the wallets. By creating the new social risk category of young people with irregular and insecure employment experiences, it is not surprising that young people simply lack the income to consume. I am certainly not a supporter of hedonistic consumption, but within the logic of a growth-driven capitalist economy it is impossible to not demand growth and still maintain social equilibrium.

The winners of innovation and technological advancement are, no doubt, the global oligarchy. By that I mean a handful of people, who use copyrights, patents and legal systems to protect their private claims on this huge wealth generation, which is really the biggest wealth transfer in our history, when we think of the Bill Gates in the world.

Apologists of capitalism may still seek to defend Bill Gates and people in his tribe, because he is partially responsible for the innovation. I cannot take this argument very seriously, because it is the joint creation of workers and their entrepreneurial bosses, which produces innovation, and the mid-level software engineers and the workers in the assembly line are certainly not paid off appropriately for their labor.

Before one goes on to praise the entrepreneurs like Louis XIV during his absolutist heyday, one should consider carefully the simple question whether it is possible for one person to earn billions and billions of dollars out of his own volition without the workers and consumers that have created the demand and supply of the product to begin with.

But let me admit that the Bill Gates of the world are not the worst creatures of contemporary capitalism. Even worse are the financiers, the Warren Buffetts and George Soros of the world. In the ideal economic system, financiers only have the role to funnel the savings of some people to the productive investments of another group. What is really happening is that productive investments are becoming a decreasingly important area for financial investments.

The vast majority of financial investment should rather be called financial speculation, where assets are bought and sold in the expectation that the value will increase. They have the fantastic effect of redistributing vast sums of money into the pockets of these financiers, whether they are managing a private equity firm or a hedge fund. What is worse is that the central banks have aided their speculative drive by lowering their interest rates to near zero, and supplying them with endless amounts of liquidity.

Needless to say, people, who don't own major financial shares in companies, and workers, who fell victim to efficiency-enhancing job cuts and wage cuts, do not benefit much from the financial sector boom. Income inequality necessarily increases. James Galbraith (University of Texas 2014) writes "For countries very high in the world income scale, as you get richer you get more unequal. And that is because your economies shift toward being dominated by finance, by banks, by technology firms, and in some cases by oil and energy firms. And when you have growth, these industries are already at the top so they get richer relatively and the inequality increases."

Even apologists of entrepreneurial capitalism can no longer deny that contemporary capitalism and the contemporary growth of wealth and income inequality is largely driven by a rapacious finance-driven growth model, the increase of private, public and corporate debt, which creates no additional value in the economy but fixes debt peonage and slavery for the workers, consumers and taxpayers of the world (financiers and corporations, who shelter their income in tax havens are not even the primary taxpayers here).

Galbraith claims that technology is not the main cause of rising inequality, while I think that there are multiple reasons why inequality is increasing, and technology is just one of them. Financial capitalism is another major cause.

But let me go back to the main question that I posed in this post: what is the effect of rising inequality, precarious employment and debt-based low economic growth on democracy? For one, we can see that the macroeconomic policy tools for governments are not as far-reaching as it used to be. We no longer have any cross-national capital controls. The lack of national regulation allows wealthy players to pick their favorite countries to park their money untaxed.

If there were such a thing as global democracy, some of these assets would be taxed and redistributed, so everyone benefits. But where is this global government? The increasing wealth of the global oligarchy also means that their means to control the political system are also enhanced. Pericles (Funeral Speech, 430/1 BC), the leader of Athenian democracy, said in his funeral speech that democracy means that the administration of the state is in the hands of the whole of the people, and not the few. But if income inequality is rapidly increasing within countries, then it is rather untenable to maintain a democratic system. Even Aristotle (1999) realized that, and said that in order to maintain a stable political system, any society needs a strong middle class.

What the ancient Greeks are telling us is that growing wealth and income inequality weakens democratic decision-making. The poor masses are not influential in politics and have to fend for their immediate survival. The collapsing middle class cannot form a counter-balance to the influence-peddling of the rich. The rich become more suspicious of the envious masses, and they draw up their barriers to protect their wealth. They buy off the political system. Is it any surprise that barely any politician wants to openly increase taxes on the rich, and the "job creators"?

The unresponsiveness of our political leaders to the needs of working and middle class people is clearly revealed in the handling of the economic crisis. We know first of all, that there is a secular development toward economic stagnation, in brief, secular stagnation, which is based on a slowdown in population growth, the creation of credit bubbles in the housing sector, the slowdown of overall productivity growth, and the growth of inequality as the wealthy have a higher tendency to save than the poor (see Larry Summers discussion in the Economist, "Secular Stagnation: The Long View", November 3, 2014).

The tendency toward secular stagnation is frantically counteracted by higher inflation, rise in state and private debt and central bank purchase of bank liabilities (see my discussion of Streeck, Liu 2014), each time followed by ever decreasing rates of satisfaction.

Logically, we should realize how foolish the hope of endless compound economic growth is. It is easier for a very small economy to grow than for a very large economy. Imagine a very uneducated society that begins to build schools to raise the human capital of the citizenry, so they can use those skills in the labor market at higher level of productivity, and another society with a fully developed educational system, where additional schooling has no or few marginal benefits. (Also see Harvey's 2010 skepticism of endless compound growth.)

Now that we have established secular stagnation as a reality of life, we should reflect briefly on what government policymakers have done to respond to the crisis. Bank bailouts and economic austerity are the only permissible medicine, which is more acutely the case in Europe than in the US, costing more jobs and livelihoods. Greece is perhaps the most dramatic example of the mishandling of the economic crisis.

One tragic fate was the image of a crying pensioner in Greece, Giorgos Chatzifotiadis. He tried to withdraw money from his pension check, and was denied each time. He decided to block the entrance to the bank and sob in despair. The police, which ironically protects private capital rather than pension rights, drags him out.

His fate is not the only fate. We have to realize that in the neoliberal present, any social rights that the working class has fought for over the last decades are put into question. The dramatic deterioration in the fiscal balance in Greece following the spike of government bond interest rates resulted in elevated rates (punitive rates!) of taxation for the working class, cutbacks in health, pension, education and social spending, and a flight of the capital of the rich, who can escape the taxman anytime.

Austerity is sold to the people as a panacea to restore international competitiveness, but after the x-th time of implementing it, failing to restore economic growth and lowering public debt, we know that there is a different agenda in the minds of policymakers: the simple redistribution of wealth into the hands of the rich. The fact that all centrist political parties accept the banker narrative of the crisis and prescription means that people are becoming more and more disaffected from the regular democratic process.

(3) The last point I advance here is to link the permanent economic crisis together with climate change, resource scarcity, wars and political conflict. We know that there are long-running political conflicts that come from resource scarcity and the decreasing ability to operate agriculture in trouble regions like sub-Saharan Africa. We know that the most war torn region happens to be the Middle East, and it is hard to find a day when we don't read about nasty killings and explosions in Afghanistan, Iraq or Syria.

Not surprisingly, we have seen a huge refugee wave, which has resulted in intense political discussions in Europe about how to halt this stream of refugees. The political optics of the situation cannot be uglier: at a time of massive austerity, people in Europe are being told that they should tolerate refugees, who inevitably need clothing and shelter financed by the state, which creates the perception of injustice.

In Austria, the government wants to shield the labor market from the refugees, because there is the old tradition of prioritizing employment for citizens, especially when the unemployment rate is elevated. But if the refuges are not allowed to work, then they will burden the welfare budgets, though I doubt that the burden is quite so heavy as right-wing policymakers claim.

But the optics is what matters in politics. Extreme right-wing forces are very much on the rise, and we need to only look at the recent elections in France (Front National) and Poland (Party of Law and Justice). Germany and Austria also have tremendous right-wing potential, even though the Nazi history makes those attempts rather muted. The FPO could gain much more power in Austria, and so does the AfD in Germany. Let us not forget Donald Trump in the US.

These are political forces, which still speak in the language of a democratic polity. But substantially, they would see no problem if a charismatic ruler were to put in place his policies with few constitutional restrictions. Whether it is banning the building of mosques or ridding the country of immigrants, these political objectives, which are somewhat popular among the frightened masses, would require quite dictatorial means to carry out. The losers are the defenders of civil liberties and democracy.

Some people say that my fears for an enlarging authoritarianism are overblown, and that from a world historical perspective, we never had so much freedom to disseminate our views so cheaply and so widely (e.g. this blog). But my view is that we already see indications of government clampdowns on civil liberties.

The famous examples are Edward Snowden, who revealed homeland security data, and Julian Assange, the founder of Wikileaks, the major platform to reveal government secrets. What happened to these two gentlemen? Snowden is hiding in asylum in Russia, because he happened to not offend the Russians, who are now at crosshair with the West because of Ukraine and Syria. Assange is hiding in the Ecuadorian embassy in London, even though he is facing extradition to Sweden for trumped up sexual harassment charges (which are linked to the US desire to have him extradited to the US to face prosecution). Snowden and Assange are the heroes, who show that the emperor wears no clothes and they are prosecuted by the US government.

One could now argue that few of us are as "heroic" as these two gentlemen, and that we commoners live a normal life without the permanent prosecution from our governments. But we need to think twice here. What Snowden and Assange have shown the world is that government surveillance is a major industry, which is growing by leaps and bounds. Every time there is another terrorist attack, whether it is 9/11 in New York or the Paris attacks recently, there is a new justification for each government to step up the wiretapping of phones, e-mails, bank accounts and other digital information portals.

The government tells us that in order to protect national security it is necessary for all of us to give up some of our privacy, because we don't want to risk another terror attack, right? How ridiculous this argument is! If the government were serious in preventing future terror attacks, they would attempt all they can to stop adding fuel to conflicts in the Middle East. They would give their youngsters in their own countries real job and educational opportunities rather than let them lie idle, and become receptive to extremist influences of any stripe.

So if we know that our governments are not really interested in preserving national security, why is this expensive security apparatus to monitor the population necessary in the first place? Loic Wacquant (2001) noted in his research that the reason why more Americans are put into prison, and why more Europeans face welfare retrenchment and workfare activation schemes, is that these measures are a way to manage social insecurity in a neoliberal political economy.

This account makes perfect sense. We don't have anything productive to do for the working masses, so we increase monitoring over them, because things will have to go wrong, right? Under communism, everyone was roughly equally poor, so the crime rate was negligible. In a flourishing capitalist society, crime rates are higher, as there will be crimes of envy, but we don't expect that much crime, because everyone has a good life. In decadent capitalist society, we expect even more crime, because the poor need to steal to survive.

Ironically, the historical crime data cannot bear out this hypothesis. Steven Pinker (2011) argued that historically there is less violence, because of the civilizing force of the central state, literacy, education and commerce. I have not engaged his thesis deeply enough to question it, but I will note that as the neoliberal economy has taken hold, people are not tending toward more crime, yet the penal state thinks that we have to be prevented from getting crazy ideas via constant surveillance.

Part of the effort of surveillance comes from the technical capacity to do so. It is harder to intercept the content of letters or face-to-face conversations than phone calls or e-mails. Another part comes from managing the social insecurity rather than taking steps to solve the root problem.

Governments tend to say that all safety measures are taken to prevent terrorist activity, but if we look at the various police clampdowns from the Seattle (WTO) protests to the Arab Spring to Occupy Wall Street to Ferguson, Missouri and lately Paris after the terror attacks, we can see that it is the goal of the states to maintain social order, or social disorder to be more precise. We may consider the police batons and the tear gas as attempts to preserve the social disorder of the status quo. Yes, neoliberalism is bad for your health, bad for the environment, bad for your wallet, but it is better for you to shut up and accept it than to rock the boat. Recall image of police getting ready to greet Black Lives Matter protesters in Minneapolis, Minnesota.

In conclusion, it appears that while democracy is a very worthwhile social endeavor, which humans have worked very hard to accomplish, it is difficult to imagine how it can be sustained over the long term given the external challenges that we are facing. Democracy is a luxury good, and not a basic pillar of life.

In the past, we did not have many forms of democracy, as the ruling classes throughout history have convinced us that in a world where life is solitary, poor, brutish, nasty and short (Hobbes 1652), we cannot afford the luxury of a democratic polity. We were being told that we need to unite behind a leader, who in peace times ensures that our grain storage works the way it should, and in times of war, ensures that we unite against a common foreign enemy. Even if we were not sympathetic to these notions, we lacked the literacy and education to question this paradigm.

All of that appears to be a joke to us today, but given the rise of right-wing populists and demagogues in the developed world, the conjuring up of real and imagined enemies (e.g. ISIS), the building up of a surveillance state, the permanent austerity and economic crisis, the resource constraint, the climate catastrophe, and the refugee wave, we can no longer say with the same confidence that democracy can weather the storms ahead.

In times of crisis, the demand for a strongman, who promises easy solutions to complex problems, will overpower the voices of reason. Democracy will be considered a nuisance, because it is too slow or too inflexible to respond to grave crises with the urgency that is required. The Roman Republic drifted into the Principate, the French Revolution drifted into Napoleon's monarchy, the Russian and Chinese Revolution drifted into the dictatorship over the proletariat, and the German Weimar Republic drifted into Nazi dictatorship.

We know that history usually does not repeat itself, but it does recur with certain patterns that are beyond our choosing.

Defending against Libertarian Critics

Posted on January 11, 2016

Below, I defend my argument against a good libertarian friend of mine (Wall 2016).

No business owner forces anyone to work for him or purchase his product. The state, on the other hand, can only exist through the use of force.

Yes, but no worker can live to escape his condition except if he became an entrepreneur, but this is quite exceptional. This concept does not exist in the US, but in many European countries, people would kill to be able to work for the government, where they are unlikely to be fired, and where social benefits are substantial. State coercion can be quite dangerous, but simply because you don't like what the hand is doing, you will not chop off the entire hand, but will try to make it better. What the libertarians also don't understand is that markets are *created* by the state. If he does not believe me he should tell me whether he feels safer doing business in Somalia (no state) or in the US (strong state).

The labor that is freed by increasing technology becomes available to be put to use in another, perhaps new, sector. Because human desires are limitless (wouldn't everyone like a personal masseuse, a yacht, a helicopter, a yacht upon which to land their helicopter, etc.?) the demand for labor is also limitless.

Yeah, that is the history, but what about the future? Where are the industries of the future? The frontier of technology carries few jobs. The managerial positions in banking and consulting have a more rentier function, and remain stable because they are connected with the powerful sectors of the economy. Most of the jobs today, especially for the lower skilled, are in retail, hospitality and health care industry, and even those are liable to automation.

Ever-increasing taxes, minimum wage laws, constant creation of artificial regulations, and bureaucratic red-tape all place huge hindrances on the market and is the true cause of a shrinking labor force.

These phenomena that he cites have a stabilizing impact on capitalist development as well as a destabilizing one, and he should perhaps consult Claus Offe's work, which I summarized (see "Book Review of Claus Offe, "Contradictions of the Welfare State" (1984)"). He argued that the welfare state exists to make labor capable to be sold as a commodity, for if they were to receive less than a minimum wage whatever the equilibrium may be, he won't survive and the capitalist would not have any more workers to exploit. The welfare state is also needed to guard against collapsing aggregate demand. Greece is much worse off in their economic crisis than the US, because they cut their pensions, while Social Security in the US remained the same.

But he is right to say that if the welfare state became too generous, it could undermine work participation, and the capitalist also would miss workers to exploit. The long-term historical development in capitalism is that the needs and requirements for the capitalist class is toward a greater state to furnish the capital investment (e.g. infrastructure, education of the population) and the consumption (e.g. civil servant salaries, or weapons purchases by the military). But, of course, the most developed capitalist countries tend to have the biggest state.

Does that mean that a bigger state causes less growth and jobs? It is hard to answer, but we would need to have a counterfactual of a shrinking state and a growing economy, and these libertarian dreamers have never shown me credible examples. Pro-austerity scholars have argued that Ireland and Latvia have slashed their public budgets in the 1990s and after the crisis since 2008, and have grown massively, but these are rather small economies which have export markets in the bigger economies, and 1/10th of the labor force left the country, which is quite a unique benefit. Most other countries have wisely not slashed their state spending share.

Inflationary monetary policies and artificial credit expansion create the unpredictable boom-bust cycle that makes the market largely unpredictable. When markets are unpredictable, business owners will postpone or cancel plans for expansion. Entrepreneurs will be less willing to take the risks necessary to create new ventures.

It is certainly true that monetary policy creates many of the financial bubbles that we have seen in the past and will see more of in the future, and I have voiced my criticism of central bank policy elsewhere on several occasions. But I am also of the view that without monetary expansion the economy would be even worse off. It is not the unpredictability in the market, which scares investors, but the lack of demand. It is the expectation of effective demand which steers investment decisions of investors. But where is the source of demand in an oligarchic economy, where so few private people own so much and so many living on their labor or those dependent on them own so little? It is the credit economy, the loan from the rich bankers to the poor workers, and the logical inability of the latter to repay the former with interest, which creates the fragility of the financial system. The central bank wants to paper over this contradiction by enforcing low interest rates, and bailout defaulting banks with huge loans, and we are all worse off for it.

But the question which we need to ask ourselves is the counterfactual. What would have happened if the central banks did not drive a credit bubble? The crisis of insufficient effective demand would have even earlier created the downward deflationary spiral, which this libertarian so awfully detests.

First, any person who is providing a service through voluntary transaction is necessarily providing value. If he wasn't providing value, the person purchasing the service would keep his money and spend it elsewhere. The decision to partake of the given service is made because the service is valued more highly than the money cost.

In his imaginary economy, every consumer has the full freedom to spend his money wherever he wants to. We can freely choose our banks, lawyers, consulting firms, tooth paste etc. Except that in an oligarchic economic system that free choice is certainly not there.

But for the sake of argument, I will accept that there are voluntary transactions. Is it fair that Mark Zuckerberg gets 45 billion dollars with his service getting more than a billion users, while his Silicon Valley food service workers get almost nothing? For the libertarian this world is fair, because Zuckerberg produced a product, which more than a billion people wanted to buy. If they did not buy it, he would not be so rich. The food service workers are producing a product, which everyone wants to buy, but it is easily reproducible, so there are many competitors for the same industry and job, so wages deserve to be low. That would be a market outcome, but not a "fair" outcome under considerations of social justice. A libertarian would ask his readers now whether social justice is more important or market justice? But that is why I think that this ideology should be exposed for what it is, namely to defend the status quo of extreme wealth and income inequality because it followed criteria of market justice. For people, who want to live in a more socially just world, this logic cannot apply, and calls for a basic income and higher taxation on the high earners is acceptable.

It should also not be forgotten that any invention cannot be the product of one individual, even though capitalist business propaganda tries to convince us this is so. Without the government developing the internet and the computer processor, neither Zuckerberg nor Jobs nor Gates would be where they are today. Without the software developers, programmers, or assembly line workers, they also would not be able to get their products on the market. The economy is an interdependent structure, and once we recognize that the accumulation of wealth lies in the hands of the few, who claim a product to be their exclusive private property, this fact should be suspect to anyone with brains.

Second, it is true that some of the professions he lists earn incomes that exceed the intrinsic value their job provides to society. Bankers and financiers especially, and lawyers and accountants to a lesser extent. These jobs are artificially protected and their salaries artificially inflated as a result of the workings of the state. He correctly states that bankers and financiers "get government bailouts, which is not available to working class people," but later states that these jobs should stop being produced altogether. Perhaps, but ultimately it is the special state-granted privileges these jobs receive that should be eliminated. Once that happens, the market can determine whether these jobs should exist, and at what salary.

To the extent that the state sets the framework conditions, e.g. bailing out banks and securing high salaries to bankers and austerity for the masses, he is right to say that the state takes its share of the blame for this huge inequality.

But I very much doubt that getting rid of the state would make things better. It was the hands-off position of the state, when it decided to reduce the burden of the tax system to regulate the incomes of executives in big firms that their incomes skyrocket in the 1980s. Libertarians argue that as long as their income increase derived from market dynamics, it is acceptable. But what is the "market value" in this example? No one needs a PhD in economics to understand it. (Quite the contrary, a PhD in neoclassical economics might even obscure understanding on this point.)

The escalating CEO incomes are preceded by the reduction in the tax burden on top executives. As long as income tax rates were high, executives decided it was better to keep most of the profits in the company and invest in plants and jobs, which tends to equal the distribution of income. When the marginal income tax was lowered, the penalties on redistributing corporate income to private executive income is lowered, so executives did just that. The shareholders also got a bigger piece of the pie, and now both the shareholders and executives conspired to raise the share incomes for the executives, and tie them to the stock market performance of the firm. That is shareholder value maximization, with the predictable devastating consequences for worker job security and wages.

In this situation, we actually need more and not less state intervention to ensure a more equal distribution of income. One can only imagine a weak state if a non-state actor is powerful enough to control the greed of the executives, and these were usually labor unions. That would be the case in Germany for instance. But the executives and government officials of course conspired to weaken organized labor, so there is no non-state actor, who can resist the greed of the executive class.

Libertarians believe that workers should keep every penny of their wages, while socialists believe workers should be subject to heavy taxation by an oligarchic government

Only the government exploits workers, not the capitalist. This assumption is entirely laughable. Of course, the government can be exploitative in their taxation, and I am the first critic of taxing people to pay for foreign wars where the working class people sacrifice their bodies and their tax money for the glory of their leaders. But taxation can also be used to pay for social programs, which are crucial for the self-maintenance of working class people. The surplus they contribute to their employer can also be used for the maintenance of the workers, because the profit is necessary to re-invest in the next cycle, so that the workers can keep their job. But a huge part of the surplus can also just be siphoned off, and there is no natural limitation as to how much profits a capitalist can make except the strength of organized labor and government regulations and taxes, and if we were serious observers of recent history, where excessive profits in certain sectors had become the norm, we know that limitations are absolutely necessary.

This constitutes little more than envy and greed. It was the business owner, who invested the initial capital to create the business, and who risked all of that capital solely on his belief that the venture would be successful; he had no guarantee that it would be.

For a capitalist economy to work the business owner needs to make some profit or the enterprise does not happen. But how much is not subject to religious or natural law, but subject to the balance of power in society. Why should the workers, who are essential for the enterprise be content with self-limiting their claims on production? Why should a few capitalists become the new feudal lords, because of their excessive wealth accumulation? How can one person out of the sweat of his labor and his investment earn billions of dollars? This is not entrepreneurialism. This is called theft.

No business owner puts a gun to the potential worker's head to accept the wage, and workers are always free to seek better and more lucrative employment.

There is a fallacy of composition in the argument. What is true for one worker cannot be true for all workers. In other words, one or some workers can get better training, better education, better networks, better jobs or better business acumen to become a capitalist himself, but not all workers combined. If the libertarian says that he does not care whether he creates good advice for 10% of the people or 100% of the people, then this assumption should be exposed, and we shall see how many people can grow to support this position. We socialists have always claimed that policies should serve all of the people, and not just a handful of people. The reader should judge for himself who is "right" or "wrong".

Libertarians are morally correct to state that it is never permissible to own another person or their labor.

Only a blind person does not see the hypocrisy embedded in this statement. He states that slave exploitation is not permissible but wage slave exploitation is permissible. If you own a slave, it is owning another person's labor. If you own a worker's fruit of production, it is not owning another person's labor. The workers at Foxconn should judge for themselves whether the Apple executives don't own their labor.

As he has demonstrated, it is through the natural progression of human labor, ingenuity, and capital accumulation that increases in production have been possible. Impeding this progression through the interventions of central planners can never be as efficient as what occurs naturally and is a large reason why mankind is still so far away from being able to provide a life of leisure to all.

Central planners are those which can bring about such a UBI scheme, but the author fails to point out whether the market will ever deliver on such a scheme beneficial to all, and if not then why not? Why should humans be slaves to machines, when machines can be made the slaves of humans?

John Rockefeller once said, "I don't want a nation of thinkers, I want a nation of workers." He backed up those words by giving over $180 million in 1902 to the government's General Education Board which was responsible for huge increases in the power and scope of "government-mandated" schools. The reasoning behind his words, and his purpose for such giving was simple. He wanted his businesses to be protected from competition. If he had workers who were also thinkers, the likelihood that one of his workers would start a competing firm and be able to produce the same goods more efficiently and cheaper was high. Libertarians will be quick to point out that if there were no state, there would have been no mechanism through which he could have carried out these desires.

If there were no state, there would be no public education at all. If you had one country where the state does not mandate schools and many other countries which do mandate school attendance, I will be curious to see how well the state-less country will train and produce the talent to compete in the global economy.

The fact that people must eat, drink, clothe themselves, and have shelter means that one has to find a way to satisfy those needs. The only moral way to satisfy those needs is to work. It is immoral to take from someone else to achieve those ends.

That is if the scarcity principle still holds true. The point of the UBI scheme is that many jobs will be eliminated, so there can at most be a decreasing fraction of the population in the active labor force, and without government induced redistribution this will result in economic collapse. The second point is that libertarians talk about the immorality of stealing from somebody else's labor, and are silent when shareholders and managers take the lion's share of what the workers produced.

Aristotelian Friendship and the Importance of Making Clear Choices

Posted on January 13, 2016

Aristotle has been one of the most inspiring philosophers in western thinking. Part of what made his writing and thinking so attractive is that his ideas spanned across a vast range of fields, and captured the daily ethical challenges that we face on this planet even today. How can we tell whether a philosopher was relevant? By citing his ideas over and over again, and still finding validity in them even after so many years that have passed.

In my undergraduate days I took a political philosophy course, where the teacher asked her intellectually rather uninspiring students whether if they went out to work for the banks, insurance and consulting companies awaiting them in the "real" world, they would ask themselves about the values of virtue, truth and justice. These were things that came more naturally to our ancient Greek predecessors than our contemporaries. Her words still ring in my head. When I interviewed her in her office for another class, she recommended me to read the Nicomachean Ethics, which I did only in part a few weeks ago. I was particularly interested in the passage on friends and friendship (also superbly summarized by Lethbridge 2007), where we realize that to live a full and happy life, we cannot rest content by philosophizing on our own, like Schopenhauer argued, but we need other human beings with whom we need to share our time and effort.

Why are friends so important? Friends are what make people happy, as they can share ideas with each other, reduce each other's pain as during the death of a loved one, but also partake in lighter moments like weddings or a sports game on television. Friendship is valued very highly by most people and is to be preferred over things like honor. People looking for honor seek something else. They seek flattery and praise. As someone is bestowed with honor, it also implies that other people may receive fewer honors. With friendship, however, the relationship between two or more people can be enjoyed for their own sake, and the friendship among people does not mean that other people are reduced in their ability to have friends (though if the same people all want that one person as a friend, there is a direct competition for the person's time and effort resources).

There are principally three types of friendships: that of utility, pleasure and virtue. Aristotle claims that the last type of friendship has the highest value and is the most durable, even though it is the most difficult to achieve. What are they? A friendship of utility is like a business partnership. Both sides befriend each other, so they can gain more connections and make more money. The relationship is fragile, because if one partner stops making money for the other, there is no more reason to maintain the relationship.

A friendship of pleasure might be two young lovers, who are following their sexual passions, and enjoy each other's company while sexual relations are active. But as time goes on, the sexual excitement weakens, and the two lovers begin to grow apart. If the one partner no longer provides pleasure, there is no more reason to maintain the relationship, so a friendship of pleasure is also very fragile.

A friendship of virtue, however, is durable, because sympathy for the other person exists even without utility and pleasure. It becomes irrelevant whether the person earns a lot of money or has sexual prowess, but one still likes to spend time with a person for their own sake. Kant said with regard to his categorical imperative that in dealing with other people, they should be treated as ends in themselves rather than as means to an end. A virtuous friendship would mean that the other person is treated as an end, that there is no expectation other than being there for the other person and partake in his or her company. If there is no possibility of disappointing the other side because of the low expectation, there is also no strong reason to break up the relationship.

But we also know that avoiding disappointment by itself does not create friendship. The mutual sympathy factor among the two people needs to be strong, and both need to be filled with a certain amount of virtue. A famous example for that are the two people in the US serving in the highest political offices in the country. Vice President Biden's son had died of a brain tumor, and Biden was struggling to maintain his son's family, so he contemplated to sell his house. (I ask why? Is it not enough to live on a vice presidential salary?)

When President Obama had heard of it, he told his vice president that he should not sell his house, and that he would personally give the vice president as much money as he needed. Is this story true or not? It is according to Biden, so we don't know for sure. But if it is true it would be a great example for a good friendship. One might anticipate that their relationship would be cordial and formal, because they meet each other regularly in the corridors of the White House, for briefings, dinners, meetings and so forth. When the job ends in 2017, both men would continue with their own private lives, and this might very well be the case. But it could also be that with the job and both of them staying in power, they got to know each other very well as close friends, and they would help out each other in times of personal trials, even though the president had no such obligation to help his subordinate. Maybe he was offering his help because if he didn't do so it would undermine Biden's effectiveness in office, and that would undermine his presidency, so it could have been a move of utility. But it can also be that they are just doing what good friends would do to each other. Biden and Obama are likely virtuous friends.

Now that I have laid out the three different types of friendships according to Aristotle, we have to analyze the importance of making clear choices with regard to making friends. You might have encountered people, who don't necessarily intend to spend much time with you, and there is a lack of ability to connect. What is the best way to deal with these people? In the case of relatives, there are no real solutions, and we have to take them as they are. For strangers, it is perfectly acceptable to just move on and lose touch. Rejections are one of the most difficult things that we have to encounter. Our partner that we thought would want to marry us reject us. The job offer that we thought we would get, we don't get. The university that we thought we could get into, we were not able to get into. The person that we thought were sympathetic does not want to maintain contact.

What to do? What often helps is to step back and take a look at the big picture: we might have been rejected by one person, but we have not been rejected by all people. With some people it is easy and evident to create good friendships, which are of the virtuous type. Wherever it works out, we should embrace these friendships, and we should leave by the wayside people who are not so sympathetic. It is somewhat of a mystery to try to understand why some people develop no strong mutual relations. It could be a lack of common interests, prejudice, suspicion or being too much of an introvert. It would also be quite troublesome if it was too easy to make too many friends, because we only have 7 days in a week and roughly 80 years of life. The amount of friends that we can make is time-limited, and the number of very good friends that we can make is even more limited, because they require the most time to nurture.

On the other hand, it is not true that most friendships are so time-intensive. The most important relationships of humans are the intimate ones: parents, siblings, spouse, and children. They absorb absolutely the most amount of time, as they should. While they bring significant benefits of being integrated in a small community and being cared for, they also come with rather heavy strings attached.

Friendships, however, even if they are of the virtuous kind, do not have so many strings attached. Take say a friend, who is constantly busy, and puts his friend at a low level of priority given work and family obligation. Because the passed over friend probably has the same kind of commitments, there is no resentment, and he or she accepts that if there is any opening in their mutual schedules they will eventually meet. (It is more troublesome if one of the friends is for instance unemployed and has much time to spare, which creates an asymmetry that can lead to tension.) The level of freedom and flexibility that exists even among good friends reinforces the impression that we have on our own volition decided to create these bonds. Whenever relations are made voluntarily, there is a greater contentment within it, while forced relations can be quite artificial. Family relations are closer than friend relations and can generate more contentment than the latter, but even for all family members there is a substantial craving to break outside the confines of the family and create free relations with outside friends.

I conclude on the note that we should carefully and strategically think about which person we want to enter into a friendship with, and how we should categorize each individual. Are they friends of utility, pleasure or virtue? There might be significant overlap between the first two types of friendship, but there is no real overlap between the first two and the third unless people who first thought they had a utility or pleasure driven friendship develop a virtuous friendship. Greater preference in terms of commitment in time and effort accords to virtuous friendships, but the first two should also be cultivated out of necessity or current need. For unsympathetic people falling outside the category, we should reconsider whether it is worth building up good relations with them or whether it is just a waste of time, such that it is better to focus on people, who are easily becoming friends.

There is no rocket science behind it, because we humans are political animals, and we decide to form friends and foe spontaneously with every interaction that we have. Traditional concepts of friend and foe are constantly overthrown by the simple reality that the world is becoming more interconnected with globalization, communication technology and affordable airfare. As Aristotle says, friends are good to have around, whether you are rich or poor, male or female, strong or weak, sad or happy, young or old.

Trump vs. Sanders: A Duel That the Establishment Denied

Posted on January 14, 2016

In a conversation with one of my former professors this past summer (in the middle of July), I had predicted that the general election would be match-up between Donald Trump and Bernie Sanders. I think I am still right. These are two figures, which are so different, yet share the same feature: they are opposed to the political establishment, which includes the media, the big corporations/lobbies and most of the mainstream politicians in both parties. The establishment politicians claim they want to make things better for most Americans, when they know that this is not true, and that a thoroughly corrupted political system, which only pays attention to the needs and interests of the mega donors, cannot produce the kinds of candidates with the campaign platforms that are truly benefiting the masses.

In March 2015, Rob Andrews, former Democratic Congressman from New Jersey, had come to campus, and predicted that the final match-up will be Clinton vs. Bush, the establishment figures facing off each other. These are two rather familiar names, as they both appeared on the 1992 ballot, except that this time it will be the wife and the son of either of these former candidates respectively. I initially bought into the logic of the establishment, and did not think that the political outsiders will get very far.

How wrong I was. In the summer, it became clear that Donald Trump rose in the polls with his biting political statements, his sexism, racism, anti-Muslim, anti-Mexican, anti-Chinese hate speech. The more hateful and controversial his statements, the more political support he would get. The establishment first denied that Trump was more than a fluke, who would collapse as soon as the summer was over. But he kept on climbing up, and never came down. For a short time, we thought that Ben Carson, a neurosurgeon just as crazy as Trump, could compete with him until errors in his campaign made him disappear in the background.

What makes Trump, whom I regard as a modern day fascist for his crude racist and envy against the weak (Muslims, immigrants etc.), so popular? It is the fact that he does not speak for the political establishment. He claims that all the Republican candidates raise money from the big banks, big pharma, big defense, big insurance, big oil and other big lobbies. It is not surprising that they are all beholden to the big corporate interests. That was certainly the case for the union-busting Scott Walker, who was set up by the Koch brothers, but quickly dropped out of the race to save him more embarrassment. Ted Cruz is the most promising of all establishment candidates, though he tries to portray himself as the representative of the Tea Party and the evangelical right. But that is being a fake outsider, because the Tea Party is bankrolled by the wealthy oligarchs, and the evangelicals under Bush were also financed by the rich, but were galvanizing the less educated, devout followers. Cruz or any other candidate for that matter would be nowhere without their mega donors behind them.

The Republican base knows this, and why should they continue to fall for this sham? Here they have a candidate, a smug, half-educated (though he graduated from Wharton), posh real-estate tycoon, reality TV star and multibillionaire, Donald Trump, who can say whatever he thinks without relying on the money of his fellow plutocrats. In his Facebook and Twitter messages, Trump emphasizes how he does not rely on money from the donor class, and he clearly gets the positive feedback from the Republican base. The rest of his status updates are empty platitudes, which ranges from demeaning his opponents or a minority, to "making America great again"- whatever that means. The policy implication here is quite obvious: the voters will not really get anything from Trump except empty rhetoric, more tax cuts for the rich, and harsher anti-immigrant policies. It does not put their kids to college, pay rent or medical bills, or give them a job, but they sure as hell will have punished the establishment.

Among the Democratic contenders, there is a little bit more optimism. Bernie Sanders has a true social democratic (though not really democratic socialist) agenda, i.e. making capitalism work for working class people (see "Sanders Is Not a Left-Wing Radical Socialist But a Social Democrat"). Sanders started with 2-3% in the polls, while Clinton had been the "inevitable" candidate with 60 or 70% voter support. She had the name recognition, which continued throughout the summer, because the mainstream media kept on accepting her as the inevitable candidate. But there is something very different today, and even Barack Obama had realized this in his 2008 bid. Essentially, the power of the internet, social networks and online alternative news media means that particularly younger voters have a much broader range of news sources, and they were certainly hungry for a political candidate, who provided better solutions to their pressing problems.

As the summer months went by, Sanders had reached 25% of the national voter support in polls, and was narrowing the gap quite substantially in New Hampshire, the second state for voting. Clinton was still 25-30 points ahead, but who would have thought that

Sanders can gain so much momentum? Then something strange happened. The summer turned into autumn, and around September the poll figures began to stagnate for Sanders. Joe Biden decided not to run. In late fall, I began to accept the narrative again that the establishment figure, Clinton, will make the race. Historically, one might say that she deserved to be the first female president after the more charismatic Obama took the limelight from her 8 years prior. But let's be careful here: no person has a natural entitlement to the presidency, and people should select the candidate that is best for the country.

On all political issues, Clinton is nowhere near as progressive as Sanders. She had formulated some progressive positions, but only after Sanders pushed them forward. When Clinton served as Secretary of State, she was quite supportive of the Transpacific Partnership and was open to the idea of the Keystone oil pipeline. When Sanders voiced his opposition, she swung against both. She told journalists that she "evolved" on these issues. She had no strong position on the minimum wage until Sanders took the popular demand for 15 dollars an hour, and she repeated the mantra but only 12 dollars an hour. She developed no clear plan for college access until Sanders pushed for free college tuition at public universities, and only then did she reveal a plan to "make college more affordable", whatever that means.

To say that this is "evolving" on issues is just plain stupid. Clinton was pressured to make concessions to Sanders, and when she made them, she pretended that her previous position did not matter. For people on the left, who are serious about political change, this is a very bad message. If she is so quick to change her position like the color of her clothes (no sexual pun intended), what will prevent her from switching back to accepting the status quo once elected? In some policy areas, that is rather obvious as is the case for he unwillingness to break up the big banks (huge campaign contributors of hers) or to create a single-payer health care system (with big insurers and pharma backing her). Clinton represents the rotten core of establishment politics.

In December, I was anxious and checked the polls, showing that even though Sanders was narrowing the Clinton lead in Iowa while building his lead in New Hampshire, he was still trailing by more than 20 points nationally. In comparison, in December 2007, Obama was trailing Clinton by an average of 10 to 15 points nationally, so there wasn't much time for catch-up, I figured. I was counting the days toward a Clinton-Trump match-up. But the latest January polls indicated otherwise. Clinton is now in serious trouble, because she gave up on both Iowa and New Hampshire, while nationally she only leads between 5-7 points. I think that national lead can quickly melt away, as Iowa and New Hampshire bring forward the political momentum. Now it is likely to say that Bernie Sanders will win the Democratic nomination for president.

People are feeling the Bern, as they come out to his events, see his social media presence and hear him speak on the most serious issues facing the country. Clinton is clearly a seasoned politician, but beyond the same-old, she has nothing to offer. We know why that is. Clinton wants to be populist enough to get the popular vote, while not being too populist to prevent offending the mega rich donors like the big banks. We know that this has been the story of the Democratic Party. As income and wealth became more concentrated, the Republican Party became a rich-people party, while the Democratic Party wanted to fake it both ways. That is what the Bill Clinton New Democrat movement was all about, and that is what Obama's hope and change message was all about.

With Bernie Sanders it is quite different. He gets earth-shattering small donations from voters, while rejecting the super PACs and other big campaign donors. With that structure in place, he could afford to offend the wealthy interests, and say what he thought was always right: break up the big banks, create a huge infrastructure project, tax the rich, single payer health care, free college tuition and a higher minimum wage. People hear that and they love it.

The pro-Hillary media establishment phalanx has tried its best to downplay the Sanders phenomenon. First, they had a blackout on Sanders. Second, they said that Sanders function is just to push Clinton to the left rather than be a serious candidate himself. Third, they tried to get Sanders to make personal attacks against Clinton, which Sanders never does because he only cares about the "issues". Fourth, they hammer Sanders on supposed inconsistencies with his issues, but Sanders dismantles substantial attacks on his policies easily. Now that he is rising in the polls, these tried strategies don't work. So now they are really covering Sanders, albeit still less than what his poll numbers would suggest. Mahatma Gandhi said, "First, your enemies ignore you, then they laugh at you, then they fight you, then you win."

The Clinton campaign flips from calmness to panic. Daughter Chelsea Clinton made cheap shot attacks against Sanders' health care plan for "dismantling" Obamacare, without mentioning that he intends to replace it with a more cost-effective and universal single payer program. Hillary Clinton tried to paint Sanders as a gun nut, which might be a smart move in a country polarized and shocked by senseless gun murders. But the strategy exhausted itself, because Sanders proudly defended his D- gun lobby voting record. Clinton then said that if the electorate wants to guarantee a Democratic president, they should vote for the moderate candidate, i.e. her. What nonsense!

The polling shows that in the key swing states, Sanders defeats Trump and Cruz by significantly higher margins than Clinton, contrary to what Clinton said. Why does that make sense? Political punditry should convince us that the moderate figures can pull more votes. Clinton is clearly the moderate politician, while Cruz and Trump are evidently on the crazy fringe to the right, and Sanders on the left. Yes, in normal political times this might be true. But we don't live in normal political times. We live in an economy where only very few people benefit from it. Many are working longer hours for lower wages, while almost all new income flows to the very rich, making the wealth distribution similar to what we had in the late 1920s. This is a politically and morally untenable situation, and people have had enough of it. They need change.

When Clinton wins the party nomination she might narrowly win the White House against Trump or she might lose against him, and that is because the left-wing Sanders supporters will be so furious as to stay home in the general elections or even switch over to Trump to air their frustration against Clinton. Most moderate Democrats will continue backing Clinton, but the Republican base and many independent voters will stick with Trump. He is anti-establishment, and she is part of the establishment. Period. To show the corrupted nature of Clinton one just needs to look at Clinton's visit of a family friend's wedding ceremony in 2005: no other than Donald Trump. How much money did Trump give to her senate reelection in 2006?

When Sanders wins the party nomination he will smash any Republican opponent. He will have the left-wing firmly on his side, and most of the independent voters and moderates, who find free college and universal health care to be more promising than immigrant bashing and xenophobia. I think Sanders will even pull some of the Republican base with him, especially in the key swing states like New Hampshire or Ohio. In the case of Trump vs. Sanders, the voters have a genuine choice between two anti-establishment figures, and that will likely drive the voter turnout. The choices cannot be any starker, because the one is a social democrat and the other is a fascist. A candidate of hope and a candidate of despair.

Electoral shakeup is the way forward in economically and politically challenging times. Democratic decision-making is hampered when neoliberal and oligarchic economic policies are the only tolerable mainstream positions (see my discussion of democracy's decline in "Democracy's Best Days Have Passed"). Anybody who begs to differ will carry the most votes. Syriza in Greece; Corbyn in the UK; Trump or Sanders in the US. If even then, the political economy does not change for the better, then even more radical solutions can no longer be precluded. Let us hope it won't get this far.

Democratic Primaries: A Battle among Generations

Posted on February 3, 2016

The Iowa caucus has shown that the US presidential elections have not yet been decided. Ted Cruz beat Trump and Rubio by a few points, though Trump is still up nationally. I still have very few doubts that anybody but Trump will win the Republican nomination. There is significantly more uncertainty among Democrats. Bernie Sanders carries half the vote, while Clinton carries the other half. More interesting, though, is to analyze precisely the voter profile on either side coming out of the Iowa caucus.

One look at the demographic breakdown clearly shows that Sanders is doing rather well among white, educated liberals, among men and among young people (figures reported in Brownstein 2016). He still struggles to make headway among minorities, Democratic party members and older voters. In a state like Iowa, where there are few minorities and many educated liberals, he is certainly as competitive as Clinton. There is also very little doubt that he will do very well in New Hampshire, which has a similar demographic profile as in neighboring Vermont, which Sanders has represented in Congress for the last 26 years.

Sanders' poll numbers in other states are not so bright. Besides New Hampshire and Vermont, only Alaska solidly feels the Bern, while in Nevada, Wisconsin, Missouri, Arkansas, Ohio and Maine, he has started to become more competitive. In many of the other states surveyed, Clinton still retains a substantial lead in the polls (see Wikipedia, "Statewide opinion polling for the Democratic Party presidential primaries, 2016"). On the other hand, I would not underestimate the Iowa effect. Even though, not all candidates who won Iowa ended up winning the nomination (Bill Clinton lost Iowa and New Hampshire in 1992), doing well in Iowa increases Sanders' exposure to the voters in other states. By now it should be increasingly becoming clear that Sanders no longer is a fluke, and that the name recognition problem, which held him back for so long, is getting smaller.

But, nonetheless, I want to focus on two issues that the Sanders campaign has to overcome if they want to lock down the Democratic nomination (especially given that the superdelegates and the entire party establishment have endorsed Clinton). Sanders has to do much better among minorities and old people.

It is fairly obvious that many of the southern states have more black voters (as much as 55% in South Carolina), and Sanders needs more of their votes. He has gotten the prominent backing of public celebrities like Cornel West and Killermike, but how much influence do they really have on inciting the Bern in the black community? Regarding policy, there is no doubt that blacks and Latinos would both significantly benefit more from President Sanders than President Clinton. Sanders wants criminal justice reform, which basically means decriminalizing some drugs and reducing the likelihood of minorities to be put to prison. He supports comprehensive immigration reform, which basically means that all illegal immigrants residing currently in the US should get citizenship. He has a very energetic jobs agenda, and free tuition and universal health care disproportionately benefit poor people, including minorities. Clinton, however, trumpets the status quo, and still gets significant minority support.

Why is that? Sanders himself claims repeatedly that minorities simply don't know much about his agenda, and I find this to be the most credible answer. It was easy to make the case to African Americans that they should support Barack Obama, who after all became the first black president in US history. But why should they support a white Jewish socialist, who comes from a white state? Never mind his civil rights record or his progressive political agenda. People just don't know much about him. In addition, blacks have a strange loyalty to the Clinton's, who backed Bill when he was presenting himself as the "first black president of the US" (even though his crackdown on crime campaign and welfare cuts disproportionately hurt the black community). But Sanders' poll numbers are clearly improving in minority communities, as they hear his message. One can only hope that he can reach out to enough voters before the game is over.

More stunning in the Iowa caucus voter profile was the finding that Sanders defeated Clinton by a whopping 84 to 14% margin among the below 30, and 58 to 37% in the 30-44 age category, while he was defeated 58 to 35% among 45-64 and 69 to 26% among seniors above age 65. These statistics matter insofar as 61% of the voters are above age 45, and only 39% are below age 45. Everyone knows that senior citizens decide elections, because as the Baby Boomers are retiring, there are more of them, and seniors have the highest voting participation rate of any age group.

The youth are overwhelmingly feeling the Bern (including this author), and they are showing up in large numbers to the Sanders rallies, while only a few middle aged and old people show up in Clinton rallies. The media reports the masses of Sanders supporters in his rallies, but in the elections they don't mean much, because the youth tend to vote in fewer numbers and there are fewer of them than older people. The youth, who are showing up in the Sanders rallies, are naturally showing up to vote, but it is questionable whether they can convince all of their less political friends and age peers to join politics. As a fairly political observer since I was a teenager, I have long noted the political apathy, which most young people around me had. That picture persisted well into my college days. Now I find more people around me being interested in politics, but that is a selection bias, because college students tend to be more politicized than the general youth. Unless the youth voter turnout can be massively increased, Sanders will have a difficult time to win the nomination.

The other strategy for Sanders would be to increasingly court the vote of senior citizens. That proposition is made difficult by the fact that old voters don't embrace change, and are more likely to support the establishment figure. The other problem is that a greater social media strategy won't work despite the much more powerful Facebook presence of Sanders, because old people are less likely to use social media than younger people. Ironically, the physical age of the candidate also does not have much of an effect on the voting behavior of seniors, because Sanders is even a few years older than Clinton. What matters are the political positions.

Seniors crave political continuity, and Clinton clearly represents this. She has said repeatedly how she wanted to build on Barack Obama's political legacy. She does not want to challenge Obamacare (i.e. no support for single payer health care). She does not want to have a massive jobs program. She does not want to raise the minimum wage to 15 dollars an hour. She does not want free college tuition. She wants to focus her efforts on carrying out a more aggressive foreign policy (though I doubt that she will want to trigger foolish wars like Bush). What is the benefit to seniors? She has not indicated any cuts to Medicare and Social Security, which are the major social programs that bolster old people. The fact that there is no good health care system for their children and grandchildren, or that there is no robust unemployment insurance programs for the younger generation does not seem to bother them too much.

There is another even more worrisome consideration for Sanders to attract the senior vote: because the Baby Boomers are better off economically than the younger generations, they tend to be more politically conservative. The Baby Boomer generation that is moving into retirement has entered the labor force during a time when the labor market was buoyant, the jobs were good-paying and opportunities for career advancement were plentiful (roughly 1960s to mid-1970s). As a result, they have been able to buy houses and have their mortgages paid off. They attended college during a time when state and federal governments still believed that most people should benefit from low-cost college, or benefit from it via the GI bill, as most men had served in the military during World War II. So they have no student debt to cripple them for a lifetime. When they retired, they still benefited from the legacy of company pensions, which are defined-benefit (i.e. they get a fixed amount of money every month). These are the kinds of cushy pensions that young workers today have never even heard of.

With all these benefits in place, it might explain why some older voters are very skeptical about the misfortune of their children and grandchildren. They don't understand how the younger generation is graduating deeply in debt, while entering a labor market, where only few positions allow a continued middle class lifestyle. Corporations have been downsizing everywhere since the 1980s, and it is increasingly difficult to climb the company ladder anywhere. This is what Sanders has been speaking to in all of his stump speeches, and young voters get it and want change.

I am not arguing that all is rosy for the old-age generation today. Many Baby Boomers had decided to retire around 2008, when the major Wall Street crash burned their pension funds, and forced them to return or stay in the labor market for longer than they had hoped for.

But the overall narrative is that to the extent that Baby Boomers have on average a better income and wealth position than their younger peers, they have much more reason to become more conservative in their views, and support establishment figures like Clinton. In fact, the political dynamic of a growing and fearful senior generation might produce even more reactionary politics. As the Wall Street managers are greedily looking forward to smash Social Security by privatizing it, senior citizens will throw their support behind potentially fascist candidates like Donald Trump. or at least they will back Clinton over Sanders, even though only the latter promotes a substantial expansion in Social Security benefits.

What seniors, of course, don't understand sufficiently is that the conservative "hold on to what we have" mentality is not going to cut it. Sanders correctly pointed out that what we have going on is not intergenerational warfare, where the old are supposedly greedily absorbing more of the economic wealth of the country, but class warfare. More and more wealth is concentrated into the hands of ever few people, who then come to dominate the political process either in the form of having billionaire candidates (like Trump and possibly Bloomberg) or billionaire-financed candidates (like Clinton and every other Republican candidate except Trump) run for public office. By voting in more of those same-old establishment figures, seniors are enabling the very policy success of the nation's oligarchs, who will not rest content with merely squeezing young people, but are also turning against the "liability" of old people.

The intellectual old people (think of college professors) might understand my argument, and I am sure that Sanders is polling better among that group than the less educated seniors. But it will prove very difficult to effect real political change if most seniors hold on to their establishment figures. Antonio Gramsci (1999: 556) wrote in his prison notebooks, "The crisis consists precisely in the fact that the old is dying and the new cannot be born; in this interregnum a great variety of morbid symptoms appear."

Why Brexit Is a Mistake
Posted on February 22, 2016

The British government announced that they would set a referendum for the British people to decide whether to leave the EU for June 23. The saga started when prime minister Cameron promised his voters that he would get a better deal out of Europe and then let the voters decide whether that deal is acceptable to them. Because he set the referendum, he thought that he would have sufficient leverage over the EU, whose leaders would be scared to see the British off from the EU. I strongly oppose the Brexit, and hope that the British people will vote to stay in. We need a better and more social Europe, not a Europe divided by nationalism and suspicion.

The recently negotiated package involved the following points:

- An "emergency brake" on migrants' in-work benefits for four years when there are "exceptional" levels of migration. The UK will be able to operate the brake for seven years
- Child benefit for the children of EU migrants living overseas will now be paid at a rate based on the cost of living in their home country – applicable immediately for new arrivals and from 2020 for the 34,000 existing claimants
- The amending of EU treaties to state explicitly that references to the requirement to seek ever-closer union "do not apply to the United Kingdom", meaning Britain "can never be forced into political integration"
- The ability for the UK to enact "an emergency safeguard" to protect the City of London, to stop UK firms being forced to relocate into Europe and to ensure British businesses do not face "discrimination" for being outside the eurozone (BBC, EU deal gives UK special status, says David Cameron, February 20, 2016)

There was a lot of fanfare about restricting social benefits to EU and non-EU migrants. The British certainly got scared when all these refugees made their way to Greece and other parts of the EU. But the scare and the treaty changes for the UK are nowhere near proportionate to the number of refugees they take into their country compared to Germany, Sweden, Austria or Hungary (see visual on https://en.wikipedia.org/wiki/European_migrant_crisis#/media/File:Map_of_the_European_Migrant_Crisis_2015.png).

The British had usually conceived of themselves as relatively aloof from the continent, and they never had to face the full force of German or French invaders in their own country (except when the Normans came in 1066). The channel protected the British way of life. The UK was also not a founding member of the European Community, which really began as an organization to reconcile France and West Germany. West Germany needed the legitimacy to recover as an economic power after the end of World War II, and France wanted to prevent an independently strong Germany, and so both spearheaded the European Community in the 1950s. The UK joined the EC in 1973.

Among the top leaders in Brussels, there never has been a British person. The architects of EU policy are France and Germany. It was these two countries which hatched out the monetary union and they also advanced the Schengen agreement and the enlargement of the Union to Eastern Europe. The only time the British really made noise was when Thatcher banged her handbag against the table and said to EU officials, "I want my money back!" She was referring to the UK contributions to the EU budget, and the UK eventually got a rebate. The official reasoning was that much of the EU funds went into agriculture, and most of these funds were given to farming intensive countries, especially France, and the UK should not have to foot that bill. In addition, the EU budget is mostly funded from VAT, which tends to be higher in the UK than in other EU countries, which naturally means higher UK contributions.

The UK is one of the main reasons why the EU is a helpless sovereign. Instead of gradually growing into a supranational entity with strong fiscal, administrative and legal power, all major EU decisions still need the consent of every single member state government. It is the intention of every UK government that this fragmentation in EU decision making remains as such in order to retain the full sovereignty of the member states. It is okay to have a Europe with different speeds, as the logic goes.

I cannot disagree more. It was one of Britain's finest political philosophers, Thomas Hobbes, who said that for a social contract to work, a country needs a sovereign, who can keep the different social forces in society under control, or else there would be anarchy. We don't have anarchy, because the nation states fulfill the role of the sovereign. If there were no EU that would be the end of the story. (Though I find it questionable how well individual nation states hold up in the global economy.)

But the danger is that the EU has some sovereign functions (e.g. a centralized currency and monetary policy), but it lacks the full sovereignty that the US federal government has, even as much legislation is determined on a state by state basis. A semi-sovereign entity results from the simultaneous will to a political union, but disagreement over details. It is ultimately self-defeating for the EU if it cannot act the way that a sovereign can. Friedrich Hayek promoted a supranational entity because the central entity has sufficient power to have sovereign rights transferred to it, but not enough power to make full use of it. Because there would always be uncertainty and disagreement about what powers the central entity has, and because there is a unanimous vote decision that is necessary (rather than majority vote), only the lowest common denominator decisions can be made. The lowest common denominator usually is related to less regulation, less state influence, and would produce the kind of market freedom that Hayekian libertarians have desired.

This discourse might sound like some abstract philosophical concern, but it is not. The Eurozone crisis and refugee crisis are good examples for why semi-sovereign power does more harm than good. If you create a monetary union without centralizing fiscal power to compensate for member state current account imbalances (usually affecting net importers), then you create a financial crisis with debt, austerity, unemployment, poverty and permanent economic crisis, as we have seen in Greece. If you don't have a strong EU government, who can impose a distribution key for the millions of refugees entering the continent, you will have a lopsided distribution of refugees.

The solution to all of this is a stronger central government in the EU, not a weaker one. It is the semi-sovereignty rather than the full sovereignty of Europe which produces the displeasing socio-economic and political results, which give credence to the nationalists and Euroskeptics. Countries with more pronounced Euroskeptics like the UK will declare the alleged power grab of the EU as the source of their problems, and will demand an exit.

Could the EU live without the UK? Yes, but it would lose an important country. But more important than any material or economic problems, a Brexit might exacerbate the political climate in Europe and make the exit of further member states more likely. The same reason has been applied to a Grexit from the euro, which was also supposed to have such negative consequences for the precedent that it sets that the euro is a dispensable currency. I am more sanguine about a Grexit, because in the absence of a better EU agreement to handle the Greek debt and economic crisis, it would have been the less painful option, and we have long not seen the last of it. I am less sanguine about a Brexit, because leaving the EU can weaken if not destroy the credibility of the entire EU project.

The economic consequences for the UK as a result of Brexit would be much more negative, because the trade agreements which are negotiated by the EU will no longer apply to the UK, and they have to attempt their own negotiations. The UK will likely want to insist on maintaining free access to EU markets, but if it wanted to do so, it would have to join the non-EU European club of countries like Switzerland and Norway, who have to submit to EU regulations without any capacity to affect the direction of these laws.

There will be a rather passionate debate in Britain about where the country should be going, and the referendum will also force the other EU member states to consider how they should advance a more sovereign EU. Unfortunately, I very much fear that the UK referendum actually makes the technocratic leaders less willing to consider further steps toward integration. Given the unresolved nature of the debt, economic, unemployment and refugee crisis, it becomes even easier for nationalists to clamor for a return to strong nation-state boundaries. A no-vote in the UK might not improve the situation at all, because it will send the signal to other European leaders that business as usual can be continued. How wrong they are.

For now, I hope that the UK will opt to stay within the EU.

Are We Living through Another Capitalist Crisis?

Posted on <u>March 7, 2016</u>

One of the running jokes on Marxists is that they tend to predict 10 out of the last 4 recessions. Basically, we expect another crisis of capitalism to unfold itself at any moment. Certainly, the number of book orders that talk about the economic crisis and the number of *Das Kapital* orders on Amazon tend to increase after every recession. People tend to have a rather short memory such that we read too much into the current business headlines, while academics since Karl Marx do not have much to say about dynamic and unfolding events, which are hard to grasp. As John Kenneth Galbraith wrote of the great financial crash.

The financial markets are characterized by...

"...*extreme brevity of the financial memory. In consequence, financial disaster is quickly forgotten. In further consequence, when the same or closely similar circumstances occur again. Sometimes in a few years they are hailed by a new, often youthful, and always extremely self-confident generation as a brilliantly innovative discovery in the financial and larger economic world. There can be few fields of human endeavor in which history counts for so little as in the world of finance.*"

(Quoted from Cross Hairs Trader, http://www.thecrosshairstrader.com/2011/05/john-kenneth-galbraith-on-stock-market-memory-loss/)

The relevant question for us as social commentators is whether we have any indication to believe that we are imminently facing another big crash, or whether that is still too early to tell. There are a number of factors, which should lead us to believe that we might be facing another big crash, though these news stories tend to get buried.

Arguably, the locus of economic power has shifted from the western industrialized country to East Asia, which means principally China. Any economic investigation should, therefore, begin in China, and then we can make more credible links with what is happening elsewhere. I found the headline that China's steel and coal plants were laying off 1.8 million workers (Phillips 2016). Since summer of 2014, one-fifth of China's foreign reserves were wiped out, because of capital flight and the government propping up the value of the currency (Bradsher 2016). What are investors recognizing? What they are reacting to is the deceleration in the Chinese rate of economic growth.

The entire motivation for the investor class to place their funds in China was that economic growth would be very high, so that the rate of investment would be correspondingly high. But the steel and iron industry are now cutting back on production and employment, because the capacity utilization rate is a paltry 67%, and there is a steel surplus of 400 million tons (Stanway 2016). The government scales back growth expectations from a 'normal' of 7.5% to 6.5-7% (BBC 2016). What this means is that Chinese companies and the government have long known that their growth has been derived from overbuilding and overproduction. It is only now that the private sector debt has doubled to 200% between 2008 and 2016 (Economist, "Red Ink Rising", March 3, 2016) that the leaders recognize that they can no longer rely on debt-financed and overproducing growth.

The Chinese government's decision to repeal the one-child policy reveals that the leaders are aware that the economic effects of demographic aging are largely negative. However, to think that motivating Chinese women to raise their fertility rate is illusory for several reasons: (1) more female education and employment opportunities implies more choices for women, and tends to lower the rate of fertility, which is below 1 in some provinces (Beijing, Shanghai, Zhejiang etc.- see birth rate map in Target Map, http://www.targetmap.com/viewer.aspx?reportId=14223) already; (2) the one-child policy has reoriented the norms of people such that a three person household with only one child is considered optimal. This also gives women more time to succeed in their careers rather than devote all their lives to nurturing, making it even less likely for them to desire more children. (3) Government policies for family and maternity leave are nowhere near generous enough to stimulate indiscriminate procreation. (4) Even if the government were successful in raising the fertility rate, they would have to do so in no time and at such a large scale to counteract their declining labor force.

A real economic slowdown in China will have and is already having severe implications for other parts of the world economy. In October 2015, the German statisticians already had to shave off 0.3 percentage points from their annual growth for 2015, because exports to China had declined (Adam 2015). Germany is hailed as the biggest and most powerful economy in Europe, but because they base more than 50% of their annual economic output on exports, they react very sensibly to swings in global demand. With the German growth engine confronting obstacles, the Europeans can bury any realistic hopes of generating significant growth, especially considering the fact that the austerity regime has created a huge

Eurozone trade surplus (primarily by reducing imports in the indebted peripheral Eurozone countries), which indicates greater reliance on world markets for consumer outlets.

Brazil had also been hailed as an emerging economy. As the largest South American economy, they play an important role in the entire Latin America region. Their growth model had been heavily reliant on the export of commodities (iron ore, sugar, soybeans etc.; see Atlas MIT, http://atlas.media.mit.edu/en/profile/country/bra/). But since 2011, the value of exports to China has roughly stagnated and now declined between 2013 and 2014 (Lyons and Kiernan 2015). They are also suffering from a corruption scandal in the state-owned oil company, Petrobras. The decline in Chinese and overall world demand implies a falling price for these export commodities, which results in economic problems.

The US economy is not so much exposed to swings in the global economy, because of a much larger domestic market. (Though they are linked to China because of the dollar reserves the Chinese hold.) The jobs situation had been broadly improving, and there are indications that the retail sector is raising wages (Lam 2016). This is the lowest paid sector in the economy, and it means a lot if these workers are getting paid more than before. But there is no illusion here: the massive jobs growth is not visible, because labor force participation rates are expected to decline. There are many young workers who are putting off employment options, because they are not lucrative enough or do not exist. The Global Minotaur is still doing fine on the surface. But any economic growth should reflect the fact that the workers have not seen their fair shake, that millennial wages are stagnant compared to their age peers in the 1980s, while the overall economic productivity has risen by 70% (White 2016).

Is there only an ethical argument to be made about productivity growth needing to be shared more broadly in the economy? Well, there is an economic argument as well, which is that broadly shared growth is a necessary condition for growth itself. So far the contradiction between private appropriation in the hands of the few and consumption growth in the overall economy can only be resolved by increasing the level of indebtedness in the economy. Student debt, mortgage debt, credit card debt reflect what is happening with debt in the private household sector. Governments having to service the needs of the capitalist class have also gotten themselves into a big debt, and now say that there is not much budgetary room for social expenditures.

Chinese debt in the private corporate sector also reflects where the short-term growth opportunities are financed from. The key lesson in the history of financial crises is that a large debt buildup in a particular sector in a particular country can have substantial ripple effects on the global economy. China's 3.2 trillion dollar in foreign exchange reserves provide an ample cushion against the market instability they are facing. But only slight changes in growth forecast might swing the investor sentiment toward further outflow. Some people argue that we need to calm down, and accept that the second largest world economy, which is exhausting its labor pool (which is getting more expensive and less competitive by the day), will not be able to produce the same compound growth rate forever. Even at dramatically rising rate of productivity, there are limitations to fast growth. But in a private capitalist economy, where the so-called "electronic herd" (Friedman 1999), is in charge, it is that same capitalist class which decides based on its collective sentiment whether, where and how much to invest.

People concerned about global stability would very much prefer the inevitable deceleration of Chinese growth to be manageable rather than chaotic. But I expect that deleveraging debt in the private sector could have a somewhat chaotic effect, and will have a massively negative impact on global growth expectations. February 2016 growth outlook (2.5%) is 0.3 percentage points lower than November last year (Conference Board 2016, https://www.conference-board.org/data/globaloutlook/). Quo vadis, capitalism? We don't know, but I take the safe bet that the big economic crash is not far off. We are biding our time, and hoping that we can finally overcome the instability which is inherent to our transient economic system of the present. If we are only waiting, then it is for Godot to come. If we want to change it, we need a counter-hegemony to capitalism.

Do We Need Free Trade?
Posted on <u>March 21, 2016</u>

What the US presidential campaign is showing is that the free trade consensus no longer holds. Bernie Sanders for the Democrats, and Donald Trump for the Republicans, both make the point that free trade has harmed the American working class, and that it is urgently necessary to cancel the various free trade agreements that were drawn up in the last 20 years. In addition, these candidates also view TPP and TTIP, which are US trade agreements with Asia and Europe, as suspicious agreements.

The question that needs to be asked is whether we should agree with Trump and Sanders, and claim that we no longer need free trade, because we need to protect US middle class jobs from cheap labor imports from Mexico, China and other countries. The labor protectionist left and nationalist right agree that importing goods from cheap labor countries undermines the interests of the US working class. They claim that a reinvigoration of the US working class and democracy requires a cancellation of the free trade agreements.

I am quite split on the trade agreements, because to the extent that different countries start to trade with each other, it is the case that consumers can substantially benefit from cheaper prices (though strangely those cheaper prices only occur at the capitalist core, i.e. in Europe and US, rather than the capitalist periphery, where many commodities are produced; another issue is whether producer prices come down faster than consumer prices, which shifts surplus income to private capitalists rather than consumers). The losers are the workers in export-competitive industries, which tends to be manufacturing and textile. But most of the jobs that are created in today's economy are to be found in the non-tradeable sector, such as transportation, education, health and retail. These jobs are rather unlikely to be offshored by companies. (Though there is a risk that shifting workers from the tradeable to the non-tradeable industries will increase labor competition in the latter sector, which pushes down wages and pushes up profits.)

But there is no doubt that free trade results in economic losses for workers, while the capitalist bosses always win, because they see their short term profits increase. It is not surprising that the stock markets are rallying when the executives can submit substantial cost savings to their shareholders, which is coming on the backs of the workers who have lost their jobs with open trade. Every standard economic textbook praises free trade, but they also add the proviso that nothing principally prevents the government from redistributing the concentrated gains of trade to the overall population either in the form of tax, public-sector hiring or social transfer benefits. But international economists tend to be silent on the political mechanism as to how such transfer is to be achieved in a political system, where the rich dominate.

I am principally in favor of free trade agreements if we have a political economy that ensures that workers who lose their jobs receive job training and new jobs (perhaps in the public sector) financed from a surtax on multinational corporations, who are reaping the rewards of a globalized labor market. But simply because this is not the case today does not mean that we have to roll back free trade and reintroduce tariffs. An economic nationalist agenda might benefit a part of the working class for a certain time, and can at most be considered temporary sand strewn at the wheels of private capital accumulation. The capitalist will find new ingenious ways to bring the free trade agenda on the table. The challenge is to negotiate free trade agreements with substantial social protections and national accountability of multinational corporations, who are trying to play one country off against another.

This is a segway to the current free trade agreement, TTIP and TPP, which are currently negotiated in secret by the US, EU and many Asian countries. Free trade agreement might be somewhat of a misnomer here, because the traditional understanding is that those agreements revolve around tariff protection. Worldwide tariffs tend to be rather low (though Japanese farmers still receive substantial protection for instance). TTIP and TPP go beyond the simple trade agreements, because they prioritize on legal protections for investors, who seek recourse when national governments decide on policies to protect their people (health, safety, environment and labor). President Obama has claimed that the US needs to take the leadership in negotiating free trade agreements, because otherwise the Chinese will do it.

This makes it seem as if Obama was really interested in protecting US national interests. But what is national interest anyway? It is the ability of multinational corporations with headquarters in the US to reap the maximum profits possible with little regard for the national interests (including their health, safety, environment and labor standards) of the countries that agree to such agreement. TPP and TTIP, therefore, directly consolidate corporate power, and create a world that is more unequal than what we see today.

What is the way forward for the left? There are basically two rational positions that individuals can hold: (1) accept the new agreements and expect the dialectics of history with growing inequality, concentrated corporate power, disenfranchised, poor, angry and unemployed masses to move forward until we create a more acceptable equilibrium condition at some future point. (2) Oppose the new trade agreements, and use that victory to mobilize for new and more progressive objectives in international trade.

Dutch No Vote on EU-Ukraine Association Agreement Reflects Anti-EU Sentiment

Posted on April 11, 2016

In a referendum, the Dutch people have voted against the EU-Ukraine Association agreement. The goal of this agreement was to get the Ukraine to accept judicial, financial and political reforms that make the country more conform to EU standards. For instance, the EU would be able to dispatch judicial advisers to the Ukraine to enforce labor or business laws. The Ukraine would also be required to modernize their energy infrastructure, and they would become eligible for European Investment Bank loans. Visa restrictions on travel would be reduced.

Most importantly, the Association agreement contains a free trade treaty between the EU and Ukraine, which would essentially allow EU countries to flood the Ukrainian market with their goods. The Ukrainian government will sell the free trade agreement as allowing Ukrainian industries to export their goods to the EU. But their export profile is heavily reliant on iron ore and wheat (Atlas MIT, http://atlas.media.mit.edu/en/profile/country/ukr/), which won't get them sufficient leverage against French or German companies, who export finished goods.

There might still be a merit for the Ukraine to agree to the Association agreement even if it came at some cost to them, because they certainly need a strong economic partner to their west, when the Russians have severed their energy and trade ties with the Ukraine. For the country to survive, it means either to lean closer to the eastern Russians or to the western Europeans. Petro Poroshenko, the Ukrainian president, is clearly pro-western, and has to bank his political capital on the rapprochement with the EU.

It is all the more irritating for him to now see the Dutch people, who don't seem to have that much of a direct stake in this agreement, vote down this agreement, which means so much to his country. A foreign ministry official in Kiev said that he found it disappointing that the Euroskeptic sentiment of the Dutch public is reflected on this Association agreement (BBC, "Netherlands rejects EU-Ukraine partnership deal", April 7 2016). The numbers bear out this suspicion, because even though 61% voted against the agreement in the referendum, only 32% of the voters participated in it. This implies that only the most politically mobilized people bothered to vote in the referendum, and the Euroskeptics (better "EU skeptics") are certainly much more and better organized than the Europhiles (better "EU philes").

I also do not find it plausible that the Dutch voters were particularly concerned about their Ukrainian brothers and sisters, and how they would be screwed with this agreement. I would also argue that the no vote in the Netherlands reflects the Euroskeptic sentiment that not only exists there, but in many European countries. It is simply that the 27 other national governments decided not to allow their people to speak directly on this issue for fear of the same results that we have not seen this Euroskeptic sentiment expressed elsewhere. It is, therefore, justifiable to analyze the no vote in terms of the Euroskeptic sentiment. Do the Euroskeptics have a good case on their hand? Yes, I think so.

Before someone condemns the Dutch voters for voting against an agreement that is not directly related to Europe as such, the same way as the British EU referendum is, we should acknowledge that there are not many other ways for Dutch or any other European voters to make their discontent with EU policies and politics heard. So any proposal that the EU officials put forward is eyed with general voter suspicion. I think the Dutch voters are right to hold the EU leaders accountable by voting against this agreement.

But what is the case that Euroskeptics can really make? It should first be noted that being a Euroskeptic does not mean being against Europe. People certainly do enjoy the freedom to travel, live and work anywhere within the 28 member states. They certainly also relish the general peace, which has prevailed since 1945, and would have been unlikely without the EU. But people are fed up about a political and economic structure that is not accountable to them and their interests. The lack of accountability can be measured on three vital issues: currency, refugees and economic/ social policy in general. It is to be feared that the lack of accountability to the public will continue as long as the EU institutions remain too weak to dispense with sovereign power.

Six years on from the economic crash in Greece (which is continuing to the present), we have seen yet again that EU leaders offer no real solutions to the Eurozone crisis. They still continue with the "extend and pretend" option, whereby the EU continues to subsidize Greek loans, which Greece will never be able to repay given the EU's insistent focus on austerity. Rather than canceling debts, breaking up the Eurozone or concentrating fiscal powers in Brussels (e.g. via Eurobonds), the EU leaders prefer to apply bandaid solutions, which make the lives of Europeans more miserable.

The refugee crisis fell on the unfortunate laps of the Europeans for which they were partly responsible, because they backed the US invasion in Iraq, which resulted in sectarian violence, civil war and the rise of the Islamic state, which spread to neighboring Syria, from which most of the refugees come from. Leaving the cause of the refugee crisis aside, one needs to reflect on the EU's poor handling of it. During the first months of the crisis, when Turkey lifted the restrictions for onward travel to Greece and the EU, German chancellor, Angela Merkel, still spoke of the "welcoming culture" of Germany, and that they can easily absorb many refugees fleeing from the war.

But this strategy backfired as the number of refugees kept on swelling to more than a million in Germany, over 90,000 in neighboring Austria and 160,000 in Sweden. Sweden restricted border access between Malmo and Copenhagen. Austria then convened a Balkan conference in February, where they mutually agreed to shut the border to Greece, and no longer allow refugees to pass through. (There probably even was a bribe from Vienna, but I can't confirm this.) Now we see dramatic scenes in Idomene, on the Greek-Macedonian border, where Macedonian police used teargas and stun grenades to stop more refugees from going north. Germany publicly condemns Austrian unilateralism, but is in reality quite grateful for the harsh border policies in southeastern Europe, as it relieves refugee pressure on Germany, which is still badly shaken from the Cologne incident around New Year, when a group of refugees molested German women on the streets.

But the question in all this is where was the EU? Here the EU clearly lacks sovereign power to do anything, and even the powerful countries like France and Germany don't have much to say. Germany, Austria and Sweden want a "fair" distribution of refugees, which requires an EU agreement. But EU agreement is based on the unanimity principle, which means that all EU countries have to agree. The Visegrad countries (Poland, Hungary, Czechia, Slovakia) are vehemently opposed to taking on any refugees. The UK being outside of Schengen only wants to take as many (or as little) as they feel like. The French might take more, but most refugees aren't going there. Of course, the preferences of the refugees also shapes where many refugees will end up in, but that makes EU agreement on a fair distribution even more important. Germany knows that it needs to a EU wide solution quickly, because the right-wing AfD is making headwinds in regional elections, which cost the SPD and CDU many seats.

The EU finally did get an agreement, but not with the distribution of refugees inside the EU, but with keeping them out by convincing Turkey to keep the refugees in exchange for 6 billion euros and EU visa free travel for Turkish nationals. While I am generally in favor of the agreement, I see it as no more than another bandaid solution, which can be torn apart if the moody president Erdogan decides to change his mind.

In the meantime, the damage is already done. Europeans, who already are shafted by the misguided social and economic policies of their governments (austerity, bank bailout, failure of public investment, high unemployment, deficit reduction), now feel threatened by the newcoming refugees, and will blame them for the lack of jobs and affordable housing. A return of nationalist sentiment that gets exploited by right-wing parties will merely accelerate the decline of the European Union, which has just seen its first serious test with the relatively "harmless" Dutch referendum (which is not even legally binding, even though the Dutch government promised to "consider" the referendum results). The next serious test is the UK referendum on whether or not to stay in the EU. If Britain leaves, then this could be the beginning of the end of the EU project. If Britain stays, EU officials bought themselves some extra time before the next referendum comes along. The EU needs reform if it wants to continue to legitimately exist.

Protest Against French Labor Law Reform Is Justified

Posted on <u>April 20, 2016</u>

400,000 French people, mostly students and civil servants, went out on the streets to protest against the labor code reform proposed by the French government (Bohlen 2016). The Khomri law (named after the labor minister) would make it easier for companies to fire workers, lower redundancy payout, and flexibilize overtime requirements, which would dismantle the standard 35-hour work week. Most full-time workers currently work longer than that, but get paid overtime at a higher wage rate beyond the standard week; under the proposed law employers can impose a maximum of 46 hours of work for 16 consecutive weeks in 3 years (see Rose and Melander 2016).

Ironically, even some employers are opposed to part of the reform bill, because it would seek to tax short-term contracts higher in order to incentivize long-term contracts (Tonnelier 2016). Trade unionists from the CGT are furious about the law and vow to fight it with mass mobilization and strikes. In their conference in Marseille, chairman Olivier Mateu, sees their opposition to the labor reform as "an opportunity to reinforce their class organization, mass, democracy and unity" (il voit dans le congrès de Marseille « l'occasion de conforter notre organisation de classe, de masse, démocratique et unitaire ».Noblecourt 2016).

The Economist ("I dreamed a dream", April 7, 2016) makes fun of the young student protesters against the law, because making it easy to fire more elderly workers would create more job opportunities for younger workers. The economist Jean Tirole claims that the onerous labor regulations, which make it difficult to sack workers, encourage firms to hire young workers only as temporary contractors, or not to hire them at all, which is reflected in the 24% youth unemployment rate. But how does the Economist know that the youth will benefit by displacing the older age workers?

Many Mediterranean countries, including Spain, Greece and Italy, have submitted painful labor reforms (in some cases under the duress of the EU troika like in Greece), but their youth employment picture is not substantially better than before. In Greece it remains around 50%, in Spain around 45% and in Italy around 40%. This to me suggests that the secret to reduce the stubbornly high youth unemployment rate is not to make it easier to displace older workers, but to create economic growth, which will feed into job creation. (Or hopefully it does, because jobless recoveries of the recent past reflect the power of current automation technology to displace rather than augment employment, of which we have only seen the beginnings.)

Critics will now object that economic growth is prevented by having older less productive workers commanding most of the jobs, while seniority rules grant them relatively the highest wages. Therefore, the profit per employee is less, and without sufficient profit, there won't be enough investment opportunities for capitalists, so there can't be economic growth. Replace these old high wage- low productivity workers with young low wage- high productivity workers, restore the rate of profit, and produce new economic growth.

First, it should be doubted whether the calculation of low productivity works out this way. Older workers still make valuable contributions to their company. Second, I have yet to see any empirical evidence, where the easy firing makes job opportunities more abundant for the young. Redistributing jobs is merely a zero-sum game, creating many economic losers, and fewer winners. Even if we accepted the argument that if old workers are losing their jobs for young workers, how long will this effect last? There might be the initial boost of productivity, and the reduction of unit labor cost resulting from the cut in wages paid to young relative to old workers. And then what happens next year?

The supply-side argument says that higher profits are a panacea to growth, but lower wages are not a panacea to create higher profits. In fact, if capitalists are merely looking for ways to push down the wage bill, they are merely reinforcing the contradiction of higher output but not sufficient markets to absorb these products. French manufacturers could increase exports to displace this contradiction, but the French trade balance has been negative since they introduced the euro in 2002, and the main reason is because their German trade partners have used the currency to their own advantage (by keeping the wage bill way below inflation, which the French companies with more militant labor have not matched).

The French president realizes that the country is trapped in this neoliberal paradigm, where low growth, high profits among M&A corporate behemoths, high debts (emanating from private households and the banking sector), low wages, insecure employment and high inequality rule the roost. Instead of daring to challenge this paradigm by either developing a new growth machine (as is tried with Canada's 3 year deficit-funded infrastructure investment program) or by opposing the capitalist growth paradigm via nationalization or a universal basic income, he helps to make the situation even worse by accelerating the neoliberal agenda.

In that situation, Hollande will not be able to get re-elected, which is reflected in his dismal poll numbers. (Can he even be considered a 'socialist' anymore?) The center-right is equally bankrupted, only offering the same old face, Nicolas Sarkozy, and dressing him up as hope and change for the country. That leaves the French people with Marine LePen, whose rabid nationalism and xenophobia does not give the French people any better opportunities, but some faint hope.

Austrian Presidential Elections and the Decline of Mainstream Parties

Posted on <u>April 26, 2016</u>

If there is one thing that the presidential elections in Austria show is that the mainstream political parties no longer enjoy the legitimacy to retain power in the 21st century. Norbert Hofer from the FPO, and Alexander van der Bellen from the Greens made it to the second round, while the SPO and OVP candidates didn't make it. One might still be able to claim that all is not lost for the grand coalition, consisting of Social Democrats (SPO) and Conservatives (OVP), because the federal president in Austria is not particularly powerful as is the case in France or in the US. The president represents the country abroad by visiting other countries and receiving foreign officials; he appoints the prime ministerial candidate, who is usually the first-ranked in the parliamentary elections; and he is the commander in chief of the army, though the administrative control lies with the defense minister and the country has not fought a war since it was founded.

The people in Austria were showing their discontent with the ruling coalition government. Some people within the leading party (Claus Raidl, OVP, in ORF "Report", April 25th, 2016) have said that the grand coalition with SPO and OVP only make sense during major changes like negotiating the state treaty or joining the EU. This statement implies that the country does not have major objectives, so the people no longer see a point to support the big parties. But those standard lines are nothing but lazy establishment thinking.

The Austrian electorate is really responding to two interrelated phenomena for which the governing parties do not have a genuine answer: the neoliberalization of the economy and the refugee crisis. As part of the neoliberalization of the economy, we have to analyze the world of work. 25.7% of the workforce are part-time employed, as of 2012. This situation mostly affects women (80%). Between 1996 and 2012, the number of low-wage workers receiving up to the tax-free threshold of currently 415 euros a month doubled to 300,000. (The poverty threshold would be about 1,000 euros a month per person). For the lowest decile of the income distribution, purchasing power declined by 40% between 1998 and 2012. Over 1 million Austrians are living in poverty, which is currently defined as an income less than 60% of the median income (numbers in Leisch

2013). This might not mean that people are missing out on basics like food or medicine. After all, these are only relative and not absolute numbers, and Austria is still a rich country, but the poverty indicator shows the dispersion of income, which is certainly increasing.

Wealth inequality is certainly increasing, as the richest 1% of Austrians (about 80,000 people) own 469 billion euros in 2013, which was larger than the GDP of 307 billion euros, and is equivalent to 37% of the national wealth (Linsinger 2013). That is great for people, who live off of their assets, but but means nothing to people, who rely on their labor. The number of unemployed people increased from 322,000 in 2011 to 438,000 in 2016. That is currently a high unemployment rate of 9.4% and a dismal 14% in the capital in Vienna (Kurier, "Arbeitslosigkeit in Österreich im März auf Rekordniveau", April 1, 2016), which is much higher than the 5% or so, which Eurostat writes about, claiming that Austria is a country with a job miracle (here is one example in Schmitz et al. 2013). The Austrian job situation, which is admittedly still better than in the more desperate parts of southern Europe, has become so dismal that there are currently more people receiving welfare (162,000) than unemployment benefits (153,000). Unemployment pays about a monthly 878 euros while welfare pays only 724 euros a month, while long-term welfare recipients only get 678 euros (DerStandard, "Notstandshilfe als Wiener Phänomen", April 24, 2016), which to me sounds like everything but a cozy hammock.

Upon reviewing the political pages, you find that politicians in the government are calling for drastic reductions in benefits for long-term unemployed people (especially from the conservative OVP) as if they were responsible for the poor job market. Cutting benefits in times of greater need will also backfire on the government. Leaders are also calling for curbing refugee welfare benefits, which would presumably sit well with the electorate, who only want welfare for nationals. In Oberosterreich, the regional government had proposed to slash the monthly welfare benefits for refugees from 914 to 580 euros (Heute.at, "Nur mehr 520 statt 914 Euro Mindestsicherung für Flüchtlinge", March 29, 2016). I find this proposal rather troubling, because it would mean unnecessary suffering for refugees without any benefit to low-income Austrian nationals, but at least the shameful government officials then have something to claim credit for.

The welfare issue intersects with the second problem, namely the massive increase in the number of refugees, which goes beyond the capacity of the country to handle them. There were 88,000 refugee applications in Austria in 2015, and only 11,000 so far in 2016 (De.statista), which reflects the harsher border policies in Austria, and the EU agreement with Turkey to keep more refugees out of the EU.

Naturally, there are the cultural difficulties of integrating a large number of people with a different language and culture, though I think that the Austrians would still be able to handle that as they had in the past. Another difficulty is economic, because the refugees, who receive the entitlement to stay, want and have to join the Austrian labor market, which is quite stressed given weak demand. Average economic growth from 2000 to 2005 was 1.7% and only 1.3% from 2005 to 2010. In 2014, growth was a paltry 0.4% (WKO 2015, http://wko.at/statistik/eu/europa-wirtschaftswachstum.pdf). That is not nearly enough growth to provoke a lot of job creation. Employers, who are looking for cheaper ways to produce things, are also investing in more technology, which tends to put a downward pressure on labor demand. I don't see the government at all being concerned about a major jobs offensive given that the finance minister is reaffirming his commitment to reduce the national budget deficit. They are also not talking about creating a universal basic income or at least increasing benefits for means-tested welfare. What they are instead doing is to double down on failed efforts toward job activation (more research of it in Eichhorst et al. 2008). Despite the growth in active labor market spending since the late-1990s, the trajectory of the unemployment rate is increasing (AMS.at 2012).

Former chancellor, Bruno Kreisky (1970-83), used to say that it is better to have a billion schilling (currency) in debt than to have one more unemployed person. He took it for granted that the state would subsidize state companies to keep them alive and retain staff. It was a very costly option, but it kept voters relatively loyal to social democracy while it lasted. As we can see, no one has been saying that today. The political price for today's situation is high.

The helplessness of the government to address these two interrelated problems of a neoliberal economy and the refugee crisis naturally proliferates the voter support for the non-governing parties. There are currently only three realistic opposition parties in the Austrian political spectrum: The FPO (nationalist), the Greens (bourgeois left), and the NEOs (bourgeois liberal). The first two of these parties have proposed their candidate for the presidential elections, and have received substantial support. The Greens, however, were trailing the FPO candidate, Norbert Hofer, by 15 percentage points, whereby it is not clear (as I hope) whether there will be a non-right wing coalition strong enough to get the Green party candidate, Alexander van der Bellen, elected.

But this asymmetry roughly reflects the general power constellation that will be relevant in the next parliamentary elections in 2018. The Greens have a stable support base of 15% as of 2013, even though that share is unlikely to grow in 2018. The NEOs similarly only have a reservoir of maybe 5-6% support, as had been the case with the LIF party in the 1990s. Van der Bellen received 21% in the first round, which means that he got another 6 percentage points from the social democrats and the conservatives, who were frustrated with the status quo.

The FPO received 20% during the 2013 parliamentary elections and 36% for their candidate Hofer. That would mean that 16 percentage points were received from SPO and OVP. But if you look at the current polls for the parliamentary elections, the needle has clearly moved, as the FPO would securely get 30-32% of the vote (while OVP and SPO each get slightly less than 25% each), see Nationalratswahl.at (http://www.nationalratswahl.at/umfragen.html). In other words, Hofer's popularity is not a fluke. While with Van der Bellen we could say that people find an old economics professor, who has been in active politics for nearly 30 years, appealing and vote for his persona rather than his party affiliation, the same cannot be said of Hofer, who had been in politics a lot less time, in part, because he is much younger than Van der Bellen. Hofer supporters are FPO supporters, and their party reservoir is in the 30+ % range.

We should not forget that the support for nationalist parties is larger, because in times of despair it is easy to seek scapegoats, especially for the lesser educated and working class electorate, while making sound policy arguments will likely only attract bourgeois voters, who are always in the minority. With the current trajectory, it is only a matter of time until H.C. Strache, the FPO party leader, will become chancellor. I don't know in what constellation that will happen. Maybe the OVP is more power-hungry than the SPO, and will join a coalition as they did in 2000, when the OVP got fewer votes than the FPO but still claimed the chancellorship, which was a first-time in the history of the republic. This time the OVP will have a less legitimate claim for the chancellorship, because the differential in votes would be much larger than in 2000.

Another alternative in 2018 would be to maintain the grand coalition, but with the support of the Greens, who will probably demand one or two ministries to back the continuation of the Faymann (SPO) administration. I am very skeptical of this constellation. Even though I am sure that Eva Glawischnig, the Green party chairwoman, would want to have governing responsibility, the issue is that the cost of keeping the FPO out of the government would get higher and higher. In 2023, the FPO could then get more than 40%, and when they get 51%, you can no longer ignore them. The reason why I project this is because I don't think that the new government will solve the old problems better than the previous one. And neither do I think the FPO can solve them, but, in fact, make it worse with protectionism and scapegoating.

Maybe the refugee crisis will quiet down, assuming there is not another war in the Middle East or another drought in Pakistan or Somalia. These are pie in the sky assumptions, but I assume that they are true for now. Then the next problem is to solve the crisis of neoliberalism of which there had been many books and some speeches by left-wing leaders (Bernie Sanders, Jeremy Corbyn etc.), but not much movement. I neither think that the Austrian nor any other government will solve the problem by itself.

Yanis Varoufakis, the much scolded former finance minister of Greece, is using his elder statesman position to argue for a united European left-wing movement (Oltermann 2016), whose primary goal it is to make the EU more transparent and accountable for the people, and then devise mechanisms to reduce debt and spur economic growth in Europe. He warns than inaction results in a post-modern 1930s, an eerie reminder of what could happen to supposedly stable democratic regimes, who can't cope with their political-economic challenges of their time, and resort to authoritarianism and fascism, as we see in Poland or Hungary today.

The Austrians will decide on May 22 who will become the federal president. Whoever wins the elections, life will continue. I doubt, however, whether political stability will return in late-capitalism. There nor anywhere else in the west.

Does Sanders Still Stand a Chance?

Posted on <u>April 28, 2016</u>

The last elections in New York, Pennsylvania and a few other states were a rout for Bernie Sanders in his run for the Democratic presidential nomination. Clinton currently has a delegate lead of 327. Of course, there were substantial irregularities in the voting process, as several ward leaders, who administered the election, were clearly favoring Clinton. But aside from that, most of the registered Democrats are still warming their hearts with Clinton, even though it is not obvious to me how she would be the best choice for the country.

Even though, Sanders has affirmed after his defeat in the last few big primaries that he would fight until the very end, moving on a rather narrow path to victory, he is now speculating as to what would happen if he were not to become the nominee, and he understands that his campaign remains a longshot campaign. But what he pointed out correctly is that independents favor Sanders by a much bigger margin than Clinton. The Democratic Party members might have a slight tendency to Clinton, but given that there are way more independents than either Democrats or Republicans (2-1), the independents are much more important in a general election. If the Democrats want to ensure a Democratic victory, they are better off with Sanders than with Clinton.

But that is not the way how it will turn out to be. Clinton now has the best chances to lock down a path to the nomination, and then confront Donald Trump in the general elections. The optics here is enormously weird, because Trump used to be a Democrat in the early-2000s, lavishing campaign contributions on Hillary Clinton when she was US senator in New York. Why would the Clinton's voluntarily show up in Trump's wedding ceremony in 2005 if there was no quid pro quo?

Now we might get the impression that as members of opposite parties confronting each other in the general elections that they are mortal enemies, but that is all show. Trump himself admitted that he gets along well with "everybody", which includes Democrats and Republicans, because only by buying up both sides can he ensure "making good deals" (i.e. ripping off the public and have the politicians on both sides support him).

240

Defenders of Hillary Clinton claim that Sanders supporters insinuate her corruption, and that there is no evidence that the campaign money she has taken from the financial industry would corrupt her views on policy. But the evidence for corruption is rather obvious: she does not support a breakup of the big banks, a 15 dollar an hour minimum wage (only accepting 12 dollars), single-payer health care and free college tuition. She repeatedly said how she wanted to build on "Obama's legacy", which basically means to change nothing. Supporting the status quo means to be comfortable with the oligarchic takeover of the economy, which she considers to be the only "realistic" path.

During a "normal" election year that would have been sufficient. But it is hard for people to see how they are living in normal times, when economic insecurity is greater than before, and billionaires make democracy superfluous. The establishment media treats Sanders and Trump as weird outliers, when, in fact, they are at the center stage, because of the corrupted nature of our political system and the growing realization that something needs to be done about it.

Another problem with Clinton is that she is clearly progressive only in those issues that do not offend the rich donor class. When she gave a speech for Goldman Sachs, she apparently praised the number of women in executive positions, without mentioning the fraud and abuse inherent in the industry. Of course, it makes you a progressive if you support women's rights and gay rights, but the capitalist class cannot care less who it is that does the exploiting. The working class should buy that brand of progressivism which is focused on identity politics, while the socio-economic issues should be conveniently ignored (see Frank's 2016 take on this). She occasionally lashes out at the rich, who have "rigged the system" in their favor, but then is rather coy about saying what to do about it, which reminds me of Obama's vague "hope" and "change" campaign of 2008.

Of course, a Clinton presidency would not be as bad as a Trump presidency, but why do the American people have to settle for less, especially if Sanders is a candidate, who finally promises to talk about the "issues"? Left commentators (The Young Turks) have already noted their pessimism as far as a Sanders win is concerned, and they emphasize the big movement that he is capable of creating which will outlast Sanders long after he stopped campaigning for the presidency. But let us not kid ourselves. If the Sanders campaign dies, so does the movement. It might get reactivated elsewhere, as people who have gained experience organizing for his campaign apply it elsewhere, but the timing of it would be quite uncertain.

The question, thus, becomes how Sanders can pave his way to the presidency in 2016. The simplest way would be to win the remaining primaries by a landslide, get most of the pledged delegates on his side, and convince the superdelegates that he has a strong case for the nomination. Then it will be Trump versus Sanders, where Sanders will have an easy time destroying Trump's empty messages. In the other case, Sanders loses the Democratic nomination for which he already stated that he did not want to be the spoiler running on an independent platform, thus splitting the Democratic vote and handing the victory to Trump. But that might be the best way forward if he does not get the Democratic nomination. It is not very clear why he would be a spoiler, because the electorate now has had a chance to see him in action and to be familiar with his ideas. The independents like him much more than either Trump or Clinton, and they are the large voter bloc that decides the elections. In a three-way race, Sanders' chances are not so bad.

I don't know whether he will decide to go down this route, but given what he stated himself that he would do much better among independents than among Democratic voters, there is principally only one way to test his idea in reality. In an election that is fought by a 1%er (Trump) for the 1%er (Clinton), would it not be ideal to have some alternative on the ballot as well?

Book Review of "A History of Chinese Civilization" by Jacques Gernet (1982)

Posted on <u>May 9, 2016</u>

I have just finished reading "A History of Chinese Civilization" by Jacques Gernet (Cambridge: Cambridge University Press, 1982 [1972]), a French scholar of Chinese history, and was very much blown away by it. What any good writer of history is doing is to integrate all elements of a country's history, i.e. the politics, the society, the economy, the technology, the culture, the philosophy, the sciences, the intellectual trends, the literature etc. I have previously read Chinese history books, but their natural deficiency is that they overtly focus on the political history, i.e. the rise and fall of dynasties and empires, the intrigues, the backstabbing, the gossiping, the wars and the peasant rebellions among others. Gernet's work does not fall into this trap. He does not hide his western perspective, but how would one do it anyway? He uses western terms like "rationalism", "materialism" and so forth to describe the intellectual currents since the days of Confucius. This is not so much a weakness as much as an attempt to lay out to western readers what Chinese civilization and history entails.

I remark on two elements of the book that I particularly enjoyed: the social and economic history and the intellectual history. This will be more descriptive rather than reflective, which expresses my profound amazement at the clarity and breadth of Gernet's scholarship (albeit not so much depth because it is difficult to squeeze all the civilization into 700 pages of writing).

The major reason why dynasties collapse is evidently because they lose the proverbial "Mandate of Heaven" as is described by Confucius and his followers. The rulers don't deliver what the people think they deserve. The persistent pattern in Chinese history is that dynasties get overthrown, because of (1) the toleration of the concentration of wealth in the hands of a few large landowners at the expense of peasants (e.g. Han dynasty, p.150); (2) the fiscal crisis of the state, which is linked to (3) the corruption and mismanagement of power (e.g. lavish court feasts) within the central government, (4) the waging of costly wars and military campaigns; furthermore (5) the overtaxation of the rural peasantry, which usually carries most of the tax burden, their exploitation by the landowners and the bankers, who lend at usurious interest rates; (6) foreign invasion (as with the

Mongols in 1200s, Manchu Qing dynasty in 1600s, western powers in 1800s and Japan in 1930s-40s); (7) famines usually resulting in peasant rebellions, (8) decentralization weakening the center (as in 1800s Qing).

Another important social and economic question revolves around the methods of production, which include changes in technological availability and the "social relations" of production. As with most civilizations, Chinese superiority emerged out of a gradual increase in agricultural productivity. Foremost in my mind is the importation of a rice seed from Vietnam in the 1000s (Song dynasty) to the lower Yangtze river area, which substantially increased the population in that region. The next stage of civilizational development is the growth in the number of large, affluent landowners, who can live off the labor of the peasants from whom the land was usurped (pp.312-3). The next stage involves the growth of the cities with the merchants, traders and the bourgeoisie. Manufacturing was developed only very late and until the the Communist takeover in 1949 was restricted to the coastal area around Shanghai and Jiangsu province. Gernet remarks that the Mongols and Song rulers (900-1200s) relied on merchants for tax revenues, while the Ming and Qing (1300-1900s) economy heavily relied on farmers (p.391).

Growing overall affluence also allowed the king to expand his tax capacity and pay for the huge court to entertain him, the large army to secure the borders and conquer new spaces, and most interestingly, develop the massive state bureaucracy involving civil servants (the so-called 'literati' 士大夫 shìdàfū as they passed complex imperial exams with knowledge of ancient historical texts to become a civil servant) and eunuchs (宦官 huàngu□n), who were castrated men, who ran the day to day affairs of government, swearing loyalty only to the king as they don't have children of their own. The strong, central Chinese state, which was first established by Qin Shi Huang (221 BC) has been the hallmark of Chinese civilization, which makes current calls for a more relaxed Communist state quite laughable.

A brief aside on an important historical question, which was first raised by a high-level Taiwanese official, who shared the anecdote of him studying in a US university many years ago and a professor asking him the question, "Why did the Nationalists lose the civil war against the Communists?" Barrington Moore (1966, "Social Origins of Dictatorship and Democracy") answered the question partly by stating that the Nationalists did not really care much about the peasant question. Most people were living on the land, surviving on a subsistence income and still being brutally oppressed by the big landowners. (Though Moore's argument states, on the contrary, that peasants were quite powerful, but I would say only to the extent that they were activated and organized by the Communist insurgency.)

Gernet adds to this by claiming that Chiang Kai-shek's (Nationalist) power base were the military and the Shanghai-based bankers (p.631, 634). The three banker families included the Soong's, Kung's and Chen's. Chiang was married to Soong Mei-ling from the Soong family, and his brother-in-law via the Soong family was Kung Hsiang-hsi, the other major banker. The bankers paid for Chiang's military academy and the wars of annihilation he was fighting against the Communists.

When the Japanese seized Manchuria in 1932, Chiang was not so much bothered by the "disease of the skin" (Japanese) as much as by the "cancer below the skin" (Communists). In fact, he did not give up assaulting Communist bases until his own generals kidnapped him and forced him to cooperate with the Communists in a united front against Japan (1936). The Communists themselves were almost annihilated by the Nationalist military campaigns, but they survived the Long March and regrouped. Mao Zedong formulated a populist campaign to organize the vast masses of peasants to fight for the Communists and be paid off by massive land redistribution hurting the big landowners (and part of the Nationalists' power base). During the Japanese invasion in 1937, Chiang's troops were routed despite heavy US support and he transferred his power base to Chongqing. The Communists organized guerilla attacks behind the lines in Japanese-controlled territory, had close support by the rural peasantry and was always able to hide against big attacks in the hinterland. The Nationalists were not so fortunate as their power base was primarily based in the big cities, which the Japanese controlled throughout the war.

When the Japanese were defeated, Chiang realized the difficulty of reconquering China, which at this point was very Communist, especially in the north, where most of the Japanese troops were concentrated. Despite receiving more loans and military aid from the US, the Nationalists were quickly defeated and expelled in the Civil War and took refuge in Taiwan. If it were not for the Korean War, where Communist China hurled half a million soldiers against the US forces aiding South Korea, the US would not have sent their fleet to the straits of Taiwan, and Chiang and the Nationalists would not have survived the end of the civil war. (There were clear invasion plans of Taiwan by the mainland.) In short, the Communists defeated the Nationalists, because the former knew how to mobilize the peasants, who if they were mobilized sufficiently were the most powerful force, while the Nationalists' reliance on the military, the industrialists and bankers in the big cities gave them only the illusion of permanent power. The Japanese invasion was also important in giving the Communists breathing room to regroup, while the Nationalists sat out the invasion with their economic power base taken by the Japanese.

Back to Gernet: Intellectual history in China is very rich, and that book was, of course, only able to scratch the surface of what intellectuals were capable of producing. Much of the basic ideas were established early on, and are summarized by Confucianism (with Mencius as most important follower), Mohism, Legalism, Taoism and Buddhism. Confucianism is foremost concerned about creating a perfectly harmonious society, which achievable by ritual behavior of the good man, respecting elders and those in power, pursuing wisdom and self-knowledge. Confucius is rather practical in orientation and is only concerned with good behavior in the current world without any mention of transcendentalism as is common in the monotheist religions of the west. Mencius agreed with Confucius. He claimed, in addition, that humans are inherently good, they merely need to be shown the good way. He sees the importance of having benevolent rulers, who are kind to the people to shape them in a good direction.

Mohism says that creating an egalitarian society based on altruistic principles would provide for the common good (some similarity to Marxism is clearly evident). Mohists reject the blind pursuit of rituals, and prefer self-reflection to attain wisdom. They also prefer asceticism and a renunciation of worldly riches. Legalists claim that the prince must concentrate power into his hands and establish a rule of law to provide for political stability. Taoists and Buddhists are much more transcendental in that they demand of followers a retreat from the world and seek salvation. Gernet, however, remarks that Chinese thinking emphasizes the "general, spontaneous order over the notion of direct, mechanical action" (p.524). In other words, rather than seeking truth in a reality outside of things (i.e. transcendentalism, reification), the Chinese thinkers accepted the truth of the worldly order. Westerners might describe this as secularism and materialism. In addition, Chinese writing, which is based on pictographs rather than phonetics, has an inherently mathematical quality, which facilitated the rise of an elite literati caste to pursue scientific and philosophical inquiry.

Does Class Conflict Promote Historical Development?

Posted on May 12, 2016

We could argue that class conflict is not important for historical development and that the changes in the social relations among classes (from landlord to bourgeoisie, from peasant to worker) are driven by external factors like technological development (weaponry and navigation to conquer faraway places, steam engine to create industries and factories) or state-centric developments (king usurping power from the landlord, enclosure or primitive accumulation, whereby peasants are kicked off the land and become city vagabonds).

I will not and cannot deny that these external factors are crucial to determine the changes in the fate of human development. But nowhere do I see that Marx had dismissed these external factors as part of his analysis in the Communist Manifesto. In the account given in the Manifesto, Marx took account of the technological changes that favored the growth of the city-based bourgeoisie. He took into account the capture of international markets via European seafaring, colonial conquests, the slave trade and general trade. Societies become more complex with trade and new technology, while feudalism relies on simplicity and stagnation. The landlord says to his peasants, "I tax your produce, and in exchange I protect you from marauding bands."

Now, back to class struggle. Is class struggle at the root of those changes? The class struggle is the undercurrent, the constant underlying development, but it is true that class antagonism does not lead to social change without technology, state centralization and colonial conquest. But to dismiss the class struggle argument we have to prove that in the absence of class struggle we would have gotten to the same social changes as with class struggle. But that is impossible to determine, because class struggle is not just an independent variable, but also a dependent variable. It is not just the cause but also the effect. The social change, i.e. the shift from landlord to bourgeoisie and from peasant to worker, is itself the manifestation of class struggle. External factors reinforce class struggles and thus forcing social change.

Critics will counter this is too broad of a definition, and that we should restrict class struggle to the violent warfare and bloody revolution among different social classes. But I ask why we should have such a narrow definition? If I am a bourgeois (businessman, merchant, financier etc.) and I make more money than the landlord, pay more taxes to the state than him, and bring the king to side with me to pass the enclosure laws that remove peasants from the land, and I open the factories to employ those landless peasants as my workers, thus depriving the landlord of his peasants, and in that process have not shot one bullet, am I engaging in a class struggle with the landlord? Yes, I think so.

So to repeat myself, *class struggle is the undercurrent of social change, but is by itself not a driver of social change.* Call it a necessary but not sufficient condition. Yes, we need the other factors to help bring it about. I think the question in the title is an odd and confusing one. I would not go as far as saying that class struggle is a cause for any change, but that it is a *permanent feature of human society* that manifests itself differently in different epochs with different state systems, technology and imperial power.

The more interesting question that we are dealing with is whether class struggle continues to play a role in today's world. Some of my classical liberal and conservative friends will deny entertaining the possibility of class struggle in the 21st century. Let me help them open their eyes a little bit.

Trade unions, who have fought hard for gains throughout the industrial revolution and into the 1970s in the west, are now in full-scale retreat, fighting rearguard battles against the resurgent capitalist class, which is reflected in declining rates of trade union membership, declining coverage of collective bargaining arrangements, growing number of concessionary contracts, social program focused government austerity measures, elevated rates of corporate profits, low corporate tax receipts in national governments and outrageous sums of money being squirreled away in the world's major tax havens. Strike activity at the workplace is reduced in much of the developed world (though China's labor actions are interesting to observe as their labor markets appear more robust), but don't mistake worker docility for worker satisfaction. What we are seeing is more and more workers are going through ever longer periods of credentialization, such that college degrees today are worth as much or even less than high school diplomas a generation ago. Zero hour contracts, part-time and low paid positions in the service sector have become our major occupation (the "Uberization" of the economy), as much of the genuinely productive work is either handled by robots, machines or by workers in cheap labor countries. If the capitalist class plundering more and more resources and shifting them away from the workers and the unemployed (of which there are more and more) does not constitute an act of class warfare, then I don't know what does.

The working class is the only class which can fight back and protect the interests of the underdog class (the '99%') because of their important role in providing the surplus labor, which is the source of all profits. But organizationally, it becomes ever more complicated to form a phalanx to oppose the unjust claims of the global oligarchy. Let us not get bogged down by the 'false consciousness' argument that the workers are too stupid to become a self-conscious class. If a company decides to shut down a plant in the rich country and move to a poor country, the decision-making power is concentrated in the corporate headquarter, while the workers in the poor and rich country see no reason for solidarity because they have no way to communicate with each other and poor country workers see the benefit of getting job opportunities, which makes them unwilling to collaborate with the workers in the rich countries.

Technology also weakens the position of the working class, which was well predicted by Marx, because we don't have so many manufacturing workers left following automation and we are transferring more and more workers into the service sector, which keeps the so-called equilibrium wage down in those industries. People are so scared and loaded up with college and mortgage debt, that they will work longer hours for lower wages and only concern about daily survival rather than the general class struggle, which is the only way to improve their lot. With automation continuing apace, the only way to return dignity to every human being and stabilize the position of the underdog class is to have a universal basic income scheme. These demands will continue to pop up among the left, and for the sake of maintaining human civilization we can demand nothing less.

The Neoliberal Coup d'Etat in Brazil
Posted on May 16, 2016

Dilma Rousseff, Brazilian president from the Worker's Party, was suspended and replaced by her vice president Michel Temer, from the officially non-ideological Democratic Movement Party (Wikipedia, "Brazilian Democratic Movement Party"). The charge that the senators levied against Rousseff is her involvement in a corruption scandal of Petrobras, the major Brazilian oil corporation. Strangely, however, she is not directly implicated in those scandals (O'Grady 2016), which could mean that she lets other people do the dirty work, and she can at most be incriminated for having knowledge of corruption but not doing anything about it.

But we know that it is impossible that corruption is the main reason for the ongoing impeachment proceedings against Rousseff. The reason is that the newly appointed president Temer is not less corrupt than Rousseff. Temer is also unpopular, as only 1 or 2% of the voters are willing to support his leadership (Reuters, "Support for Rousseff's impeachment ebbs in Brazil poll", April 9, 2016). Temer is accused of taking 1.5 million US dollars in bribes from a construction company that contracted with Petrobras. And that is just one of the dozens of allegations that are waged against the current president. Even worse, 60% of all the parliamentarians, who are supposed to prosecute president Rousseff, are also under corruption investigations, including the speaker of the House and the president of the Senate (detailed allegations can be found in FoxNews, "3 men in line for Brazilian presidency accused of corruption", April 19, 2016). The people, who are supposed to carry out the Rousseff investigations are themselves very corrupt politicians, which reduces the credibility of the entire investigation. It can't be corruption that these politicians are concerned about, but finding a pretext to get rid of Rousseff, a democratically elected leader of Brazil (as even the Economist, "Brazil's political crisis: time to go", March 23, 2016 argues).

I do not mean to blindly defend Rousseff, as there are many people on the streets, who are justifiably upset about corruption, a declining economy (GDP declines to 1.7 trillion in 2015 from 2.6 trillion dollars in 2011, Statista, http://www.statista.com/statistics/263769/gross-domestic-product-gdp-in-brazil/), rising inflation (over 10% in 2015 compared to 3% in 2006), growing unemployment (at nearly 11%

compared to 8% in 2015) and rising budget deficits (from -3% in 2013 to -10% in 2015) and debt (from 52% in 2013 to 66% in 2015- all Trading Economics, http://www.tradingeconomics.com/brazil).

But it is questionable what the agenda is behind the politicians, who want to get rid of Rousseff as quick as they can. Temer is a trained lawyer with friendly ties to US corporations and acting as a spy to the US embassy (see Wikipedia, "Michel_Temer#Investigations" and footnotes that direct to Wikileaks cables). His finance minister is Henrique Mereilles, a trained banker and former central bank chief, who has noted his preference to "not raise taxes" and emphasizing the "priority to balance public finances" (O'Grady 2016), which basically means austerity for the masses. His appointment has resulted in the rallying of financial markets in Brazil (Biller 2016), revealing the confidence that the investors have in him to carry out the neoliberal program of austerity for the masses and payoff to investors. Deutsche Bank already predicts that Petrobras, steel, bank and commercial property bond rating will substantially improve with the new government at the helm (Parra-Bernal 2016). The new chairman of the central bank, Ilan Goldfein, is an adviser to the IMF and the World Bank with a PhD from MIT (Ynetnews 2016), thus ensuring the continuity of anti-inflation monetary policy.

This new government consists only of old white men as opposed to the more diverse cabinet of Rousseff (RT, "'Brazil's new all-white, all-male government shows what's at stake'", May 16, 2016). But that is by itself not a problem as long as their policies are halfway consistent with the needs and interests of the ordinary Brazilian people. We can already see signs of that not being the case.

Rousseff's ouster was nothing short of a neoliberal coup d'état, because Temer was very quick in announcing measures to privatize postal services, transport, power and insurance companies that are currently held by the state to raise sufficient revenues to reduce the budget deficit. This is a move that was never contemplated by Rousseff (Fortune, "Brazil Is Reportedly Considering Selling State Assets to Raise Cash", May 16, 2016). The selling-off of state assets during a financial crisis results in very low selling prices, which promise substantial profit for private investors, while both the state and the public users of these services lose out in the form of lower state revenues, higher consumer prices and lower quality of services. That was the experience of post-Soviet Russia, which sold highly valuable state companies for dumping prices to oligarch cronies in the 1990s.

The second part of Temer's policy involves cuts to pensions and axing the civil service by 4,000 employees (Buenos Aires Herald, "Temer claims support for austerity in Brazil", May 14, 2016). It is not clear how these workers, who will lose their jobs, will be added onto the private sector payroll, when the overall unemployment rate is increasing. Some people might claim that new employment is created by reducing the tax burden on businesses. If the government was serious in its intentions to curb the budget deficit, it will not reduce taxes, and so there is no net benefit for private companies, who see no reason to hire new workers anyway. As far as pension cuts are concerned, one can only imagine what would happen to senior poverty if people had to work more years and/ or face lower pensions. Many of the gains of the previous government, including a reduction of absolute poverty by 28 million people (!) or 15% of the total population (Croix 2012), could be reversed if the investor-friendly austerity mantra gets implemented.

If Rousseff's ouster were only about corruption, we could expect that the caretaker president would keep the economic policy steady, but the fact that he does not shows the neoliberal intentions of the new government. Temer is given 180 days in the constitution to rule as he desires. People are not happy about the new government, but they might still be surprised about these chaotic political events and don't know what to expect from the new government. That is probably the reason why the new cabinet tries to enact their "painful medicine" (as if neoliberalism were a cure for anything) as quick as they can before people on the streets restore another left-leaning government.

The Walmartization, Uberization and Facebookization of the Economy

Posted on May 19, 2016

If I had to describe what I consider to be the frontier of today's economy and labor market, I cannot help but think of the impact that three big and powerful corporations have on the lives of Americans and other western people. Of course, it is too simple to consider only three companies' practices (Walmart, Uber and Facebook) and make logical inferences of the whole economy. But, on the other hand, I am convinced that theorists of monopoly capitalism (see old advocates in literature cited in Sweezy 2004 as well as more contemporary ones Stiglitz 2016) make the claim that a few big companies set the trend for the economy and the labor market, so that we can make logical inferences to the wider economy from the three companies' practices. I will describe each of these concepts in turn, and then make a case for why the rise of these three companies are making the lives of consumers and investors amazing, but the lives of workers very miserable. The rise of these three companies partially explains the proliferation of millionaires and billionaires as well as the growth of wealth and income inequality that the likes of Bernie Sanders have railed against.

Walmartization

Walmart is the largest private-sector employer in the US, and has about 1.4 million employees under their payroll. It is very natural to take them as the first example of where the economy is going. As they set very low wages, that has a knock on effect on other companies in the retail industry, who don't see themselves compelled to raise their own wages. There is now some evidence that with a somewhat tightening labor market, the Walmart management is now forced to slightly raise the base pay, which at 10 dollars an hour is still not significantly higher than the minimum wage of 7.25 dollars an hour. Workers at Walmart are notoriously mistreated as they work an insufficient number of hours at rather low wages. They don't have a trade union to protect their interests, which is indicative of the larger economy, where only 11% of the workforce (7% in the private sector) is unionized.

In Walmart, it is common practice to boot out workers, who had been employed longer than 10 years, because their pay has increased so much, and they can easily hire a new worker off the street at a lower wage. Because there is not much training involved, the turnover costs are perceived to be low. Economically, we have to question the logic of everyday low wages (being the flipside of their slogan "everyday low prices"). Costco is treating their workers much better and pay higher wages, which results in greater employee motivation and lower turnover, which means a higher productivity to offset the employer cost of higher wages. It is quite pathetic that the Walmart management pays itself outrageous compensation, make a substantial profit, and pay their workers so little that they rely on Food Stamps and Medicaid to survive. The taxpaying middle class (corporations pay only a small share of total taxes), therefore, is forced to subsidize Walmart's and other low-wage employers like McDonalds' profits through the social benefit programs, which Jacobs et al. (2015) estimated to cost $152.8 billion.

While consumers may relish the convenience of 24-7 access to a consumer paradise, a quasi-one-stop shop for all the retail commodities that the heart desires, the rise of Walmart has been devastating to the interests of workers, who have to rest content with low wages and no influence over work decisions. Ironically, the workers here are still relatively the best off.

Uberization

Since the rise of Uber, the taxi business is no longer the same. Consumers can now order a taxi through the webapp and private people, who decide to hire out their car and earn some extra income, pick them up and drive them to the desired destination. Because the app bypasses the bureaucracy surrounding traditional taxi companies, who restrict taxi licenses to a few individuals, the price of a hired car ride is much lower with Uber. Some Uber drivers, who voluntarily like to earn some extra money, have also spoken quite positively about their driving experience. They may be the secondary earners of the family and know very well how to drive the kids to school and to the soccer match, and are quite happy to drive strangers, who can even pay them an income.

But while the experience is mostly positive for customers, the case for drivers is more ambiguous. There has been a class action lawsuit among California and Massachusetts Uber drivers against Uber for classifying the drivers as independent contractors, where costs like fuel and maintenance are not reimbursed and benefits (health and pensions) are not paid by the company. Uber decided to pay the $100 million settlement, accepting the cost of doing business, as long as the drivers continue to be classified as independent contractors rather than the workers that they really are (Levine 2016).

Why would I make the claim that Uber drivers are really workers in a dependent employment relationship? It is clearly difficult to make a purely legal claim out of it, because both sides will hire lawyers to make their case and quote the right passages of previous court cases and statutes. This is really a moral claim more than anything else. If workers are independent contractors, we assume that these individuals can easily handle the risks within the industry, i.e. car breakdown, sickness. If workers are dependent employees, we assume that these workers cannot handle the full risk, and a substantial portion of the risk is carried by the employer, who pays substantial health contributions if the worker gets sick or is responsible for the car repair when it breaks down.

Any reasonable society will try to apportion most of the risk to the entity, which is capable of carrying the largest burden, which is usually the employer. Individual workers usually don't have enough resources to bear all the risk. What would be the problem of shifting the risk to Uber? The executives and shareholders, who are swimming hand over fist in cash, might get a little bit less money, but they are then also bearing the full responsibility of the risk, because they can bear it. Sacrificing some money in exchange for the well-being of the drivers cannot be too much asked. Yet if we delude ourselves that the neoliberal economic paradigm is the only correct paradigm, we might say otherwise.

But let us leave risk aside for the moment, and focus on the share of the fare that goes to Uber: it is usually between 20 and 25%, while some locations go as high as 30% (MacMillan 2015). Uber claims that this share is calculated based on the supply and demand at any given market, which makes it seem as if the market were justly allocating the spoils. Of course, it is not. Given the fact that Uber's taxi (not 'ride-sharing', which sounds too Orwellian to me as it implies a free service provided to a friend or family member) undercuts the prices of traditional taxis, they do generate a greater market demand, and so more taxi drivers will have to switch from the traditional taxi company to Uber, simply as a matter of survival. That situation gives an enormous market power to Uber. That to me sounds like a monopolization or cornering of the market, though Lyft is one alternative provider (though that's about it). How better can that market power be used if not for raising the share of the fare claimed by Uber?

Private investors have gotten themselves a gold mine, while customers have cheaper transport options available. For the Uber drivers and the millions of independent contractors in other companies, eking out a precarious existence (e.g. adjunct instructors in universities, nursing home workers), the innovation has been everything but beneficial. But there is an even worse example yet to come.

Facebookization

We are all guilty of it. Many of us are wasting a substantial amount of our waking time on the phone or on the laptop to check Facebook updates of our friends and the message inbox. We want to see the cute baby photos of friends and family members, who recently became parents. We want to see the cat which makes weird faces; the Donald Trump video, where he is insulting another group of people; the political stories that make people like me angry every day. When Zuckerberg founded Facebook in 2004, he understood that an important market niche in the World Wide Web was the human need for social connection. We cannot imagine nowadays to not using Facebook to stay in touch with old friends and family members, who live in a different part of the world, and whom we thought we might not see again. Facebook also allows us to narcissistically project our own viewpoint of the world to the friendship network and join our favorite tribe (called 'group'). We post our status updates, our views, videos, links, articles and comments. So from the consumer standpoint, being a Facebook user is the best thing since sliced bread.

Now we turn to the world of work. We shall begin with the 7,000 employees, who staff the headquarter in Menlo Park outside of San Francisco in California. This is in the middle of Silicon Valley where almost the entire innovation in the computer and internet industry is happening. Google, Apple, Facebook and others are vying for the top Ivy League graduates to hire programmers, engineers and marketing personnel to staff their offices, and it is a true privilege to work for any of these big Silicon Valley companies, as the pay is high, the benefits are great, the perks are substantial (e.g. free food, laundry, gym) and the creative downtime (once a week) is enormous. Surely, there are downsides to the many perks, as for instance free food at the workplace encourages employees to stay at their desks and continue working rather than enjoy the sunshine in a patio of a Bay Area restaurant. In that sense, there is an enormous stress capacity, but the perks are still substantial, right?

But I wanted to make a different point, which is to look at the number of employees and compare it with the number of users. 7,000 paid employees for more than a billion users. That is a lot of users, and that is a lot of money there. The Facebook founder is not nearly content enough. Zuckerberg speaks good Mandarin and loves traveling to China, mainly to convince the authorities to admit Facebook to their country and unlock another market of more than 1 billion people.

But notice that I say 'users' and not 'consumers'. In the case of Walmart and Uber it is clear that the consumers are just 'devouring' the service and not contributing any value toward it, which is done by the workers. In the case of Facebook users it is not the case that they are just consuming the service, but also contribute value to the company by posting, commenting and contributing content. Before you shout me down and say that posting on the Facebook wall is no more value creation than me giving an impassioned lecture to my friends in a pub, I have to say that the difference is that in the latter situation there is no exchange of money but in the former there clearly is. (We are talking here strictly in terms of economic value and not social or cultural value which involves sentiments and gaining knowledge, which is economically invaluable.)

If I give a great speech in a pub, which my drunk mates will forget the next morning, they have not paid me a nickel for that speech. That also does not happen if I post on the Facebook wall, but money exchanges hands, because the content is taken by Facebook, packaged up and sold to advertisers, who then pay the proceeds to Facebook if they want ads showing up on users' walls. If I like skiing, then I will see skiing products. If I like watching movies, I will see movie recommendations. If I like clothing, I will see clothing commercials, and so on. Facebook monetizes the content that the users put out, and in that sense people are producing value without getting compensated for it.

Does it matter for the average Joe? Yes, very much so. We have these huge centralized networks (read 'monopoly'), which no one wants to destroy because we relish the benefits of having all the people that we know in our lives be part of that great network, and we have a very concentrated ownership pattern with few formally paid (albeit well-compensated) employees. Mark Zuckerberg is now among the richest people in the world ($45 billion the last time I checked), and he showed off that he was giving most of his money away to charity when his daughter was born. (What he did not say was that the Zuckerberg-Chan foundation also serves as a useful tax shelter to avoid inheritance tax.) The collectivity is paying Zuckerberg for the privilege of using his network, where lots of economic value is created, but only very few get to benefit from it.

In such a dystopian world, there might be one little positive element, namely that if we get so frustrated in the world of work, because of the low pay, we at least get the right amount of free entertainment (chiefly Youtube and Facebook), though it will not really pay the rent or food.

Conclusion

I summarize that the three major trends in the economy and the labor market that I see today are captured in the three major companies Walmart, Uber and Facebook. Each of these companies provide a boon for consumers and investors, but provide penury and insecurity for workers. Walmart workers face low wages and job insecurity. Uber workers face low payment and uncertain contracts with enormous individual risks. Facebook users create economic value but get nothing themselves.

As most of us can scarcely rely on rent or dividend income for survival, we must go out in the labor market and try our luck there. Given the uncertainty of the labor market, we can no longer believe that jobs will be safer or better in the immediate future. That cannot happen without a substantial degree of class struggle, which can result in positive outcomes for workers. For instance, states like New York have substantially increased the minimum wage.

But even if workers, who through their strike can temporarily stop surplus accumulation in the capitalist class and redistribute some profits back to them, are successful in wresting hard-fought compromises from their employers, these gains are most likely to occur in the Walmart sector, and with sufficient legal changes (assuming that judges do not continue to be bought and paid for by the 1%, as they usually are) even the Uber sector. In the Facebook sector (which includes Google as well, among others), it is much more difficult to realize, because most users don't see themselves as creating any economic value, and those, who defend Zuckerberg's mountains of sugar (pun intended for my German-speaking friends), claim that he deserves all the money because of his innovative idea to establish Facebook in the first place. If that narrow private property principle were in place when Penicillin was invented, that inventor would have been very rich today, yet he refused to patent it for the common good. And without Zuckerberg's engineers, who helped develop the network, and users, who give live to the network by using it, he would not have anything today.

For those of us, who are constantly concerned about creating economic and social justice, there is a deep dilemma wrought by modern technology. If we decided to pay Facebook users for their postings, how much should each post get paid? For what length? For how many likes? These are tricky questions, which I think should, therefore, not be resolved within the framework of a market economy, which would have been more understandable with more traditional labor markets.

In short, we need to have a universal basic income paid to all citizens, so the users can continue providing the content which creates economic value but not necessarily payment to the value creators. We can pay for that by taxing the mountains of cash in Zuckerberg's hands and those of other fellow oligarchs (especially in finance). As Yanis Varoufakis says, it is an illusion to believe that wealth is privately created and publicly appropriated, as neoliberal discourse suggests, when, in reality, wealth is publicly (i.e. commonly) created and privately appropriated. In a world where it is difficult to discover the new frontier of work, where labor participation continues to remain low, where globalization and automation make the nice and good jobs scarce, there are few other options to create a better society than with a basic income.

Why the Grading and Examination System Is Harmful for Students

Posted on June 2, 2016

One of the major differences between the American and the British education system is that in the American it is easier to score high than it is in the British system. I have just received some grades for an assignment for which I had 38 out of 100 points. The grading process is not entirely transparent. The supervisor sat across the table from me, when she returned me the assignment and said with teary eyes that after looking at the assignment twice, they still could not award me sufficiently more points to pass me. There was some shock in me, which has to do with the fact that I barely receive failures. I have to submit an improved assignment in a few weeks.

During my undergraduate days, I would easily score well, but I had decided that I would not concern myself too much with the grading system, because it would distract me from my own research interests, for which it is difficult to assign grades. If I wanted to study Japanese economic history between 1945 and today, who was to tell me that my work should have a good or a bad grade? If I received the good grade, so be it. Validation is uplifting initially, but loses its appeal after a while. If I received the bad grade, it could mean that the powers that be did not approve of the quality of my work, but for the student it meant that I should feel worthless about myself, even though that is never said explicitly anywhere.

The negative feedback effect of the grading system is blatantly obvious. It is because a student had received a poor grade that he shall feel ashamed of himself, and either try better the next time to please the teacher and to please the system or give up on academics altogether. In that sense, millions and billions of talented and curious individuals are rebuffed from the education system, because they had not produced the kinds of answers that the system wants to hear. Ironically, the teacher told me that part of the reason why I failed was because of my chronic desire to finish the work quickly and "tick the checkbox" rather than do the work slowly and methodically. Apparently, I should not be ticking the checkbox, when, in fact, the system was about "ticking the checkbox" (i.e. submitting a work that pleases the eyes of the examiners).

What was even more disturbing was that class mates and teachers reinforced what Durkheim (1912) had called the "sacred". In fact, the only way how an institution can survive is by the members of the group repeating and reaffirming the rules. A church would stop existing without prayers and songs, and apparently a university would stop existing without exams (which I will dispute later). The students would stress out about how well or poorly they performed, and in their hope to unload some of their anxieties, they would speak with their class mates about the grading system and how they could make it out well in the assignment and the exam. By hearing the other students' worries, one begins to doubt one's own ability and get focused on how to perform sufficiently, not to enlarge the mind but to please the requirements in the system. The teachers are also reinforcing student anxiety, ironically and especially when they want to be helpful to their students; for instance by answering student questions about the process of doing well. I had one entire seminar wasted because students kept on asking questions about the process, which includes exams and thesis work, while the intellectual content of the course was the side show.

The entire anxiety derives from the artificial environment of the grading system. We know that the pressure is entirely artificial, because one year from now no one will worry about this assignment or even this course. There will be some bits and pieces of the course material, and there will be a memory of the people in the course. The guy, who always came in with the tie and suit and could blabber on endlessly. The girl, who had a charming smile and was always helpful. It will be a hodgepodge of conversations and encounters, but not the checkboxes that we had to tick off. Life will be remembered, not our survival. I am looking at the Facebook photo of my former employer with co-workers after the last day of work. He had to dissolve the retail store, which the headquarters decided to close for lack of profitability. But rather than talk about the business aspect, he spoke sentimentally of a farewell from his co-workers. The profit motive lacks a heart, but the people working in it don't.

Defenders of the grading system now claim that grades are very important to ensure that student learning is happening. But that assumes that student learning only happens with grades. The reality is that student learning can happen in a variety of settings, and learning is no worse under an alternative system without grades.

This begs the question of what the functional relevance of the grading system is. It could very well be that grading was introduced because it was the simplest way to ensure compliance with learning objectives, and then took a life of its own. But I find this path-dependence explanation too simple, because it neglects the social-psychological effects on students. It turns out that students, who are so focused on the process of securing good grades, are also very focused on getting promoted in the firm, receiving a high performance review, and pleasing the capitalist bosses. If people are so focused on the process, they lose sight of the big picture, i.e. of the relevant philosophical question that a liberal education teaches you: what for? Why should I struggle hard to jump over that next hoop? How does society benefit from me being competitive and securing a higher spot against others?

What is quite interesting is that my current program very much emphasizes the collaborative spirit, because there is no curve grading (which assigns a maximum quota of A grades), and so we are encouraged to meet each other and help each other to perform well. I do have a reasonable relationship with department mates in a way that did not exist during my undergraduate days. On the other hand, because the grading system is the underlying disciplining force of the program, I and the other students are still trapped like hamsters in a wheel. I encountered a department colleague recently, who was waiting outside the room to be called in and receive his assignment grades. He looked exhausted with a blank stare and focused on his grades, which was very different from the day before when we debated intellectual topics and he was heated, energetic and engaged.

What is profoundly sad is that academics itself is not immune to the process-centered hamster in a wheel phenomenon. One demography professor once told me with shining eyes that the greatest thing about being an academic (as opposed to a management consultant that he was before) is the freedom to research any topic, and the fact that no one can force you to choose a topic. Well, that is true, but as I pointed out previously ("Discontents of Academic Life"), there is a big distinction between older and younger faculty in that the younger faculty- facing much greater publication pressure and being methodology-driven (rather than phenomenon-driven)- are very process-centered technicians rather than wide-eyed scholars and intellectuals. Technicians are, no doubt, smart, but they are never in a position to ask the philosophical questions, only to do and not to think. One should only imagine what would have happened to human discovery if those technicians were reviewers and read manuscripts of Hobbes, Hume, Locke, Rousseau or any other thinker in those peer-reviewed journals today. They would reject their manuscripts for not being "rigorous" enough.

This rather depressing critique begs the question: What would be the content of an ideal education system? For a start, there should either be no exams, or those exams should be filled with comments for improvement for future reference. Had I received comments of improvement rather than the grade, I would have actually learned how to apply the method correctly rather than feel an empty frustration. By dropping the exams with grades, an important structural disciplining force gets dissolved, but is then replaced by self-discipline. It is true that self-discipline will vary among students, but if you look at the Montessori schools, children are more alert and

262

disciplined than in normal schools, because students are allowed to ask and answer their own questions with the guidance of teachers, but without control or force. Students will be naturally curious and want to find out what happens all around them and why it happens (read the personal account of Deweyite education by Noam Chomsky 1983). As Freire (1972) writes, knowledge should be co-creative rather than one-sided and enforced by the teacher on the student.

Wilhelm von Humboldt said himself that the knowledge that one discovers on his own will be remembered better than anything that is forced via exams. My most pleasurable experiences in Oxford have nothing to do with my course work, which for the reasons I listed above are rather frustrating and disappointing, but a mixture of listening to classical music (on the radio and even live at the Sheldonian theatre at low cost), writing this blog, reading non course-related books, watching movies, eating good food, meeting friends, seeing beautiful women smiling, having intellectual discussions with friends (including in Facebook chat groups), and going to external talks and seminars with Q&As. Even though it did not matter at all what I learned or retained from these conversations and seminars, I retained a lot more information than from a class lecture that is graded.

The most pleasurable academic experience- ironically with grading- was in the liberal arts honors program at my community college. I remember that there were some students, who were stuck in the grading paradigm, and asked the honors faculty about their grades. The students were rebuffed by the faculty, who said that they will receive the grades at the end of the term, when the college system finally requires them to input the grades. There was a mid-term and final exam, which the faculty emphasized were not "strongly evaluative". I have heard of some students receiving B's, but most students got A's in all the five courses, which were taught in a block. There were only two semesters of honors, and I wished it could be there for the full four semesters. It was a night and day contrast to return to the "normal" college class. Honors students were encouraged to ask and answer questions and craft their own arguments rather than regurgitating the textbook knowledge to teachers in exchange for a grade, so they can quickly forget everything they learned after the exam. (Okay, crafting your own argument is not possible for all subjects like math for which there is right and wrong).

I just pick out four fascinating things that I experienced in the honors program. First, there was a female English teacher in the program, who was very sociable and enjoyed sharing her candid feelings of which I just highlight two: she first reassured us that we all already have A's and now the question is what to do next, how to use that freedom of mind to write good commentaries of texts and discuss them with others. What a great feeling, but that great feeling naturally dissipates and is displaced by the desire to understand why Homer is relevant for us today, and what the ancient Greeks and ancient Chinese had in common. The second was her candid observation that it did not even matter if we kept the notes from the lectures. We might as well throw them away and never look at them if we did not want to. No teacher had ever told me that before, as notes are usually prerequisites to writing good exam papers.

The second fascinating experience was to stumble into the office of an honors professor and seeing him read a book by Bertrand Russell (1994), who wrote about early childhood education and the importance of imbibing in children a thirst for learning and a lack of fear to discover the world for themselves. The third observation were my constant political debates and discussions with my department chair, who challenged and attacked my assumptions with quick wit and sharpness. The fourth experience was another faculty member taking us to the Metropolitan Museum of Arts in New York, where he told us before we got off the bus that we could decide to wander New York on our own or take the free guided tour with him (he is an art historian by training) inside the museum before wandering off on our own for the lovely day trip (which I attended twice, always duly stopping by at the legendary Strand bookshop at 12th Street and Broadway). Before honors, I had the inclination of an intellectual. After honors, I could not be anything but an intellectual.

My intellectually most stimulating time during my undergraduate days at Penn was taking the graduate sociological theory course with a world famous sociologist (Randall Collins), who despite his towering intellect (see the many books and articles he published and the thick skin on his forehead right above his eyebrows if you believe in body language) was humble, welcomed his students for one-hour one-on-one meetings. Rather than him lecturing you, you would lecture him, and he would take meticulous notes on his yellow notepad, which no other professor had ever done in front of me. When you were finished, you would have a conversation with him, where he gives his insights, but lets the student be in charge of his project. In class he would give a lecture during the first hour, and then would let the students make their comments for the rest of class (another 2 hours), and he would comment on every single student comment, so it was always dialog oriented. It is small wonder that his sociological theory would have so much reach and power. He was constantly engaging in dialog with students to gain a new perspective and a new insight. The only requirement in that class was to submit a 10-20 page paper at the end of the class dealing with any sociological theory of our choice. No stupid exam.

If I convinced you that abolishing the grading system makes sense, the next question is: Would free-thinking individuals pose a danger to society? There is no doubt that in a grade-less world, students would compare themselves with their former selves and try to do better than their former selves rather than compare themselves with other students and be constantly anxious and frustrated about themselves (rather than the system, which actually creates the anxiety and frustration). There is also no doubt that students, who ask the philosophical questions, are also more difficult to suppress and oppress by the powers that be (it is for instance more difficult to crush teachers unions than, say, retail unions). In that sense, the free-thinkers are a threat to the power structure, but that does not imply any danger to society.

I don't know whether it is feasible to overthrow a system which so many people believe has worked so well for them (if they are deluded enough to believe it, though there are material benefits for paying deference to the system). There are counter-hegemonic sources of inspiration, primarily Paulo Freire, Noam Chomsky, Bertrand Russell, Wilhelm von Humboldt and John Dewey, but they can convert no more than a few intellectually-minded people, who have little to offer to counter the system. Even if I wanted to shield my children from the pernicious effects of mainstream education, they would still have to be exposed to it unless I am so rich that I can enable them to live in an isolated hamlet meeting only fellow bon vivant intellects. It is also true that it is much easier to swim with the stream than against it, which my limited punting experience in Oxford taught me.

One of my good friends and faculty during my undergraduate days organized critical seminars with his students, so they could analyze how the oppressive capitalist system worked out in their everyday lives. His advice was to pick a job to make a living, but to always retain the intellectual freedom in one's mind, because that is the only life worth living after discovering the light. As Bertell Ollman (n.d.) put it, the first step toward liberation is knowledge of what is wrong with our present education system.

I Endorse Abstention for the US General Elections

Posted on June 8, 2016

Bernie Sanders was banking all of his hopes on winning California, which went to Clinton in overwhelming numbers (56 to 43%). If Sanders had won California, he would have had a very strong case to win the Democratic nomination by tying with Clinton in the pledged delegate count. His loss implies that his chances to win are essentially nil. His chances were certainly diminished by the media calling Clinton as the winner prematurely, thus demotivating potential Sanders voters to go to the polls. There is one more symbolic primary next week in Washington DC. In his latest speech, Sanders announced that he wants to fight for every single delegate, though his language was vague enough to suggest that he would either officially drop out by the DC primary or go to the Philadelphia convention and commit to a "floor fight", which is the audacious proposition to convince the majority of the superdelegates to flip their vote from Clinton to Sanders.

That proposition is rather strange, because Sanders strongest case until recently was that the superdelegates are undemocratic and do not reflect the real interests of the voting base. The implication is that they should be abolished. But you can't demand the abolition of the same institution for which you hope that it will get you the nomination. Sanders will now argue that the superdelegates should support him, because the polls indicate that he has a higher chance of winning against Donald Trump than Clinton.

The reason for that is obvious for any reasonable person to see: in this election, voters are so sick and tired of establishment politics and the same-old, which does not deliver, either on jobs, affordable health care, a college education or a retirement. The bedrock of the American Dream is destroyed by foolish government policies that exacerbate inequality and don't solve the issues that burn in the eyes of the voters. Clinton is the establishment, and Sanders and Trump are not. Sanders has the good policies, while Trump does not.

There is no suggestion at all that Trump would solve these aforementioned problems any better than Clinton. His outrageous racism, plans to build a wall to Mexico and "make them pay for it", introduce a 35% tariff on Chinese imported goods and to "remove the lines" between states on the health care market either lack feasibility or don't solve any of our problems. Trump is a buffoon, but a clever buffoon, who can so easily manipulate the masses, rile them up and focus their anger on the political establishment and some new minority group. What Trump knows better than any other candidate is how to use the 24/7 news cycle in his favor. Make an outrageous statement, the viewers will like it, the media will cover it, and the advertising money will keep pouring in.

Also, his messages are so simple, you barely need any secondary education to understand it. Bernie Sanders tries to explain why inequality is bad for the society and the economy, and the professors and students in the audience will clap enthusiastically in his rallies, but it is more difficult to reach the masses in that way. When Trump shouts "Crooked Hillary" everyone understands that. In a country of intelligent people, Trump would stand no chance, but that is not the nature of society nor of democracy during uncertain political times.

What it means for the general election match Clinton vs. Trump is that Clinton will be associated with the status quo that does not work for the people, and Trump will be considered the guy, who will shake up things. That puts the odds in Trump's favor. The optics for Clinton cannot be worse. I don't particularly care about her e-mails or Benghazi, or other right-wing fabrications, which don't really matter to the general public. What troubles me are her policy positions. She wanted to go into Libya and then even Syria. She believes strongly in regime change. She wants to retain Obamacare despite the escalating costs and the threat it thus poses to the financial security of Americans. She supported the TPP, a trade agreement, as secretary of state, and now opposes it. She did not talk much about the minimum wage until Sanders brought it up (and now she has every reason to downplay it for the general election). Her proposal for "debt-free" college are quite nebulous and don't go as far as Sanders' plan.

With the Democratic nomination wrapping up and both sides preparing for the general election, we can see the contours of what will happen in the fall. The Democratic nomination process was filled with policy ideas during the debates, mainly propelled by Sanders, who has a laser-sharp focus like a union organizer with a clip board rattling down the progressive agenda that Americans need. Let's focus on the issues, and forget the soap opera part of politics, which is the way how the corporate media earns its daily bread.

What we will see in the fall will be nothing like that. In Clinton's foreign policy speech (June 2, 2016), all she did was attack Donald Trump for being a lunatic and a danger to US national security. I don't necessarily want to contest those claims (except that Trump does not shoot as straight as he talks and pretends, but leave that aside), but simply point out what the irony in this situation is. Clinton will not have to waste a second talking up a progressive agenda, as she did when she was on stage with Sanders. The progressive agenda is not the natural instinct of Clinton. As I argue, it is something much more basic: the lust for power. This is the only golden thread that I can see to connect all her policy decisions. Clinton tries to win the elections by saying that Trump is worse than her. That will wonderfully distract from the status quo oriented policies that she had always intended to pursue. It is the fear of the greater evil rather than the hope for better policies that should motivate the voters in the fall. In an election among the lesser evils, the voter turnout will be very low, which has potential bad outcomes for both sides, but maybe a small advantage for Republicans.

For those on the left the question is what to do next? What should Sanders do next? I certainly don't discourage him from taking up the "floor fight" at the Democratic National Convention in Philadelphia, and see how far he gets with his rousing speech. But again, the optics is bad for Sanders. He could make the case that superdelegates should vote the same way that pledged delegates vote, but because Clinton has nearly 400 more pledged delegates than Sanders, it would still hand the victory to Clinton. The only way he could win at this point is to essentially convince all the superdelegates to back him, but that would be very unlikely and as undemocratic as when he complained about the premature superdelegate support for Clinton (at 10-to-1). Sanders, the political independent, who joined the Democratic Party only last year to run for the presidency, now faces a bitter dead-end with the Democratic Party.

The only way for him to stay in the race would be to run as an independent, but that is very unlikely given that he used up his political capital trying to run within the Democratic Party. Sanders is still an incumbent US Senator and has two more years to his term. If his health holds up (which I don't doubt it will), he will be handily re-elected (maybe even unopposed) for a third term in 2018. Sanders' political future is not at stake, though he has used up his opportunity to become president. Rather it is the progressive movement, which now has to take a backseat in 2016 presidential election politics. Given the bad choices on both sides, I recommend an electoral abstention.

Some people will now criticize me by saying that such electoral cynicism will make it less likely to have the lesser evil (Clinton) elected, and could make us end up with Trump. This is a probable nightmare scenario, though in the best case scenario president Trump will be some fits of blustering, and embarrassment to the country, but no big change in policy, because the rest of the political system does not support his tantrums. I quite frankly don't see how Clinton can be considered the lesser of the two evils. The difference is that Clinton is predictably evil (neocon, status quo, growth of inequality), while Trump is unpredictably evil (a tinge of fascism and also the growth of inequality). People are not given any good choices, so the left has to hope that the Congressional races have more promising candidates, or for 2020 and 2024, when popular anger and frustration will be even bigger than what we see today.

Responding to a Critic of the Universal Basic Income

Posted on June 9, 2016

The following is my reply to Robin Wilson's (2016) article.

My critique in his argument is that a universal welfare state (which he postulates) does not contradict the universal basic income. He is right that the number of jobs is as much a social function as it is a technological function, as the proliferation of "bullshit" jobs (see David Graeber) shows. But that provides no justification for continuing on that path (and even if so, job creation happens too weakly for the less-skilled workers).

What Wilson also gets wrong is to believe that people will live on the hammock once they get the UBI and that that would contradict socialist ideals of everyone working. Yes, working is fine, but not employment for its own sake or capital accumulation, when much of the necessary labor gets automated. It is false to assume that humans will stop working with a UBI.

Humans are creative enough to invent things and try things out except now it won't be about survival, but about personal pleasure and communal welfare. Put Youtube videos online, write a blog, volunteer in old people's homes, find the cure for cancer. Whatever. To deny this capacity of human beings in the absence of a paycheck is rather foolish. It is even more foolish to hold onto a coercive laborist political economy at which core lies the exploitation of man by man, which is what his romantic version of "socialism" does not mention.

Brexit: What Comes Next?

Posted on July 10, 2016

Two weeks after the shock of the Brexit referendum result, we have to evaluate carefully where the UK and Europe stand today. The country had decided 52-48 to exit from the European Union, but there are two important remarks to be made: first, if we look at geography the majority of people in southern England, especially around London, Cambridge or Oxford, Scotland and Northern Ireland have opted to stay in. It is rural England that is lesser educated and in a more precarious economic position that voted to secede. Second, young people (those below 50) overwhelmingly voted to stay in. It is the more educated younger people, who see a direct benefit in visa free travel in Europe, and taking European integration for granted. The older people being more scared of immigrants and economic uncertainty voted for Brexit.

Now it is possible to construct a discourse around the follies of democracy, that we cannot entrust important decisions to be made by the plebeians, who don't know what is good for them. There is probably evidence for the idiocy of David Cameron to haphazardly announce a referendum in order to quiet the Tory backbenchers, who were getting nervous about UKIP becoming more influential and taking Tory voters away by making a scare around EU immigrants and the evil EU bureaucracy. It has cost him his political career. But scoffing at democracy won't help us here, because at least when we shift away temporarily from the parliamentary reality of representative democracy via a referendum, we get the barometer of what people generally think of their political leadership.

I argue that Brexit was not so much a knowledgeable decision by voters about "reasserting their national sovereignty" or stopping the flow of EU migrants. It was purely an anti-establishment vote. The political establishment told the people to vote for Remain and so people wanted to show the middle finger to the establishment by voting contrary. I don't necessarily think that people were too convinced that all the migration or economic problems (low-paid jobs etc.) are going to disappear with a Brexit vote. All the plebiscite wanted to show was that they needed better leaders and better policies, so that people can have a positive future to look forward to. The British people are not given that, and ironically it will only get worse with Brexit, because Britain is in no position to solve the challenges of inequality, precarious labor and economic uncertainty on their own.

Let us consider the economic and political fallout of Brexit. I do not pretend to have the insight into a crystal ball, but a few thoughts are in order here. Economically, we have seen the pound devalue, but these are short-term events triggered by an investor sell-off. What Thomas Friedman had called the "electronic herd" is playing wild somewhat, but I expect that storm to settle down. The European Commission demands quick Brexit negotiations, while the UK is more interested in taking its time to start the negotiation because they are in a strategically weaker position. The quickness of the negotiation is justified by the economic uncertainty that would accompany negotiations that drag into the future.

Would Britain get a bad deal from the EU? That would naturally depend on the power of negotiators, but I very much doubt that the divorce proceedings will be bloody, because the UK and the EU need each other. A punitive EU would not be beneficial for German exporters, who have already complained about the rough wording used by Juncker, who said he wanted to make the negotiations with the UK so tough as to deter other countries from considering leaving the EU. But why would people want to leave? What Juncker and other EU officials still don't get is that EU policy itself contributes to discontent against the EU. The EU is too weak to do good (as in providing social policy or fair refugee distribution) and misuses the few strengths for bad (fiscal compact, mishandling of Greek bailout cum austerity). An institutional halfway house like the EU will breed more political discontent, which will be the beginning of the end of the EU project.

Schulz and Juncker declare in an interview that they are committed to the European idea, because they don't want to witness another European war. But the problem is that as time passes, the no war argument is not enough to galvanize support from the masses, especially as the last survivors of the war generation are dying and so does the memory of the war. What the EU needs is a vision of something positive: good jobs, strong social welfare, more cultural exchange. I don't think that in the immediate future there will be further referendum that would result in a disintegration of the EU, but as time passes the inhibitions of right-wing groups will become smaller. If we have another Greek-style situation, then we could have a resurgence of anti-EU sentiment, which will bury the EU institutions. Ironically a resurgence of protectionism and nationalism might worsen the economic situation sufficiently to justify another fascist strongmen conquering living space abroad.

On a more positive note, the right-wing populists are being decimated the same moment that they reached their triumph. It has always been like that, because anger without good policy uncovers you as a charlatan once you get what you want. UKIP was the standard bearer of right-wing populism and they have campaigned vigorously for a Brexit since the beginning, and they had one-third of all the UK seats in the EU parliament, which was the biggest parliamentary faction for the UK. Their leader Nigel Farage was beaming with happiness in his EU parliament speech, because he was successful. But he did not and could not use this "success" of Brexit for his own political advantage. He resigned as UKIP leader the day after the referendum, and said he would back the next UKIP leader, who he hopes to do great things for the country. But whom is he kidding? UKIP has only one seat in the UK parliament (and a moderate figure at that!). Their power base had been the EU parliament, where the winner-take-all electoral system did not apply and allowed them to get many seats. Also, UKIP was a one issue party and now that they got Brexit, they have nothing that will go for them. Farage sees his mission accomplished. The British ship will steer into heady waters, and the instigator quietly bows down as a private citizen, who "never wanted to be a career politician" (he served for 17 years in the EU parliament, which makes him very much a career politician).

The Tories are also a joke. Boris Johnson and Michael Gove were the fratboys from Oxford, who wanted to serve their own political ambitions with their Brexit push, as they were hoping to punch out their party rivals, David Cameron and George Osborne, who campaigned for Remain. But when they won, they both lost. Gove declared his non-confidence in Johnson, who immediately withdrew his bid for Tory leadership. Gove announced his leadership candidacy only to be dissed by his party in favor of Andrea Leadsom and Theresa May.

Farage, Johnson and Gove were the trio that campaigned hardest for Brexit, and they blew their political fortunes with that. The reason is quite obvious: their promise to throw out immigrants and redirect 350 million pounds a week that go to Brussels to the NHS were empty and could not be kept. The negative economic fallout, which the Brexiters were silent about, is already recognizable in the falling value of the pound, which is only the beginning of what will happen to the economy. It is obvious that none of them want to captain the ship, which is what Michael Heseltine had suggested, and I very much support that proposal. Let the Brexiters figure out what to do next, but they abandoned ship prematurely.

Whichever of the two (Leadsom and May) will be prime minister will have an unthankfully hard task to accomplish. May campaigned for Remain, but said she will respect the voter decision and negotiate the Brexit. There is naturally a lack of credibility. Leadsom campaigned for Brexit, but she is an unknown political animal around Westminster. She blithely thinks that Britain can retain access to the goods and service market without personal free movement, which would be anathema to the EU, which rightly sees the four freedoms as inseparable (goods, services, capital, people/labor). So there is inevitably another credibility gap with her leadership bid.

The Labour Party is in apparent disarray, because the Labour MP's accuse Jeremy Corbyn of not campaigning vigorously enough for Remain, even though most Labour voters had backed Remain. But that is no more than a cheap excuse. What is really going on is that the moderate Labour MPs were searching for a pre-text to get rid of Corbyn and his left-wing ideology, which they fear would not get him and the Labour Party elected, so they can't get their cushy cabinet jobs back. But the Labour MPs are misreading the signs of their times. There are many people who want real political change, who don't want to be fed with more New Labour and Tory conservative policies that do not serve them.

In any case, Corbyn's predecessor, Ed Miliband, had made it easy for people to join the Labour Party by paying a nominal membership fee of 3 pounds. Within days of the Labour MPs coup attempt discovered, Corbyn's supporters appealed to the public to join the Labour Party to back Corbyn, which promptly resulted in an increase of Labour Party membership to more than 500,000 (it was as low as 176,000 in 2007). With such a groundswell of popular support, the Labour MPs cannot defeat Corbyn, at least not directly.

Their only hope to get their moderate candidate as leader is to do what the Financial Times had suggested in an Oped (Ganesh 2016): split into a separate faction, thus making Corbyn be part of a Labour party without the parliamentary infrastructure. That would be a high-risk strategy. A left-wing faction split the Labour Party in 1983 with the founding of the Social Democratic Party, which did not get any support from the voting public and ensured Tory rule until Tony Blair came to power. Who would now vote for the moderate Labour Party?

Besides, one should consider what had galvanized the public and convinced so many to join or rejoin the Labour Party: it was the election of Jeremy Corbyn. Corbyn rightfully presents himself as the tribune of the people by forcefully advocating on their behalf against austerity and for public investments and the welfare state. A moderate faction of a Labour Party forming their own party would doom them to failure, and would ensure another two decades of uninterrupted Tory rule, precisely the outcome the anti-Corbyn Labour MPs fear about Corbyn at the helm.

In the meantime, the Labour grassroots should not stay asleep by only galvanizing people to back Corbyn in a leadership election, which appears increasingly likely. They also have to use their numbers to pressure the centrist Labour MPs to fall into line or risk deselection. The next challenge would be to recruit new parliamentarians, who would support a more progressive agenda. Critics of Corbyn claim that he is preaching an outdated economic and political model. What these critics don't mention is that the Corbyn support largely derives from the failure of government policy to deliver real benefits to working people.

Brexit can be interpreted as a political renewal for Europe. Let no crisis go to waste, as a Chinese proverb says. But the odds of that being true get diminished by the day because we don't know what renewal means.

US Elections: Vote However You Like
Posted on July 23, 2016

In my last post on the US presidential elections I had advocated for electoral abstention ("I Endorse Abstention for the US General Elections"). I have received some feedback since publishing this post. The liberal left says that abstention is tantamount to silence your own voice, and it would be better to support Jill Stein from the Green Party instead. The moderate left tells me that Clinton is a much better candidate than Trump, and even the most hardcore Bernie supporters have to rally behind Clinton to prevent Trump. And then there is the Republican base and a group of largely disenfranchised working-class whites, who enthusiastically back Trump, as they had when Trump easily defeated the other Republican "establishment" challengers (a very bad label to have in this presidential year). Who is right?

I argue that all of them are right. I will make a case that any choice in this election is defensible. This is a weakening of my original position toward abstention. But I don't exclude abstention as an acceptable choice of action.

Abstention

I still make a case that given that both major parties have appointed unappetizing choices, one way to show discontent is to abstain and look for more promising congressional races this year or the presidential elections in 2020. Let us carefully consider again the choices facing the American people:

Trump is an obnoxious, opportunistic celebrity billionaire, who is riding on a wave of anti-immigrant, anti-Muslim and xenophobic hate. His foreign policy is toward retrenchment and weakening US military presence abroad, which is quite acceptable. But he supports cuts to Social Security and other important social programs, and his tax policies are regressive to the benefit of his own billionaire class. Under Trump, there is little doubt that the little guy gets a little spectacle in the form of anti-immigrant and anti-trade agreement policy (which does not solve the economic insecurity at the root of the insurgency), while the billionaires get the actual economic goodies.

Clinton is a power-hungry and self-absorbed leader, who takes the most opportunistic position based on what might sound popular. Her style is way more constrained by the spin doctors than Trump, which makes her more of a traditional "establishment" politician. In domestic policy, she would keep the Obama course steady, which basically means that current economic and social policies and their distributional consequences (bailout for banks cum austerity for the masses resulting in more income and wealth inequality) are frozen into place. To be fair, Sanders was able to wring out a few concessions from Clinton, such as the free college pledge for families earning less than 125,000 dollars. But I have the inkling that Clinton is banking on the short-term memory of the public. She appointed Tim Kaine from Virginia as her running mate, who is considered to be a moderate Democrat in the Senate (Govtrack.us). After the magic of the DNC in Philadelphia has passed, she will switch back to "moderate" (i.e. don't rock the boat) policy positions, and continue distracting from her own unpopular policy positions by pointing to her opponent. "Donald, is even worse than me!" I accept the label that Clinton is probably (though not definitely) the lesser evil.

Vote for Trump

I personally do not recommend anyone to vote for Trump, because it would be similar to the cataclysmically stupid Brexit decision of the British electorate. But let us not forget why Brexit happened. I don't think people were aware of the economic fallout, but that Brexit was about the anti-establishment vote mixed with a sense of xenophobia. The Leave side campaigned on the promise to restrict EU migration to prevent social benefit transfers to them. This claim is not factually sustainable, because EU migrants tend to be young and healthy and contribute more taxes than they get in benefits. But base emotions of the frightened English electorate swayed the vote in favor of Brexit. But it was not the EU alone, which caused economic suffering (which they surely did with their anti-deficit mantra), but the Tory government, which substantially slashed social programs and local council funding. Voting for Brexit was a way of getting back at Tory government.

Back to Trump: we have the same xenophobic sentiment, which my elite-university educated friends (from UPenn, Oxford and Princeton) decry as being foolish and short-sighted. I largely concur with this view, but we must not talk down on the little guy, who has not seen his income rise. In fact, his income has decreased. And these people are maniacally afraid of anyone, who can take their jobs and benefits. Trump offers no real solution to the little guy, but he is speaking to the little guy, because he offers to do "something". He appeals to the little guy by being "self-funded" and not having to rely on billionaires to run the election. Indeed, his campaign was rather cheap, and he took advantage of free media coverage by making one outrageous statement after another.

But what does he offer? Rage, rage, rage. He has not promised to reform campaign finance (as Bernie Sanders did). Now, it turns out that for the general election, he wants to take money from Republican-backing rich people, largely to defray general election campaign costs, which he does not want to bear. Remember when he declared bankruptcy four times, so he could let others pay for his businesses gone bad? Now he does not want to pay the full cost of his campaign, inviting his fellow billionaires in the game. The fact that his tax and economic policies undoubtedly will benefit the 1% fits into the picture.

But at the end, it doesn't matter to his loyal voters, consisting of the disenfranchised white working class, and even some from the colored working class. I know people in my neighborhood, whose economic prospects are everything but bright, gloating about Donald Trump. Yeah, he is a strongman who will fix it for us. They don't know what to say when you press them on how he will fix things. "He will get rid of immigrants and Muslim terrorists." Yeah, right.

There is only one rational reason to vote for Trump: he is an anti-establishment figure and establishment politics has been disastrous for the working class. Hillary Clinton will cozy up with the powerful from Day 1, and so much the little guy understands about her.

Vote for Clinton

Voting for Clinton is probably a choice of the lesser evil. This cannot be emphasized enough. She will continue Obama's domestic policy agenda, which is to make incremental changes to the health care or education system. She won't mind inheriting a largely Republican Congress and will talk up compromise. Whether she gets anything done is not as important as the fact that she will be able to return to the White House once more. If Hillary makes it for two terms in the White House, the Clintons will have occupied the presidency longer than any other couple had. Clinton is the establishment, there is no way around it. Her domestic social policy agenda, however, could be compromised, and she might be ready to cut Social Security as a "grand bargain" (but for what?). She will be willing to let health insurance companies get richer coming at the heels of her own failed health care revamp in 1993. She might not advocate strongly for a rise in the minimum wage. There are a lot of things that are quite awful about the status quo, which she will be unenthusiastic to challenge

The one thing that would concern me the most about a Clinton presidency is that she is much more willing to use military force around the world to maintain US global dominance and pursue her "humanitarian" agenda of "regime change". That was in full display during her stint as secretary of state in the first Obama term. She argued forcefully for the no-fly zone in Libya, which Obama granted and now regrets looking back at it. She argued for another no-fly zone and potentially ground force invasion of Syria, which Obama wisely declined on grounds of lack of congressional approval. The US, nonetheless, engages in airstrikes in Syria, which inflames the conflict and proliferates the refugee wave to Europe (and some of the recent strings of terrorist attacks in Paris, Brussels, Nice and Munich). If Clinton was commander-in-chief back then, more parents of active-duty US soldiers would have to carry their sons and daughters home in caskets. I am ironically more afraid of Clinton having access to the nuclear codes than Trump, who is unenthusiastic about foreign wars.

The only rational reason to vote for Clinton is the same as she said in her speeches: "Donald is worse than me."

Vote for Jill Stein

Stein is the Green Party candidate. Without having read the entire Green Party agenda, we can simplify and say that she supports virtually all of Bernie Sanders positions: infrastructure jobs, energy efficiency and sustainability, military spending cuts, free college tuition (cancel student debt, going farther than Bernie), Medicare-for-all health care etc. Supporting her makes absolute sense from a policy standpoint. But the politics of supporting her is difficult. She is not part of the two-party system. She is not invited in presidential debates. She has a very small budget. She has virtually no name recognition outside the educated left (academics, civil servants, college students), and even those from the educated left might be wary of "wasting" their vote on her. Her chances of victory are virtually zero, which is also why Sanders has refused to entertain running on the Green Party ticket (as does his brother Larry in the UK). He also thinks that supporting a third party would split the left vote and hand the victory to Trump.

The rationale for supporting Stein, however, is more basic: her policy positions are the only one among running candidates that make sense.

Conclusion

I have given you four choices, and I think they are all legitimate choices: abstain, vote for Trump, Clinton or Stein. I refuse to give more weight to one choice than the other, because we have a disappointing selection of candidates with realistic chances to win the general election. The American people deserve better.

The Turkish Coup and Its Fallout

Posted on July 25, 2016

10 days ago a group of Islamist-inspired military generals and colonels took it upon themselves to overthrow the government of Turkey. The coup largely failed because only a core of maybe 1,000 officers participated in the coup, while enough others vowed loyalty to the current government. Erdogan, returning from a vacation in south Turkey, called on his supporters to take to the streets and prevent the tanks from taking the political buildings, largely with success. The police immediately cracked down and imprisoned the coup plotters. The coup collapsed in less than 24 hours, taking the lives of 200 people. The financial markets recover (RT, "Turkey back to business as usual with purges nearly over - PM", July 25, 2016). But Erdogan's pushback is harsh. He already fired more than 60,000 academics, judges, soldiers, prevented them from going abroad, and imprisoned and tortured thousands of soldiers suspected to have taken part in the coup against him (Hughes 2016; Bernish 2016).

Erdogan and his followers suspect that a group of Islamists is responsible for the coup (Rodrik 2016). (But are all of the civil servants he fired part of that Islamist group? I think he also just wanted to get rid of any of his critics.) They are followers of Fethullah Gulen, a Turkish cleric, who has been in exile in the US since 1999 after falling out with the then-government. Ironically, Gulen was an ally of Erdogan's AKP, itself considered to be moderate Islamist. Erdogan found the coalition with the Gulenists quite useful, because he wanted to get rid of the Kemalist-secularist establishment, which has pervaded the civil service in Turkey, and replace them with his Islamist loyalists. The secularists have now been largely purged.

But the Erdogan and Gulen faction were always separate power-bases, and the two fell out of favor, when Gulenist civil servants and prosecutors (appointed by Erdogan himself) decided to prosecute people close to Erdogan (including his son) on corruption charges in 2013. Erdogan took revenge by closing down Gulenist schools, which were previously supported by the government. He then went on a purge of Gulenists in the civil service with the exception of the military. There were plans to purge Gulenists from the military staff too, and they probably found out about these plans and decided to risk the coup to get rid of Erdogan before they got to the chopping block (Akyol 2016).

But who are the Gulenists? Gulen does not seem to have a coherent political philosophy, and his Islamic ideology is considered to be moderate Sufism (according to Wikipedia "Fethullah Gulen"). I don't think that his political ideology is as important as the fact that he wants to influence Turkish politics and work to get rid of Erdogan, who himself has the desire to stay in power for as long as possible (prime minister from 2003 and president since 2014). Erdogan has replaced the quite independent-minded prime minister, Ahmet Davutoglu, with the loyalist Binali Yildrim. He is proposing to amend the constitution to transform Turkey from a largely parliamentary to a presidential republic, concentrating more power into his own hands. When it comes to policy initiatives, no one hears of the prime minister, only Erdogan.

But even worse than the presidential power grab is the decision to purge the Turkish civil service from Erdogan's opponents. Erdogan cannot tolerate to have Gulenists in positions of power, who will rival his power in the future. But by carrying out such a massive Stalinist purge, he is also risking to undermine his country by depriving it of technically competent civil servants. Stalin decided to purge his foes (including many former friends) from the Red Army, who were then brutally crippled when the Nazis invaded them a couple of years later. The only capable general to emerge in the battle against Nazi Germany was Georgy Zhukov, one of the few survivors of Stalin's purge. Most of the generals left in charge were political appointees and junior officers, who had little battle leadership experience, which partly explains why they were routed by the Germans in the initial years of the war. (The Soviets largely won the war with US material support and because they had much larger number of military reservists to call upon than the Germans.)

Turkey is not fighting an existential war with another country, but it is fighting quite a brutal war in the southeast of the country against the Kurdish PKK, who have long called for autonomy if not independence. Erdogan, therefore, needs military loyalty, which might have made him rather reluctant to vengefully purge the military from Gulenists. There are no longer any inhibitions to purge Gulenists since the coup.

But the war against the PKK is another strange twist of fate for Erdogan, which I think was foolish and unnecessary. Turkey had largely abandoned the war against the PKK and negotiate a peace settlement since 2012. Then in June 2015, the Kurdish-based HDP under the leadership of Selahattin Demirtas surpassed the 10% mark (quite a high threshold) to receive 80 seats (13%) in the parliamentary elections, thus diminishing Erdogans AKP majority. Some CHP (Kemalist, secularist) voters had apparently defected to HDP to weaken the AKP, which had been in power for over a decade (since 2002). Every normal democrat would consider this to be a win for democratic pluralism. Erdogan saw it as a threat to his power. He immediately called for new elections and suspended peace talks with the PKK, which was linked to the HDP. The November 2015 elections reduced HDP vote to about 10%, but they still had 59 MPs. These MPs now have their immunity revoked by Erdogan, which resulted in some physical clashes in the Turkish parliament, creating a sham of democratic institutions.

In July 2015, an ISIS-affiliated group detonated a bomb, killing 20 Turkish Kurds, who promptly accused Turkey of supporting ISIS. The PKK assassinated two Turkish police officers in revenge. Erdogan found his casus belli against the PKK. On the military front, Erdogan deployed 10,000 Turkish troops to the southeast of Turkey, pummeling the PKK stronghold around Diyarbakir, which turned into a ghost city following weeks and months of fighting between the military and the militants. PKK can at most be weakened but unlikely to be defeated, because the PKK is a guerrilla organization, hiding in the villages and in the mountains and striking Turkish troops (who are clearly visible with their military gear) when they are the most vulnerable.

The Kurds are also in an unusually strong position securing strongholds in neighboring Iraq and Syria, which has to do with the western military interventions in Iraq and Syria. The logic is as follows: under Bashar al-Assad and Saddam Hussein, the Kurds in Syria (10% of population) and Iraq (15% of population) could never have hoped to have their own province or state, and were subsequently oppressed and disadvantaged in resource access. Then the US invaded Iraq and the reward for backing the US in overthrowing Saddam was to get a province in the northeast of Iraq with the capital Arbil. The Kurds now had their autonomous province and their share of oil revenues.

That proved crucial when the Islamic State made gains in Syria and threatened the Rojava, the Syrian Kurds, in the northeast of Syria. Iraqi Kurdistan deployed the Peshmerga (with US financing), crossing Turkish territory, i.e. receiving the explicit backing of Erdogan, who find Iraqi Kurds to be a valuable ally to rout Assad as opposed to Turkish Kurds, who threatened his power in Ankara. The Syrian Kurds held their ground, and whatever post-ISIS arrangement will be negotiated, the Syrian Kurds now have their own little territory. All that naturally gives a moral boost to Turkish Kurds, who are more inspired than ever to have regional autonomy since the resumption of military hostilities last year. Erdogan has played with fire unnecessarily, and would be better off to return to the negotiating table with the PKK.

What is going to happen next in Turkey? Will we see another military coup? It could very well be the case. But what is more likely over the short term is that the massive internal purge will result in a consolidation of power for Erdogan. After the failed coup against Hitler in July 1944, Hitler was as secure in power as he never had been and could now only be removed by complete Allied annihilation which happened in April 1945.

Erdogan is similarly interested in power consolidation. He never had a liking for free-roaming journalists, and was prompt to imprison 42 journalists, who apparently threaten "national security" (Butler and Sezer 2016). L'etat c'est moi- I am the state, proclaims Erdogan, which is not uncommon for authoritarian rulers. He calls for the reintroduction of the death penalty, which he cancelled in 2004 as a precondition to initiate talks on Turkish EU membership.

But that effort had been put on ice long ago. First, many European governments are wary to accept a majority Muslim nation into the EU. Second, European countries did not want to deal with the crisis in the Middle East, which they would have to engage in with Turkey in the EU, because it borders all the other crisis countries. Third, Erdogan sees himself in a strong position now that he controls the border to the EU, where most refugees are headed. The EU showered Turkey with concessions, primarily visa-free travel for Turkish nationals in the EU (not yet implemented) and 6 billion euros in EU subsidies to stem the refugee tide. EU appetite for more refugees is unlikely to be increased after the string of terrorist attacks in Belgium, France and Germany, some of which were carried out by refugees. Erdogan can cancel the refugee agreement with the EU anytime he wants to.

The EU will talk tough about the many human rights and freedom of speech rights violations by the Turkish government, but they really don't have much leverage against their NATO partner. I would not find any EU intervention helpful either. Turkey is facing a constitutional crisis following Erdogan's consolidation of political power, but the Turks have to figure out themselves how they want to manage the situation and restore democratic institutions, which is unlikely to happen with Erdogan (only 62 years old) at the helm. I wish them the best of luck.

Why I Don't Believe in the Private Housing Market

Posted on <u>August 4, 2016</u>

After two and a half weeks of desperate housing search, I have finally found a simple, small room in a rather dilapidated house inside Princeton, where I will take up residence in connection with my doctorate program that begins in the fall. I don't want to waste any space to say how happy and relieved I am to not have to worry about organizing housing for the rest of the month. Let me instead use this opportunity to blast the private housing market. My argument is that the private housing market does not reflect the individual need for housing, but the lucky encounter between buyers and sellers with the assumption that tenants have the ability to pay the rent. Housing should better be organized in terms of personal need rather than open market availability. The best way to achieve this is not by prohibiting private housing, but by expanding the sphere of public housing.

To illustrate my point, I shall explain how my housing predicament was created to begin with. (This story also provides my impetus or this article.) I had written to my department, asking them when the deadline for the campus housing would be. I had delayed my acceptance to the program for a year, so I could study in Oxford. I was told that I did no have to worry about housing for another year. Then the department asked me about my whereabouts in January, and I replied that I would like to stay informed about the requirements for housing, and I was assured that I would be informed in due time. I heard nothing, and did not further investigate. A friend had asked me in July where I lived in the fall. I shrugged my shoulders, not knowing where I ended up in, and he suggested me to check the on campus housing website at the university, where I found out that I had long passed the on-campus housing deadline.

I immediately sent an email to the department, who confirmed to me that the on-campus housing deadline had long ago passed. I was about to panic. Unlike Oxford, I realized that Princeton had an opt-in housing system (i.e. no housing unless I applied for it) rather than opt-out in Oxford (where I was offered housing upon acceptance). Oxford, which had a private rental market largely unaffordable to the public, took good care of its students by providing on-campus accommodation to virtually any student they accepted. Oxford knew how to organize housing based on social need. Maybe this nice situation had made me oblivious of the harsh housing reality in the US.

Back to my Princeton situation: The department secretary referred me to two websites affiliated with the university and they happened to be my best bet. I networked like crazy by asking anyone that I encountered about my housing situation, and most were naturally not really able to help. I really wanted to bypass the housing market, where I was a random college student desperately looking for a place to live in what is largely a seller's market. In other words, there were many buyers (mostly students and some junior college staff) and not enough sellers, so landlords could easily ignore potential tenants they found unsympathetic.

Encountering the housing market was a complete nightmare, as it was hard to fit the mutual requirements. First, many sellers I contacted did not bother to reply to me. Others replied but lived too far away from campus. Another took my call and visit but had 4 other tenants applying, so I was passed over. There were other landlords, who rented out for a short period of time, another that already rented out until January even though I needed to move in September, and another who only took female tenants. One person wrote to me to share housing near campus that would have cost me a fortune. Another potential landlord first invited me to visit him, but then passed me over after his friend referred another person to him. Sorry, buddy. Eventually, I was lucky enough to find a place in the campus vicinity (a rare feat in the college town). I wonder where I would be now if I had less luck, less networking skills or could not impress on a potential landlord. In the private housing market, these skills and luck are essential.

Proponents of the free market will now either seek to find fault with me, because I have not looked for housing early enough, or did not network properly, or they will blame the lack of good search resources (though there are plenty including apartments.com and craigslist) or the government for having too strict zoning laws. The logic in the latter point is that the government makes it difficult to convert more rural land into residential areas, and thus tilt the market balance in favor of landlords (scarce housing, many tenants). There is some case that can be made for the latter, especially given the reality that more wealthy people than ever acquire property to rent to people, who cannot currently afford a mortgage to buy a house. "The haves in our society are renting homes out to have-nots, and they've been able to do that at increasingly high rents." (Clark and Woolley 2016)

But I question why we have to put the market logic front and center in housing when there are better ways to allocate housing, i.e.

based on social need. Among college students, there usually is no expectation that they should worry about housing by negotiating with sketchy landlords, who can easily rip off gullible college students. The universities create on-campus housing and shield their college students from having to deal with the open housing market. There is still a modicum of a market because the colleges usually offer different tiers of housing with the most expensive housing offering the most frills (e.g. with balcony and separate bathrooms).

Really poor people, who would face homelessness without government housing assistance, usually don't have to deal with the housing market either, because in most cases, where there is substantial social housing, they are allocated a guaranteed place to live. Vienna, Austria (my home town) has a rather extensive social house-building history stretching back to the first two decades of the 20th century (Narefsky 2015), allowing public apartment tenants to pay an affordable 400 euros a month in rent (compared to double the value in the private rental market).

The US does not really have good social housing, but they do provide subsidized rents for low-income people, who still have to search for a private landlord. This arrangement sort of guarantees housing to low-income people, but after volunteering for a self-help organization in Philadelphia, I had heard of many stories of low-income tenants, who were brutally ripped off by private landlords, who claimed rent on top of the government housing voucher from their tenants. The only thing these financially haunted tenants can do is to either find a way to pay up or to organize in a tenant organization with other tenants in a similar situation and fight back against the abusive practices of their landlords.

People, who believe in minimalist government intervention, will probably be okay with retaining certain protections for low-income people, seniors, students and other vulnerable populations, but would not want to change the housing situation for the rest of the society. But I would challenge this position, because I think housing should not be another commodity, which should be up to the individual to be consumed like a car. A car and a house have very different values attached to them, namely that the former is a choice and the latter is not. The lack of choice tremendously increases the market power of the sellers. At least in big cities, where public transportation is ubiquitous, people could choose not to buy a car and instead rely on buses and subway systems to be mobile. But housing is not really a choice. People need housing, and those who lack it (the homeless) show every day in a tangible way how unjust the society is. For goods that are clearly so important and essential to have a decent life, it is morally reprehensible to expose people to a market, which will never guarantee them a place to live where they need it.

I define housing as a social right. Let us assume that you don't challenge this argument (because if you do, then we just have to agree to disagree, and my T.H. Marshall social citizenship pep talk will not work), there are some practical objections that can legitimately be raised. Firstly, some might claim that if housing is a social right there is no end to the level of entitlement that can be granted to people. How big shall the house be? Are we giving out apartments or luxury mansions to the working-class man? But we should not make ridiculous caricatures here. I am highly skeptical of houses in densely populated cities, where land is scarce and zoning laws should not be weakened, which could result in fewer public parks and a more stressed out community (think of traffic jams and the lack of open-air relaxation opportunities). I also don't think that we can afford such an expansive entitlement policy if people continue to choose to live in big cities (for which there are many justifiable reasons, including access to good jobs and education). People living in more rural areas, on the other hand, should have no problems in building houses, because the land is relatively cheap.

It is not too much to be asked to want to guarantee a modest-sized apartment to all people, who need it. I would not advocate the abolition of the private housing market (those people thinking they can get something better and want to search for it in the private housing market, should go ahead), but I would substantially increase the supply of public houses. This step would most naturally reduce the requirement for people to search for houses. Initially, there will be huge investment costs for the government, and there will be substantial pent-up demand, because people will seek to flee the oppressively expensive private rental market once the government increases the stock of affordable public housing (which should be need-oriented and not profit-oriented, which ideally lowers the rental cost to building and maintenance costs). But these are short-term transition costs that are well worth bearing.

One of the most business-friendly places with hundreds of multinational companies headquartered in that city-state is Singapore, which incidentally leaves most of the land and housing ownership to the government of Singapore. It is only via the central coordination of the scarce land and housing that it is feasible to grow the island country from about 2 million people, when it got independent in the 1960s, to over 5 million people today. (The land reclamation from the sea, which grew the country's square miles, certainly helped too.) My only objection in Singapore is that while the housing market is largely publicly controlled, the method of acquisition is still privately and individually organized, because housing is financed from private savings (using the CPF funds) (Whiteman 2016).

I learned about another interesting housing model in Spain's Marinaleda, a small town, which has been controlled by a Communist government for many years. While much of the city policies are rather conventional capitalist (e.g. the need to attract outside businesses to make investments in the city), they distinguish themselves from other cities with their housing policy. Essentially, all the inhabitants of the town are guaranteed a house. When someone wants to build a house, they get the empty land allocated by the city government, which then supports the individual and his family with the material costs (cement, brick etc.). The labor to build the house is provided by neighbors, who will do it for free in return for other favors, e.g. have that neighbor help them build their house. When the house is finished, it is the individual, who owns the house, and they have no debt or mortgage on their shoulders. That is quite a feat for a working-class person (Burridge 2013).

It is true that this is a rather rosy image of how housing policy can be handled, because not all people are as sociable and helpful as the people in that Spanish town, who have tremendous trust in each other. I think there will be a lot more logistical and trust problems if we try to replicate a more socialist housing policy on a national or international level. But I would just put forward the potential and proposition to expand the public housing policy to enable people to have a place to live regardless of their circumstances. Erik Olin Wright (2015) wrote that there are four modes of anti-capitalism: smashing, taming, escaping and eroding. He said that smashing and escaping is difficult, so we have to try taming (Keynesian economics) and eroding (find alternative structure to layer on top of existing structures) capitalism. A more aggressive public housing strategy would do both.

Wars Have Become Rare with Nuclear Weapons

Posted on <u>August 15, 2016</u>

One of the major benefits in living in today's world is that despite the rise of so-called Islamic terrorism, see the recent attacks in France, Germany, Pakistan, Iraq, Syria, Turkey and other places, we do live in a more peaceful world. Steven Pinker (2011) has said that violence has decreased because of the growth of the state (monopoly of violence takes power of violence away from private individuals), growth of commerce (trading creates opportunity and makes societies averse to physical destruction), feminization (stronger role of females in society reduces violent tendencies), cosmopolitanism (idea of a global society based on literacy, common language, transport and communication technology, greater mobility, mass media) and an "escalator of reason" (people becoming more educated and thus favoring less violence). I would argue, in addition, that the continuing existence of nuclear weapons will continue to make war unlikely.

In large parts, we do observe a reduction in the amount of national resources that get wasted on wars. When the state began to centralize (e.g. Roman or Chinese empires), the foremost duty of the state was to provide their citizens with protection against predators, who could steal the crops on which people relied on. Naturally, the state bureaucrats, the king and the soldiers that were hired by the citizens came at the price of freedom. "Hired" is perhaps an unlucky terminology, because oftentimes the strongmen simply imposed themselves on society, and it was better to pay taxes to the strongest lord with the best military or else be preyed upon by an even worse lord. State spending records in Europe during the 1600s to 1900s reveal that upwards of 70% of the state expenditures were devoted to military spending (Mann 1986: 483-90). This kind of military spending was certainly a necessity in a rather Hobbesian international (dis)order. In Mann's words, "A state that wished to survive had to increase its extractive capacity over defined territories to obtain conscripted and professional armies and navies. Those that did not were crushed on the battlefield and absorbed into others." (ibid., 490)

Pinker and other theorists (Mueller 1989) have stated that wars and other structured forms of violence have become much rarer and more limited in scale, but an examination of European history would certainly question that premise (critique of the peace thesis is made in Cowen 2011; Gray 2015). War became increasingly more violent as time went on, at least until 1945. One may think of the 30-years war, the Napoleonic wars or finally the two world wars. One war became bloodier than the next, because the Europeans developed more sophisticated military weaponry and technology to effectively kill more people. And once this technology became available, one diplomatic mishap was all that was needed to result in war.

We started wars as skirmishes among hunter, gatherers, who used primitive tools like stones and bare fists as weapons. The Aborigines in Australia used boomerangs to hunt for food, but also as a weapon. The Bronze Age (5000 BC) implied the first use of daggers and swords. The Chinese developed the trebuchet (primitive version of canon and artillery) in 500 BC, and later gun powder in 800AD. The Greek hoplites (infantrymen) used spears to conquer territories. The Chinese developed the firearm around 1200, which were in widespread use after about 1500. Firearms became automatic in the 1850s (Gatling gun) after which it was no longer possible to fight open-field wars. In 1914, the British fielded their first tanks, and it was Hitler Germany in World War II, which used tanks and airplanes strategically for the Blitzkrieg, allowing him quick initial territorial conquests. The most important innovation, however, has been the nuclear bomb, which fatefully detonated in Hiroshima and Nagasaki in 1945 (Marshall 2009, Wikipedia "History of the firearm").

Military technology is still developing apace. The drone started in the early-2000s and was used for limited operations by the US military, but since Obama became president entire secret wars had been waged with the drones (Yemen, Pakistan, Afghanistan etc.). War became covert and small-scale. But the many technologies of killing that we have developed ever since the end of World War II do not have the same big impact upon war-making as during the previous wars. Vigilante violence by individuals had been curbed with the rise of the central state, but what if the central state that is constantly equipped with new means of mass killing is the perpetrator of violence? Young men were conscripted to fight in wars with weapons that became increasingly deadly. And yet, Hitler, Mussolini and Hirohito were the last perpetrators of large-scale war. The subsequent wars (Korea, Vietnam, Afghanistan, Iraq)- mostly with US or Soviet intervention- still demanded many victims, civilian and military, but had nowhere near the scale of the world wars.

I would argue that the existence of nuclear weapons makes war on a grand scale rather unlikely. In the midst of the Cold War, Henry Kissinger (1957) published a book, where he stated that nuclear weapons had made a war among the great powers (US and USSR) unthinkable because it would result in mutually assured destruction (literally 'MAD'). He also argued that in order for the US to maintain their predominance in the world (i.e. beat back the imperial ambitions of the USSR), the US would have to support proxy wars, such as in Vietnam or in African states, support their allies, make some territorial gains without losing to the other side.

One would think this to be rather cruel inside-the-beltway thinking (alas, Kissinger was promoted as national security adviser and secretary of state under Richard Nixon), but what he was saying was rather profound. Rather than sacrificing US soldiers on the frontlines close to home, they would now either be sacrificed overseas in some non-central frontier (i.e. Vietnam rather than say West-Berlin) or would not have to fight at all, because military aid and CIA operation handles it all. No wonder US imperialism is rather unique in its rather limited scale. That is also how high US administration officials like Samantha Power can get away with their "humanitarian" US intervention (read: war) claims in different conflict zones concerning "vital interests" to the US (no contradiction here?).

The saber-rattling, conflict orientation is still clearly evident among the great powers, but I don't think they will result in substantial political destabilization in the immediate future. Two current situations require more detailed commentary: the Ukraine and the South China Sea.

Ever since the Maidan protests in Kiev in 2014, the Ukraine has essentially been ripped away from Russian domination. A pro-Russian government was replaced by a pro-western government, where high EU and US officials were rather triumphant in celebrating the "victory of democratic forces" (i.e. pro-western). And that is despite the fact that the previous president- with all his corruption and faults- was democratically elected. The Russian Bear that had long eyed NATO expansion to the former Warsaw Pact states as a threat to its national security thought that the same could happen to the Ukraine. In fact, I had met a Ukrainian diplomat, who thought that the long-term future of her country would be in the European Union and NATO. It is not very surprising that the countries with historic grievances against Russia (i.e. Poland and the Baltics) are the most adamant supporters of the westward integration of the Ukraine and request more NATO troops and equipment to counter the Russian "threat".

With the background that Putin had long considered the Ukraine to be an essential part to Russian national security he deployed Russian soldiers covered up as East Ukrainian independence fighters into Luhansk and Donetsk provinces, and he formally annexed Crimea, which was part of the Soviet Union, as was the Ukraine. But what did Putin really want to achieve with these pieces of land? Maybe he wanted to intimidate the Kiev leadership, so that they would reduce their overtures to the West. One thing that certainly happened was that the war in the East Ukraine deterred foreign investors, which is what Ukraine desperately needs. Putin pursues a scorched earth policy in the hope that the Ukraine will return to the Russian orbit.

The EU and the US had imposed sanctions on Russia, but the EU is nowhere near as united as the US on Russia policy. Part of the reason is that the US does not trade much with Russia, while the EU has vital economic interests with Russia and EU companies would favor a quick end to sanctions. The Baltic states, Poland and the UK tend to be the most hawkish on Russia, while Austria, Italy and Germany take a more conciliatory tone and favor an ending of sanctions. So far, Putin has not been able to take advantage of these internal divisions in Europe, though he is doing all he can with his multilingual state TV station RT. I think that without US pressure, the EU-Russia sanctions would long ago have been lifted. As they continue to exist, they were designed to make Putin suspend his intervention in the Ukraine. But while the Russian ruble is sinking and the economy is stalling (also amid falling oil prices on which the Russians depend for export revenues), the Russian determination to hold onto their stake in the Ukraine has not declined.

The latest unfortunate development has been the NATO commitment to increase their troop contingent in Poland and the Baltics and reinforce informal cooperation with the Ukrainian military, which is another part of saber-rattling from the West to make the US defense contractors happy. Russia might respond to this provocation by deploying more airplanes on the Baltic border, but I don't see this to be a strong option. NATO spends more than ten times what Russia spends on the military, and there is no comparable military ally, who would come to their aid. But western options are also limited, as no one would risk a hot war with Russia over a small strip of land in the Don bass. The crucial point here, however, is that if Russia were a small, defenseless country without nuclear weapons as Saddam Hussein's Iraq, a more neocon US president would have long ago gotten rid of Putin. Big power battles in today's world revolve around small skirmishes and proxy-wars rather than direct military confrontation.

The South China sea involves another interesting amalgamation of powers. Since Xi Jinping rose to power in the Chinese Communist Party, he has formulated a forward-looking foreign policy, declaring to enforce the 9-dash-line, which covers a broad swath of the South China Sea. The origin of this sea claim was in 1947, when the nationalist government ruling the mainland drew a map involving an 11-dash line (see history in Wikipedia "Nine Dash Line"). But back then China lacked the naval power to enforce these claims. It is only in the last twenty years or so, in which a growing economy fed the Chinese state with sufficient resources to modernize the weaponry of the military and create a modern sea fleet. In the early days of

China's economic opening, its foreign policy remained rather limited. Being factory to the world was more important than participating in foreign wars, which confirms Pinker's postulate that commerce reduces the likelihood of war.

But as China gradually became the second-biggest economy of the world (in PPP terms, it even surpassed the US in 2014 to be the biggest economy), it was unlikely to continue a self-restrained foreign policy. It is true that China has harbored no ambitions to interfere in the foreign affairs of other countries (why would they want to meddle in the quagmire of the Middle East). It is also true that their history has made them prone to minimize interaction with foreign barbarians (i.e. everyone non-Chinese). If the British had not discovered the opium addiction of the Chinese, they would never have been able to trade with their Chinese counterparts. The British wanted their silk and tea, and the Chinese didn't want anything from the British. How daring is that?

But what about today's foreign policy? China has greater ambitions and wants to show that by developing military bases in the South China sea. The only trouble with that ambition is that there are other countries (Taiwan, Malaysia, Philippines, Indonesia, Vietnam, Brunei) that are opposed to Chinese expansion plans. All these countries have set up their own bases along the largely unpopulated Spratly islands, mainly in response to Chinese ambitions and island claims. The Philippines went as far as staking a case in the Permanent Court of Arbitration, which sided with the Philippines in condemning the Chinese island reclamation policy in the South China Sea.

But a UN-sanctioned court stands naturally no chance against the behemoth in the room. The only power that can defend the Southeast Asian countries against Chinese land claims is the US. They have beefed up their deployments in Japan, Korea, Australia, Singapore and the Philippines (the latter kicked them out in the early-1990s only to beg them to return a few years later). Recently, Congress had lifted a weapon export ban to the former enemy Vietnam. The US also entertains military cooperation and bases in Central Asia (Tajikistan, Kyrgyzstan, Pakistan and Afghanistan), which implies a complete US encirclement of China. The "pivot to Asia" strategy, whereby the US administration shifts its focus from the Middle East to East Asia, really is about containing China. I am as skeptical about US policy in Asia as I am in Eastern Europe.

This is about saber-rattling, posturing and showing who the biggest kid on the block is. It is rather unclear what the cause and effect is: does US deployment in Asia follow China's expansive territorial claims or does Chinese sea claims follow from US encirclement of China? A mix of both appears the most plausible. Given China's growth trajectory and the US fighting a rearguard battle as a more slowly growing nation, the conflict potential remains substantial, but both powers possess nukes and unlike US-Russia, for US-China the economic stakes on both sides are much higher because China supplies both the goods as well as the credit to the US to keep the dollar strong and the Walmart shelves fully stacked with cheap goods (rising Chinese production prices shift that dynamic now). But as with Russia, a military confrontation is off-the-table because of Chinese and US nukes.

The relevant policy question is thus whether it makes sense to demand a nuclear-free world. I claim it makes no sense, because the possibility that rulers can kill people in other countries without impunity because we no longer have MAD will return in such a nuclear-free world. It is also not feasible to eliminate nuclear weapons, because the technology already exists, and someone will keep the plans for continuing to build it. A few rogue countries, like North Korea, want to use nuclear weapons as a tool to get more food donations from the rich countries. We are best off with allowing a few big powers to keep their nuclear weapons arsenal intact, while reducing the continued proliferation of these weapons to minimize the risk of idiots claiming control over nukes. The decline of war implies the decline of violence and a greater deal of safety for the world's population. Prudent policy choices can keep it this way.

How to Help Low-Income People out of Poverty
Posted on August 17, 2016

One of the biggest problems we are facing in reducing poverty is how to reduce in-work poverty. Structural trends in the labor market make in-work poverty a real problem. They range from the rise of low-wage work, deindustrialization (and the loss of good-paying manufacturing jobs), the rise of service-sector work with insufficient stability (low wages, low hours, unpredictable schedules etc.), to the digitalization of work (Uber, Mechanical Turk, Task Rabbit and others).

Policy discussions that aim at reducing in-work poverty essentially have two solutions in mind. Each of these solutions really has their advantages and disadvantages. One is to raise the minimum wage and the other is to increase the negative income tax, which is called Earned Income Tax Credit (EITC) in the US. I argue that we have to consider other options to alleviate poverty as well, most importantly the universal basic income. But for now, let us reflect on each of these two solutions.

The minimum wage is the minimum amount of wage per hour that can legally be paid to a dependent employee by his employer. That is currently 7.25 dollars an hour in the US, though some jurisdictions have a higher (but not lower) minimum wage.

The rationale behind raising the minimum wage is that workers get paid so little because capitalist bosses can take advantage of the weak bargaining power of their workers (take say Walmart, where unionization drives had been largely unsuccessful) and pay their workers only a small fraction of what they produce. If there were no minimum wage at all, there would be workers that would get paid only 3 or 4 dollars an hour, and workers that are desperate for any kind of employment and not knowing any better places to turn to will accept that low wage. In economic theory, a minimum wage is justifiable under the premise of a monopsonistic labor market, which implies one or few employers and many workers. This imbalance tends to favor employers, who can threaten workers with easy replacement if they ask for a higher wage. In this case, the employer is using his political power to hold down his workers' wages, and a higher minimum wage merely transfers the rent that otherwise accrues to the employer back to the workers.

Critics of the minimum wage claim that it is an undue intervention in the labor market, which could hurt low-wage workers, because by artificially raising the wages, the number of workers employed is being reduced. The effect is to eliminate low wages, but also to eliminate many low-wage workers from the labor market altogether or push them into the shadow economy. I would counter that this equilibrium condition assumes that there are no excess rents, which firms collect. But it is true that in a minimum wage that is raised too high (e.g. more than 50% of the local median wage, see Dube n.d.), adverse effects on employment will offset other advantages of a hike (like reduced turnover, higher productivity and less firm rents). A July 2016 study of the Seattle minimum wage (Seattle Minimum Wage Study Team 2016) finds ambiguous effects of a hike to 15 dollars an hour, which has been carried out in several steps. The number of business closures has not increased, the employment rate of low-wage workers was reduced slightly, the overall paycheck for low-wage workers increased but they faced small reductions in hours worked.

This evidence seems to propel the view of the critics of the minimum wage, who think that fixing wages in the labor market above the natural rate will result in less employment and fewer hours of work. Starbucks, for instance, promised to raise the wages for its workers, but coupled that with the use of scheduling software, which cut the number of hours for their workers, so they ended up with less pay even as their hourly wage increased (Durden 2016). On the other hand, Starbucks might be a poor example to pick, because they belong to the type of large firm, which collects excess rents from their workers, and could probably easily afford to pay their workers more money.

Market liberals are skeptical about the minimum wage, but they instead tend to be very favorable toward the negative income tax (e.g. Milton Friedman, see Allen 2002). In the negative income tax, low-income earners would not pay any tax, but would receive tax credits. To quote the example in Allen

If, for example, the threshold for positive tax liability for a family of four was, say, $10,000, a family with only $8,000 of annual income would, given a negative tax rate of 25 percent, receive a check from the Treasury worth $500 (25 percent of the $2,000 difference between its $8,000 income and the $10,000 threshold). A family with zero income would receive $2,500.

Since the Reagan administration, the most prevalent form of the negative income tax has been the Earned Income Tax Credit (EITC), which provides most tax benefits to low-wage earners with dependent children (those below the age of 24). The program has been sold as a way to encourage work among able-bodied individuals without distorting the labor market. Let us take a simple example to illustrate this point: there is a low-wage worker, who produces 15 dollars an hour in value to his employer. The employer pays him the minimum wage of 7.25 dollars an hour. If the federal government hiked the minimum wage to 15 dollars an hour, the net profit would shrink to zero, and the worker would have to be laid off. Turning to EITC: If that worker is the primary earner in the family, then having an EITC scheme, which would subsidize his meager earnings by 5,000 dollars annually, would go a long way toward paying part of the rent and other living expenses he faces without changing the nominal wage. There is no need to lay that worker off and his poverty is alleviated. The advantage of the EITC is clearly that there is no assumption about the worker productivity that needs to be made in order to reduce poverty (high productivity would presumably result in a wage high enough to prevent poverty).

But there are problems with a negative income tax, because in the ideal world we imagine that employers don't react to the creation of a negative income tax, i.e. they don't change the wages of their workers knowing that the scheme exists. But we know that they do react to negative income taxes by paying their workers below subsistence wages even if they could afford to pay them more. Karl Polanyi (1944: 81-89) had been a major critic of the British Speenhamland law, which was a form of poor relief similar to the negative income tax. The poor workers would be subsidized by municipalities so they can at least afford bread. Once the law was implemented, the employers milked the law by deliberately paying below subsistence wages, knowing that their workers would receive a top-up from the municipality. The growing burden of low wages implied that municipalities would not be able to fund generous top-ups, and they were eventually forced to reduce the top-ups, which created misery among the workers. The law was later replaced by a no less draconian poor law, which created workhouses to treat the "undeserving" poor that were otherwise "unwilling" to work.

If we think about what Walmart is doing in today's economy, it can't be much different from what employers did in 19th century Britain. Walmart is taking a classical "low-road strategy" (Kalleberg 2011) of paying their workers very low wages, even though they could easily afford to pay them more given their huge share buybacks. Traub (2015) writes,

If Walmart redirected the $10 billion per year it has authorized for buybacks toward investment in human capital, it could provide its 825,000 lowest-paid U.S. employees a raise of as much as an additional $7.67 per hour without raising consumer prices by a penny. On top of the $10 an hour Walmart has already committed to, this would more than pay for the $15 an hour Walmart workers are calling for.

Instead, Walmart continues to pay low wages to their workers, knowing that they get Food Stamps, Medicaid and EITC from the taxpayers. A report by Jacobs et al. (2015) finds that the US taxpayers are subsidizing Walmart, McDonalds and other low-wage employers to the tune of 152.8 billion dollars per year. Only a part of that goes to EITC, which is the focus of this post, but it is clear that employers, who have the ability to milk the government and middle class families, will do so without impunity.

I have now shown that neither the minimum wage nor the negative income tax are ideal solutions to alleviate poverty at the minimum social cost among working people. The minimum wage is a direct intervention in the labor market and has the capacity to reduce the rent going to employers, but has the risk of making labor too expensive to hire, which is a genuine fear in largely unproductive service sectors.

The negative income tax can bypass the direct labor market intervention and this risk, but will encourage employers to pay their workers too little. Here the risk is that to eliminate poverty either the tax benefits have to be so large that the government program becomes unsustainably expensive (also politically difficult to sustain because middle class people don't benefit from the scheme and will be likely to attack it, which is the logic of the paradox of redistribution, see Korpi and Palme 1998), or the government has to sacrifice their poverty reduction targets. The employer incentive to underpay workers results in a lack of incentive to invest in high-productivity jobs, which would entrench the low pay trap of these workers. In that sense, even the negative income tax does not escape the trouble of intervention in the labor market.

My critique of the minimum wage and the negative income tax by no means implies that I would want to end these two programs. In the absence of better policy alternatives, it would be cruel to downgrade these two programs regardless of what the efficiency effect is. Any government policy to improve the lot of the lower class deserves support if we care about reducing poverty. But we have to look at pro-poor policies as a package consisting of a combination of different policies. I conclude with four ideas: productivity investment, public-sector jobs, unionization and the universal basic income.

We need to invest in the creation of higher productivity jobs out of which higher wages can be easily paid. Again, we assume that there is no mechanism by which employers can prevent the payment of higher wages despite sufficient productivity (e.g. Walmart). There is naturally a risk with high-productivity sectors, which is that they don't offer that much employment opportunities. There is only so many cars that a country needs, and yet this is a sector where productivity enhancement has been an important part of the operation, resulting in fewer total jobs in the industry. That is why we have long employment lines in the fast food joints and school janitorial positions.

Part of the credential narrative ("get an education to get a better job") is precisely the expectation that workers can easily shift from low to high productivity jobs. We know that our society is now actually suffering from overcredentialing, i.e. too many highly educated people but not enough jobs for them. The labor market only supports so many accountants and lawyers. Culturally, it is also questionable to demand of so many people to be "smarter" and be more "adaptable" to the needs of the more "complex" labor market. The Atlantic has called this discourse rightfully "the war on stupid people" (Freedman 2016).

Part of the reason why China was able to lift out so many people out of poverty is not because they have accelerated education credentialing (which did not pick up until the late-1990s, long after the economic reform of the 1970s), but because they became the factory of the world, offering so many landless peasants low-skilled factory jobs. If our solution to the in-work poverty problem is work-centric, then the expansion of low-skilled (but probably subsidized) work is what we would need. Expanding high-productivity sectors with high levels of employment is likely only feasible if we can suddenly find new markets to penetrate.

Another work-centric solution would be to increase public-sector employment. The logic would be as follows: first, the government would mainly create jobs with a living wage. Second, because the public now competes for workers with the private sector, the private sector will now also have to raise wages to stay competitive. Again, I expect that the rent function in the private sector decrease. The complaint about public sector jobs is not so much the increase in debt, because the government could increase taxes on the rich without taking out that much debt. Instead of wasting tax dollars on subsidizing low-wage workers, the state could use some of that money for direct job creation instead. The real complaint is of a rather political nature as Michal Kalecki (1943) remarked: basically, capitalists hate the heightened political power accruing to the working class as public-sector job creation swells, undermining the collective class power of the capitalists. In Kalecki's own words,

[T]he maintenance of full employment would cause social and political changes which would give a new impetus to the opposition of the business leaders. Indeed, under a regime of permanent full employment, the 'sack' would cease to play its role as a 'disciplinary measure. The social position of the boss would be undermined, and the self-assurance and class-consciousness of the working class would grow. Strikes for wage increases and improvements in conditions of work would create political tension. It is true that

profits would be higher under a regime of full employment than they are on the average under laissez-faire *[emphasis added], and even the rise in wage rates resulting from the stronger bargaining power of the workers is less likely to reduce profits than to increase prices, and thus adversely affects only the rentier interests. But 'discipline in the factories' and 'political stability' are more appreciated than profits by business leaders. Their class instinct tells them that lasting full employment is unsound from their point of view, and that unemployment is an integral part of the 'normal' capitalist system.*

Even if capitalists would benefit from full employment following public job creation, they don't like the political aspect of strengthening the interests of the workers. I would say that public-sector job creation has to return as a tool to reduce poverty and provide opportunities to more workers. The capitalists will get used to their somewhat diminished stature, and, in any case, some capitalist will make investments if the profit is large enough.

Strengthening the political hand of the workers is precisely what is needed in today's economy, where most young people don't even know what a labor union is or does. The rising political consciousness of the working class would be associated with the creation of new labor unions. Unions have been in precipitous decline since the end of World War II. I don't think it has to do with a substantial change in American values (though values certainly shift in the absence of unions). Their decline is associated with the shift from industrial to service employment and the concomitant difficulty of organizing the latter into unions. Nascent efforts like those in Walmart are easily crushed by ruthless human resource practices, like shutting down an entire store trying to unionize. Unlike port workers (the Longshoremen are notorious for their strikes and high pay), most service-sector jobs don't have a bottleneck position, i.e. their strike does not shut down commerce, so the bosses can ruthlessly go against workers trying to unionize. Union weakness was perfectly exploited by employers eager to increase their profit share. The shareholder value maximization and escalating CEO pay would be inconceivable in a world where unions still had a substantial say in corporate governance (Lazonick 2011).

But these aforementioned solutions are still very much focused on work and the labor market, while technological innovation that is labor-saving has the contrary effect of making it increasingly difficult to find employment opportunities for the masses. Needless to say, structurally greater unemployment (or a decline in the labor force participation rate expressing the same) puts a downward pressure on wages, as more workers compete for the few scarce jobs. Some people might say that Frey and Osborne's (2013) prediction of eliminating half of all jobs because of automation is exaggerated.

But even if their claim is exaggerated: just eliminating 10 or 20% of all employment opportunities would have substantial knock-on effects in the economy, which will be too slow in finding the people new employment. It would also be questionable to arbitrarily find them work just so they can work. To some extent, our crazily GDP- and employment-growth focused economy has resulted in the proliferation of goods and services, which do not necessarily enhance collective well-being (e.g. every year a slightly different smartphone). We are really creating a lot of make-work rather than useful jobs, and our creativity would have to take another turn in equipping people with new make-work as much of the useful employment is taken up by robots.

We have to sever the tie between employment and income, and only the universal basic income can accomplish that goal. It would be a substantial economic investment, and I have argued elsewhere that we could afford it and it would not have adverse effects on incentives for work, but would liberate people to choose their own employment, whether it is paid or not ("Should We Support a Universal Basic Income?", "Disputing the Scarcity Principle", "Responding to a Critic of the Universal Basic Income"). The real innovation in social policy would not be to tinker with the existing regimes of poverty reduction, though it beats an alternative of inaction, but to promote the universal basic income.

Is the Affordable Care Act Good Legislation?

Posted on August 18, 2016

Aetna had decided to pull out of many states, and refuse to offer health insurance on the exchange. Some suggest that this was because of disputes between the US administration and Aetna, who refused a merger with Humana. (How crazy is it that so few companies have so much power over the national well-being of citizens?) United Healthcare, the biggest private insurance company in the US, had decided earlier this year to rescind their insurance offerings in many markets. This would suggest that the hoped for advantage of creating a competitive market place in the US health insurance industry will not work out. The overall question, however, is whether the Affordable Care Act (ACA) as it stands is good legislation. I argue that while it is better than repealing the legislation, there is no insurance system that is better than a single-payer, Medicare-for-all system.

To decide whether it is good legislation, we may look at the overall cost of health care, which has grown at less than 4% per year between 2008 and 2013. Studies suggest that the 2015 health care cost growth projections (2014-9) come at 2.6 trillion dollars lower than the 2010 baseline estimate when the Affordable Care Act was first passed (Robert Wood Johnson Foundation 2016). This might sound like good news, but the report also suggests that the slower growth may also be linked to the recession, which essentially means that people skipped necessary medical care because they could not afford it. Even as people want to increase their consumption of health care by acquiring insurance via the exchange (which before the ACA did not exist), people face higher deductibles (Lorenzetti 2016), which also tends to reduce the consumption of necessary medical care. Even employers are increasingly shifting to high-deductible plans (ranging from 1,300 to 13,000 dollars a year) to offload the responsibility of health care to individual workers. 84% offer high deductible plans, and one-third of employers offer only high-deductible plans (Mercado 2016). In any case, the share of workers covered by their employer's health care plan decreased from 65 to 63% from 2009 to 2015 (Kaiser Family Foundation, "Visualizing Health Policy: Eligibility and Coverage Trends in Employer-Sponsored Health Insurance", May 3, 2016).

Critics of non-cost-sharing health care (as would be the case for generous employer plans or single-payer in most industrialized countries) warn of the moral hazard involved in it. The idea is that people will over-consume medical care if they don't have to pay for it. But I am not really convinced of this, because young and healthy people are unlikely to go to the hospital or the doctor just for the heck of it, and even if they did, it is better to be safe than sorry when it comes to personal health. The bigger problem actually accrues to the high-deductible, high cost-sharing health insurance options which reduce medically necessary treatment. To the extent that this would reduce the use of preventive health care, it actually raises the cost of health care by delaying treatment.

The ACA that is focused on the exchange tends to favor the growth of high-deductible plans, because healthy individuals seeking to sign up look for the cheapest option (Abelson 2016). Insurers react to this collective behavior by increasing the premiums, because healthy people cluster in some cheaper health care plans, and the sick cluster in the more expensive plans. As more healthy people shift to cheaper plans, the cost of the sick insurance pool increases, resulting in more and more healthy people to shift to ever cheaper plans. The cost will rise so exorbitantly that the sick health plans will be ultimately dissolved. Health care economists describe this situation as adverse selection.

Kaiser Permanente looked at the premium increases, and they go up by an average of 4.4% in 11 states, but taking into account the tax benefits and subsidies that go to low- and middle income people the premium increases was only 1.2% from 2015 to 2016 (NCSL 2016). But these numbers tend to cover up large variation, ranging from a 13% decrease in premiums to 25% increase. Rhode Island and Indiana are among the few markets in the survey, where health premiums are expected to decline, while many other states (DC, Tennessee, Oregon) will expect substantial premium increases (Kaiser Family Foundation, "Analysis of 2017 Premium Changes and Insurer Participation in the Affordable Care Act's Health Insurance Marketplaces", July 28, 2016). In Colorado, one insurer has requested to increase their premium by 41% (Gazette 2016). No wonder, there is now a ballot initiative there for single-payer health care. Also, premiums cover up the share of health spending coming from deductibles, which is increasing. The average deductible for people with employer-provided health coverage rose from 303 to 1,077 dollars between 2006 and 2015 (Claxton et al. 2016). 24% of non-elderly households cannot pay for deductibles when they need the health care (Altman 2015). Dissatisfaction with annual deductibles increased from 32 to 46% from 2014 to 2016 (Kaiser Family Foundation, "Survey of Non-Group Health Insurance Enrollees, Wave 3", May 20, 2016).

My prediction on costs is, thus, of a more skeptical nature. The market exchange relies on the availability of sufficient number of insurers to keep the prices competitive, but the market failure of adverse selection, where the sick self-select into high risk pools, has not been resolved with the ACA. In fact, the existence of multiple tiers (bronze, silver, gold) of health care plans would actually favor such adverse selection. Expect more large, profit-oriented insurers to withdraw from the market and/or raise prices. The rise of high-deductible plans is only seemingly limiting health care spending, because to the extent that medically necessary care is prevented, overall health outcomes would be worse. To the extent that overall health care costs keep on growing (which experts do not preclude even with the ACA), there are additional costs that consumers will face. The government, using the subsidy system, can shelter low- and some middle income people from the added cost burden, but increasing tax liability will make the health care issue come back to haunt the politicians in not too-distant future.

But cost is not the only thing that matters: the ACA has reduced the number of uninsured from more than 50 million to less than 30 million. The failure of the ACA is that because the law is focused on the exchange, subsidies, penalties and the mandate, there is no universal coverage, which a single-payer plan could easily mandate, akin to the British NHS system. The 20 million people that did receive health care coverage are a combination of additional Medicaid recipients (for people below 133% of the federal poverty level) in states that chose to expand it (i.e. not in some Republican states), and the new people benefiting from the exchange.

What is more difficult to measure is whether the ACA had positive patient outcomes. We might say that it is too soon to tell, but there are comparisons between Medicaid-expanding states (Kentucky, Arkansas) and those that did not expand it (Texas), showing that low-income people in the former states experienced better health outcomes than the latter (Sanger-Katz 2016). It goes almost without saying that people with health insurance tend to report greater health than those without it, because the latter are more likely to have access to a primary care doctor and actually visit the doctor when they need it. But the peculiar thing to me in here is that the health benefits are most clearly visible in the public provision of health care (Medicaid) rather than in anything that private insurance companies would provide.

I am not suggesting that it is not possible to produce good health outcomes with private insurance, but that it is simpler to accomplish in the public-sector than in the private-sector. Because of the market failure that is inherent in the health care system (insurers not knowing how to price the insurance correctly given the differing health profiles of the patients), and the administrative bloat and profit motive, the private health insurance system will always be less efficient than a single-payer, Medicare-for-all system. Walter Tsou, former Philadelphia health commissioner, told me that he predicts that the ACA will not be able to hold down the cost increases that are inherent to a private insurance industry. If this thing falls apart, do we have a good alternative on the pipeline?

Republicans have made clear that the ACA is a failure, and I partly agree with them, but their solution is even more insane. They want to repeal the ACA and replace it with nothing. The more sensible Republicans will talk about additional tax breaks so people can pay for their own health care, but given that the problem is supply-side driven (i.e. private insurers eager to hike prices for profit), there is no real mechanism by which costs would be contained or a guarantee that people can receive insurance in the absence of Medicaid expansion or an exchange.

The obvious solution is to create a single-payer, Medicare-for-all system. It would get rid of the administrative bloat and profiteering (Medicare only spends 2% on administration compared to up to 30% in the private insurance business), while guaranteeing to all people universal health care. The Wall Street Journal (Meckler 2016) has disingenuously attacked Bernie Sanders' single-payer health care proposal for costing 15 trillion dollars, and therefore becoming unaffordable to the federal government.

First, the spending is spread over 10 years rather than 1, which puts the annual cost at a more manageable 1.5 trillion dollars. If that sounds like a lot of money, we have to question how the figure is calculated to begin with. Second, even if that figure were true, the Journal conveniently chooses to ignore the tremendous savings that businesses and individuals generate from not paying for private insurance. If the deductibles and co-payments of tens of thousands of dollars disappear and become replaced by a few thousand dollars in tax increase, then the American people are generating net savings. I know that people don't operate on economic foresight- no understanding of behavioral economics needed. But people have to realize the potential of providing universal health care at a lower cost, because there is a clear loser of single-payer: the private insurance industry.

The United States has the audacity to be the only country in the industrial world that does not guarantee health care to all people as a right. Yet, fully 58% of Americans say that they favor a federally–funded health care system over the ACA (Newport 2016). The discourse is based on how do we tinker with the ACA so that it saves some more lives and saves us just a little bit of money, and ranging to how do we repeal the ACA? As Chomsky writes, "The smart way to keep people passive and obedient is to strictly limit the spectrum of acceptable opinion, but allow very lively debate within that spectrum." We can do better than that.

EU Requiring Apple to Pay More Corporate Taxes Reflects Economic Nationalism
Posted on <u>August 30, 2016</u>

The EU commission had ruled that a sweetheart tax deal offered by Ireland (EU member country) to Apple, where it can save billions of euros in taxes, is illegal, prompting a fine of 13 billion euros which amounts to ten years of back taxes and interest. The US administration fumes in anger, and sees an undue targeting by the EU commission against a US corporation. A senior US Treasury department spokesperson said,

"The Commission's actions could threaten to undermine foreign investment, the business climate in Europe, and the important spirit of economic partnership between the U.S. and the EU."

Kottasova (2016)

Can the US effectively punish the EU? It is certainly much harder to do against a 27 country juggernaut, whose economy and population are larger than the US, than against individual European states. The EU uses its size to enforce their position, and the US is best poised to retaliate by targeting EU corporations active in the US (not that I endorse it, just laying out the likely options). It is unlikely that US corporations refuse more foreign investment into the EU, because the market is so huge and the infrastructure capacity is enormous.

Who is right in this dispute? It is hard to tell, but there is no doubt that the EU and the US both practice economic nationalism, because the US does not want the EU to take tax money from a US corporation even though that US corporation was doing business in the EU. Josh Earnest, a White House spokesperson, referred to the Commission's decision as a transfer of funds from US taxpayers to the EU, because US corporations can claim a tax credit for every dollar in tax paid to an overseas, non-US entity. The 14.5 billion dollars in additional Apple-EU taxes would be deducted from the Apple-US taxes, such that Apple will pay only pay 35.5 billion dollars to the US (Newman 2016).

Whether all of that is just depends on the level of business that Apple carries out on both continents and what the respective tax rate is in each jurisdiction. The US has rather high statutory corporate tax rates (39%), but the effective rate is rather low (13%). Corporate tax take as share of total government revenues declined from 32% in 1952 to 10% in 2013 (Americans for Tax Fairness, http://www.americansfortaxfairness.org/tax-fairness-briefing-booklet/fact-sheet-corporate-tax-rates/). The EU has lower nominal corporate taxes (range from 0 to 35%, whereby Ireland gives away the most corporate tax deductions; Estonia has 0% corporate taxes). Implicit (net) tax rates on corporate income have declined in many European countries as well (-32% in Slovakia from 1995 to 2010, -57.1% in Latvia, -13.3% in Netherlands, see Table 81 in Eurostat 2012). The multiple tax rate structure in the EU actually works in favor of Apple and other multinationals, because they can do business all over the EU and report taxes in the low-tax country (which the EU hopes to change with their ruling).

So in all developed countries, the corporations are paying a smaller proportion of their net income in taxes. The only rationale for lowering the tax capacity of countries is that they hope to attract more foreign business investment and that by facilitating greater corporate profits some of that wealth will trickle down in the form of jobs and more economic growth. At this point, we should realize that trickling up the wealth does not result in trickle down, but the neoliberal consensus has fixated lower relative taxes on corporate income and higher taxes on consumption and labor income. It is this peculiar corporate-friendly regulatory structure which increases the disparity in wealth and income between the rich 1% and the rest of society.

But some might say that the EU commission's decision to stick it to Apple could turn this situation around. However, the EU is not discussing how to restore higher corporate tax rates. Many Eastern European countries coming out of communism would refuse to alienate their foreign investors and are unwilling to impose higher taxes. The other problem is that the US treats the EU decision as a zero-sum game, because the gain to the EU taxpayer translates into a loss for US taxpayers. While Apple appeals the EU decision, they might be hoping that the US treasury will be willing to let that decision go through, and the US then hopes to retaliate on Volkswagen (as they had with the emissions scandal) and other EU-based corporations doing business in the US.

In order to create rational corporate tax policy, it would be important to prevent economic nationalism and zero-sum games on the backs of taxpayers of one jurisdiction. A transnational corporate tax agreement would make sense, but it would be difficult to negotiate because the low-tax countries have to hike corporate taxes, and Ireland, which has banked much of its economic fortune on low corporate taxes, would scream in resistance. But the interesting thing is that small countries can easily be defeated if the will exists. For instance, Switzerland was considered an unbeatable haven for foreign dictator, businessman and illicit money and the bank secrecy laws are as holy as the Bible to Christians. But then the US applied some pressure on the Swiss authorities to release the bank data of wealthy US nationals, and they immediately caved. A similar force of pressure must be exerted on low-tax corporate jurisdictions like Ireland.

Besides, the US might, for instance, scrap or at least reduce the foreign tax credits and thereby allow a double taxation of corporate income. Apple investors will be furious, but we should not forget that Apple had 203 billion dollars in cash in 2015 (La Monica 2015), and is the most highly valued firm in the world. It is really pathetic to still complain about world hunger and crumbling infrastructure when there is plenty of available capital circulating in the world.

If the US would really change the tax law to allow more proceeds to be taxed then this would substantially change the way how corporations are treated, and would facilitate more corporate accountability to the public. It is small wonder that the corporate bosses are doing their best to negotiate the TTIP and TPP in secret without consultation of the public, because they want to rewrite the rules to facilitate the least amount of environmental, product safety and labor regulations, while creating a pro-corporate tribunal to arbitrate trade disputes against national governments and the public and in favor of corporations. For the corporate bosses and their government official cronies to have their way, democracy has to be effectively neutered.

For people, who celebrate the EU move to tax Apple as a first step to curb corporate power, we should not deceive ourselves, because it reminds me of the SEC fining US banks for selling fraudulent mortgages to clients, while the banks merely consider the fine as a cost of doing business. If the fine amount is less than 5% of total income generated under the fraudulent scheme, then the fine is no more than a bribe to government officials so they shut up. Any poor person deciding to rob the bank and being caught by the police has to pay back the entire amount stolen plus a fine, some jail time and a criminal record, while no banker has been put to jail or had to give up their business to my knowledge.

The big corporations have hired the best lawyers and former top level government officials to ensure that they would not have to face such a high tax bill. My hope is that the struggle between top EU and US officials does not take place solely on the backs of working people, who duly pay all of their taxes, but that more government revenue can be generated by corporate taxes so that we can finance the things which we all need to provide for good social policy, while also enabling these corporations to have their markets to continue earning profits. Socializing these corporations and making their revenues benefit all people would be the most desirable goal in the long run, but we still have a long way to go before reaching that objective.

References

Abelson, Reed. 2016. "Cost, Not Choice, Is Top Concern of Health Insurance Customers." New York Times, August 12.

Adam, Nina. 2015. "German Exports Register Steepest Decline in Almost Seven Years." Wall Street Journal, October 8.

Akyol, Mustafa. 2016. "Who Was Behind the Coup Attempt in Turkey?." New York Times, July 22.

Allen, Jodie T. 2002. "Negative Income Tax." Library of Economics and Liberty.

Alter, Charlotte 2015. "Millennials Are Setting New Records—for Living With Their Parents." Time, November 11.

Altman, Drew. 2015. "Health-Care Deductibles Climbing Out of Reach." Wall Street Journal, March 11.

AMS.at. 2012. "Aktive Arbeitsmarktpolitik in Osterreich." Arbeitsmarktservice. http://www.ams.at/_docs/001_Aktive_Arbeitsmarktpolitik.pdf

Aristotle. 1999. Politics. https://socserv2.socsci.mcmaster.ca/econ/ugcm/3ll3/aristotle/Politics.pdf

Barnard, Anne, and Karam Shoumali. 2015. "U.S. Weaponry Is Turning Syria Into Proxy War With Russia." New York Times, October 12.

BBC. 2016. "中国两会：全国人大定下新一年□□增□目□ [Zh□ngguó lianghuì: Quánguó réndà dìng xià x□n y□ nián j□ngjì z□ng cháng mùbi□o]." March 5.

Bernish, Claire. 2016. "Erdogan Purges 60,000 Positions After Failed Coup, Shifting Turkey Into Totalitarianism." Mint Press News, July 21.

Bernstein, Eduard. 1899. Evolutionary Socialism. https://www.marxists.org/reference/archive/bernstein/works/1899/evsoc/

Biller, David. 2016. "Meirelles Fans Would Do Well to Remember Brazil's 2015 Bond Bust." Bloomberg, May 15.

Binderup, Charles. 1937. Congressional Record-House 81-2528. March 19. https://en.wikisource.org/wiki/Page:Congressional_Record_Volume_81_Part_3.djvu/154

Blair, Tony. 2015. "Jeremy Corbyn's politics are fantasy – just like Alice in Wonderland." Guardian, August 29.

Bohlen, Celestine. 2016. "Crippling Strike in France May Have Been About More Than Labor Law." New York Times, April 4.

Bradsher, Keith 2016. "中国外□□□急□□水，人民□面□下行□力 [Zh□ngguó wàihuì chúbèi jíjù su□shuǐ, rénmínbì miànlín xiàxíng y□lì]." New York Times, February 19.

Brownstein, Ronald. 2016. "The Great Democratic Age Gap." Atlantic, February 2.

Burridge, Tom. 2013. "Marinaleda: Will 'free homes' solve Spain's evictions crisis?" BBC, June 2.

Butler, Daren, and Seda Sezer.2016. "Turkey detains 42 journalists in crackdown as Europe sounds alarm." Reuters, July 26.

Chomsky, Noam. 1983. "Personal Influences." In Chomsky Reader. https://chomsky.info/reader01/

Clark, Patrick, and Suzanne Woolley. 2016." Landlord Nation: Boomers' New Retirement Plan Is Millennials Paying Rent." Bloomberg, August 4.

Claxton, Gary, Larry Levitt, and Michelle Long. 2016. "Payments for cost sharing increasing rapidly over time." Peterson-Kaiser Health System Tracker, April 12.

Clinton, Hillary Rodham. 2004. Living History. New York: Simon and Schuster.

Cortwright, Joe. 2014. "Young People are Buying Fewer Cars." City Observatory, April 22.

Cowen, Tyler 2011. "Steven Pinker on violence." Marginal Revolution, October 11.

Credit Suisse. 2015. "Global Wealth Databook 2015." http://publications.credit-suisse.com/tasks/render/file/index.cfm?fileid=C26E3824-E868-56E0-CCA04D4BB9B9ADD5

Croix, Sarah de Sainte. 2012. "Brazil Strives for Economic Equality." Rio TImes, February 17.

Dabla-Norris, Era, Kalpana Kochhar, Nujin Suphaphiphat, Frantisek Ricka, and Evridiki Tsounta. 2015. "Causes and Consequences of Income Inequality : A Global Perspective." International Monetary Fund. https://www.imf.org/external/pubs/cat/longres.aspx?sk=42986.0

Delapaine, Joe. 2015. "Libya, imperialism and the refugee crisis." Liberation, May 4.

Democratic Underground. 2013. "Young People More Likely To Favor Socialism Than Capitalism: Pew." February 11.

Denning, Steve. 2014. "The Surprising Truth About Where New Jobs Come From." Forbes, October 29.

Desjardins, Jeff. 2014. "A Forecast of When We'll Run Out of Each Metal." Visual Capitalist, September 4.

Diamond, Jared. 1997. Guns, Germs, and Steel: The Fates of Human Societies. New York: W.W. Norton.

Doeringer, Peter, and Michael Piore. 1970. *Internal Labor Markets and Manpower Analysis*. Cambridge: Harvard University Press.

Dorell, Oren. 2015. "Foreign businesses stream into Iran as sanctions may end." *USA Today*, June 4.

Drajem, Mark, and Mark Chediak. 2014. "Pentagon Warns Climate Change Will Intensify Conflict." *Bloomberg*, October 14.

Dube, Arindrajit. N.d. "Proposal 13: Designing Thoughtful Minimum Wage Policy at the State and Local Levels." Hamilton Project, Brookings.

Durden, Tyler. 2016. "Something "Unexpected" Happened After Starbucks Raised Minimum Wages." *Zero Hedge*, July 1.

Durkheim, Emile. 1912. *The Elementary Forms of the Religious Life*.

Easley, Jason. 2014. "Bernie Sanders Wants To Know If You Are Ready To Stand Up And Fight The Koch Brothers." *Polititicus USA*, November 12.

Eichhorst, Werner, Otto Kaufmann, and Regina Konle-Seidl (eds.). 2008. *Bringing the Jobless into Work?*. Berlin: Springer.

Esping-Andersen, Gosta. 1990. *The Three Worlds of Welfare Capitalism*. Princeton: Princeton University Press.

Eurostat. 2012. "Taxation Trends in the European Union." https://ec.europa.eu/taxation_customs/sites/taxation/files/docs/body/report.pdf

Frank, T.A. 2016. "Why Democrats Are Becoming the Party of the 1 Percent." *Vanity Fair*, April 20.

Freedman, David H. 2016. "The War on Stupid People." *Atlantic*, July/August.

Freire, Paulo. 1972. *Pedagogy of the Oppressed*. Harmondsworth: Penguin.

Frey, Carl Benedikt, and Michael A. Osborne. 2013. "The Future of Employment: How Susceptible are Jobs to Computerisation?" University of Oxford.

Friedman, Thomas. 1999. *The Lexus and the Olive Tree*. New York: Farrar, Straus & Giroux.

Fukuyama, Francis. 1992. *The End of History and the Last Man*. New York: Free Press.

Galbraith, James. 2014. *The End of Normal: The Great Crisis and the Future of Growth*. New York: Simon and Schuster.

Gandel, Stephen. 2015. "America's biggest job market problem is uniquely American." *Fortune*, July 2.

Ganesh, Janan. 2016. "A Labour split will win over dispossessed Remainers." *Financial Times*, July 4.

Gates, Bill. 2014. "Why Inequality Matters." *Gates Notes*, October 13.

Gatzke, Marcus, and Mark Schieritz. 2015. ""I'm the finance minister of a bankrupt country"." *Zeit*, February 4.

Goodman, John C. "Single Payer Health Insurance: Why Bernie Sanders Just Doesn't Get It." *Forbes*, April 20.

Gorz, Andre. 1999. *Reclaiming Work: Beyond the Wage-Based Society.* Cambridge: Polity Press.

Graeber, David. 2013. "On the Phenomenon of Bullshit Jobs." Strike Magazine, August 17.

Gramsci, Antonio. 1999. *Prison Notebooks.* London: ElecBook. http://courses.justice.eku.edu/pls330_louis/docs/gramsci-prison-notebooks-vol1.pdf

Gray, John. 2015. "Steven Pinker is wrong about violence and war." Guardian, March 13.

Habermas, Jurgen. 1962/1991. *The Structural Transformation of the Public Sphere.* Cambridge: MIT Press. http://pages.uoregon.edu/koopman/courses_readings/phil123-net/publicness/habermas_structural_trans_pub_sphere.pdf

Hanauer, Nick. 2014. "The Pitchforks are Coming... For Us Plutocrats." Politico, July/August.

Harvey, David. 2010. "The Enigma of Capital and the Crisis this Time." Paper presented at the American Sociological Association Meetings, Atlanta, Georgia, August 16.

Hobbes, Thomas. 1652. *Leviathan.*

Hughes, Chris. 2016. "Thousands of Turkey coup prisoners 'raped, starved and hogtied'." Mirror, July 24.

Isidore, Chris. 2013. "Buffett says he's still paying lower tax rate than his secretary." CNN, March 4.

Jacobs, Ken, Ian Parry, and Jenifer MacGillvary. 2015. "The High Public Cost of Low Wages." UC Berkeley Labor Center.

Kalecki, Michal. 1943. "Political Aspects of Full Employment." MR Zine. http://mrzine.monthlyreview.org/2010/kalecki220510.html

Kalleberg, Arne. 2011. *Good Jobs, Bad Jobs: The Rise of Polarized and Precarious Employment Systems in the United States, 1970s to 2000s.* New York: Russell Sage.

Kennedy, Liz. 2013. "Stop the Next Citizens United." Demos, September 10.

Kirell, Andrew. 2015. "Donald Trump Rails Against Cutting Social Security, Medicare During GOP Summit." Mediaite, April 18.

Kissinger, Henry. 1957. *Nuclear Weapons and Foreign Policy.* New York: W.W. Norton.

Korpi, Walter, and Joakim Palme. 1998. "The Paradox of Redistribution and Strategies of Equality: Welfare State Institutions, Inequality, and Poverty in the Western Countries." American Sociological Review 63(5): 661-687.

Kottasova, Ivanaa. 2016. "EU hits Apple with $14.6 billion tax bill." CNN, August 30.

Lam, Bourree. 2016. "What Costco's New Wages Say About the Health of the American Economy." Atlantic, March 5.

La Monica, Robert L. 2015. "Apple has $203 billion in cash. Why?" CNN, July 22.

Lazonick, William. 2011. "From Innovation to Financialization: How Shareholder Value Ideology Is Destroying the US Economy." In *The Political Economy of Financial Crises*, edited by Gerald Epstein and Martin H. Wolfson. Oxford: Oxford University Press.

Leibovich, Mark. 2007. "The Socialist Senator." New York Times, January 21.

Leisch, Wilfried. 2013. "Immer mehr arbeiten prekär." Arbeit&Wirtschaft, April 15.

Lethbridge, Ty. 2007. "Aristotle and His View of Friendship." The Wire Blog, December 14.

Levine, Dan. 2016. "Uber drivers remain independent contractors as lawsuit settled." Reuters, April 22.

Linsinger, Eva. 2013. "Vermögen der reichsten Österreicher doppelt so groß wie angenommen." Profil, August 3.

Liu, Larry. 2012. "Social Democracy vs. Democratic Socialism." Mr. Liu's Opinions, December 21.

Liu, Larry. 2013. "Why it is Disappointing to be on the Left, While it Remains an Inherent Necessity." Mr Liu's Opinions, June 10.

Liu, Larry. 2014. "Book Review of Wolfgang Streeck "Buying Time: The Delayed Crisis of Democratic Capitalism" (London: Verso, 2014)." Mr Liu's Opinions, December 29.

Liu, Larry. 2015. "The Decline of Centrist Mass Parties and the Rise of Right-Wing Populism (RWP) in Europe: Case Studies of Neoliberal Reform and Immigration in the UK, Germany and Austria." mimeo. http://www.academia.edu/12081506/The_Decline_of_Centrist_Mass_Parties_and_the_Rise_of_Right-Wing_Populism_RWP_in_Europe_Case_Studies_of_Neoliberal_Reform_and_Immigration_in_the_UK_Germany_and_Austria

Lorenzetti, Laura. 2016. "U.S. Will Spend $2.6 Trillion Less on Health Care Than Previously Estimated." Fortune, June 21.

Lyons, John, and Paul Kiernan. 2015. "How Brazil's China-Driven Commodities Boom Went Bust." Wall Street Journal, August 27.

MacMillan, Douglas. 2015. "Uber Tests 30% Fee, Its Highest Yet." Wall Street Journal, May 18.

Magness, Philip, Robert Murphy. 2014. "Challenging the Empirical Contribution of Thomas Piketty's Capital in the 21st Century. " Journal of Private Enterprise (2015), 15(2).

Mann, Michael. 1986. *The Sources of Social Power Volume 1. A History of Power from the Beginning to AD 1760*. Cambridge: Cambridge University Press.

Marshall, John. 2009. "Timeline: Weapons technology." New Scientist, July 7.

Mason, Paul. 2013. *Why It's Kicking Off Everywhere: The New Global Revolutions*. London: Verso.

Mason, Rowena. 2015. "Labour leadership: Jeremy Corbyn elected with huge mandate." Guardian, September 12.

Meckler, Laura. 2015. "Price Tag of Bernie Sanders's Proposals: $18 Trillion." Wall Street Journal, September 14.

Mercado, Darla. 2016. "Expect your health insurance costs to rise in 2017." CNBC, August 11.

Mitnick, Joshua. 2015. "Netanyahu Calls Iran Deal 'Historic Mistake'." Wall Street Journal, July 14.

Monbiot, George. 2015. "Greece is the latest battleground in the financial elite's war on democracy." Guardian, July 7.

Moore, Barrington Jr. 1966. *Social Origins of Dictatorship and Democracy: Lord and Peasant in the Making of the Modern World*. Boston, MA: Beacon Press.

Moseley, Fred. 1997. "The Rate of Profit and the Future of Capitalism." Review of Radical Political Economics.

Mueller, John. 1989. *Retreat from Doomsday: The Obsolescence of Major War*. New York: Basic Books.

Nader, Ralph. 2014. "Ralph Nader on GOP's 2014 Wins: Democrats Can't Use Citizens United, Voter Restriction Laws as Alibi." Democracy Now (interview), November 6.

Narefsky, Karen. 2015. "The Case for Public Housing." Dissent, November 20.

NCSL. 2016. "Health Insurance: Premiums and Increases." National Conference of State Legislatures, May 6.

Newman, Rick. 2016. "US taxpayers could end up covering Apple's back taxes in Ireland." Yahoo, August 30.

Newport, Frank. 2016. "Majority in U.S. Support Idea of Fed-Funded Healthcare System." Gallup, May 16.

Noblecourt, Michel. 2016. "La CGT se radicalise pour sortir de sa crise." Le Monde, April 16.

Obe, Mitsuru, and Rob Taylor. 2015. "Japan Says It Could Join China-Led Development Bank." Wall Street Journal, March 20.

O'Connor, James. 1973. *The Fiscal Crisis of the State*. New Brunswick: Transaction Publishers.

O'Grady, Mary Anastasia. 2016. "Brazil's Chance to Save Itself." Wall Street Journal, May 15

Ollman, Bertell. N.d. "Why So Many Exams? A Marxist Response." Dialectical Marxism. https://www.nyu.edu/projects/ollman/docs/why_exams.php

Olson, Mancur. 1965. *The Logic of Collective Action: Public Goods and the Theory of Groups*. Cambridge: Harvard University Press.

Oltermann, Philip. 2016. "Yanis Varoufakis launches pan-European leftwing movement DiEM25." Guardian, February 10.

Parra-Bernal, Guillermo. 2016. "Deutsche sees Rousseff ouster boosting Petrobras, Brazil bank debt." Reuters, May 16.

Peralta, Eydar. 2015. "6 Things You Should Know About The Iran Nuclear Deal." NPR, July 14.

Perkins, John. 2014. "An Economic Hit Man Speaks Out: John Perkins on How Greece Has Fallen Victim to "Economic Hit Men"." Truthout, September 11.

Phillips, Richard. 2015. "Donald Trump's Regressive and Retrograde Tax Plan." Tax Justice Blog, June 22.

Phillips, Mat 2016. "China just announced one of the largest single layoffs in history." Quartz, February 29.

Piketty, Thomas. 2014. *Capital in the Twenty-First Century.* Cambridge: Belknap Press.

Pinker, Steven. 2011. *The Better Angels of Our Nature: Why Violence Has Declined.* New York: Viking.

Polanyi, Karl. 1944. *The Great Transformation: The Political and Economic Origins of Our Time.* Boston: Beacon Press.

Powers, Richard Gid. 1998. *Not without Honor: The History of American Anti-Communism.* New Haven: Yale University Press.

Robert Wood Johnson Foundation. 2016. "Executive Summary: The Widespread Slowdown in Health Spending Growth Implications for Future Spending Projections and the Cost of the Affordable Care   Act." http://www.rwjf.org/content/dam/farm/reports/issue_briefs/201 6/rwjf429930/subassets/rwjf429930_1

Rodrik, Dani. 2016. "Is Fethullah Gülen behind Turkey's coup? (with update)." Dani Rodrik Weblog, July 23.

Rose, Michel, and Ingrid Melander. 2016. "French students, unions protest against labor reforms." Reuters, March 9.

Russell, Bertrand. 1994. *On Education.* Hove: Psychology Press.

Sanders, Bernie. 2014. "An Economic Agenda for America: 12 Steps Forward." Huffington Post, December 1.

Sanger-Katz, Margot. 2016. "Obamacare Appears to Be Making People Healthier." New York Times, August 9.

Schmitz, Kerstin, Lorenz Lassnigg and Rudolf Strahm. 2013. "What are they doing right? 3 cases." European Lifelong Learning Magazine, 3 April.

Schrager, Allison. 2015. "Men are both dumber and smarter than women." Quartz, July 9.

Schumpeter, Joseph. 1942. *Capitalism, Socialism and Democracy.* London: Routledge. http://digamo.free.fr/capisoc.pdf

Seattle Minimum Wage Study Team. 2016. "Report on the Impact of Seattle's Minimum Wage Ordinance on Wages, Workers, Jobs, and Establishments   through   2015." https://evans.uw.edu/sites/default/files/MinWageReport-July2016_Final.pdf

Simon, Mallory, and Ray Sanchez. 2015. "U.S. gun violence: The story in charts and graphs." CNN, December 4.

Smith, Helena. 2015. "Greek finance minister Yanis Varoufakis replaced as leader of debt talks." Guardian, April 27.

Standing, Guy. n.d. "Basic Income: A 21st Century Economic Right." http://www.guystanding.com/files/documents/CDHE_Standing.pdf

Standing, Guy. 2011. *The Precariat: The New Dangerous Class.* London: Bloomsbury.

Standing, Guy. 2015. "The Growing Precariat: Why We Need a Universal Basic Income." Singularity Hub, March 30.

Stanway, David. 2016. "China overcapacity problems worsen over 2008-2015: EU chamber." Reuters, February 21.

Stiglitz, Joseph E. 2016. "What's holding back the global economy?." World Economic Forum, February 9.

Streeck, Wolfgang. 2014. *Buying Time: The Delayed Crisis of Democratic Capitalism.* Brooklyn: Verso.

Sweezy, Paul M. 2004. "Monopoly Capitalism." Monthly Review 56(5). http://monthlyreview.org/2004/10/01/monopoly-capitalism/

Tonnelier, Audrey. 2016. "Loi travail : derrière la surenchère de Gattaz, des tensions au sein du patronat." Le Monde, April 20.

Traub, Amy. 2015. "How Walmart Could Afford to Pay $15 an Hour." American Prospect, November 25.

Trent, Katherine, Scott J. South and Sunita Bose. 2012. "The Consequences of India's Male Surplus for Women's Partnering and Sexual Experiences." http://paa2013.princeton.edu/papers/130180

University of Texas. 2014. "Professor James Galbraith on the Link Between Inequality and Financial Instability." http://lbj.utexas.edu/news/2014/professor-james-galbraith-link-between-inequality-and-financ

Varoufakis, Yanis. 2011. *The Global Minotaur: America, the True Causes of the Financial Crisis and the Future of the World Economy.* Vauxhall: Zed Books.

Varoufakis, Yanis. 2012. "From Ponzi Growth to Ponzi Austerity." Yanis Varoufakis, May 31.

Varoufakis, Yanis. 2015. "A New Deal for Greece – a Project Syndicate Op-Ed." Yanis Varoufakis, April 24.

Wacquant, Loic. 2001. "The Penalisation of Poverty and the Rise of Neoliberalism." European Journal on Criminal Policy and Research 9: 401-412.

Wall, Jared. 2016. "Freedom is Everything – A Libertarian Refutes a Socialist's Concept of Freedom." Emancipated Human, January 7.

White, Gillian B. 2016. "Can Millennials Undo What the Recession Did to Their Earnings?" Atlantic, March 3.

Whiteman, Hilary. 2016. "Luxury hotel? No, Singapore's new-generation public housing." CNN, February 28.

Wilson, Robin. 2016. "Universal Basic Income: A Disarmingly Simple Idea – And Fad." Social Europe, June 9.

Winkler, Elizabeth. 2015. "China's One-Child Policy May Be Making the Country More Violent." New Republic, June 27.

Wright, Erik Olin. 2015. "How to Be an Anticapitalist Today." Jacobin, December 2.

Wong, Kristina. 2015. "GOP candidates take turns bashing Obama's Iran deal." Hill, August 6.

About the Author:

L, Larry Liu is a doctoral student at Princeton University (sociology) with previous degrees in comparative social policy (M.Sc., University of Oxford, 2016), sociology and economic policy (B.A., University of Pennsylvania, 2015), and liberal arts honors (A.A., Community College of Philadelphia, 2012). He blogs, reads newspapers, magazines and books in the social sciences and humanities, rides the bicycle, travels, and values good conversations with friends, food, music and a passionate defense of social justice. He is resident in Philadelphia, PA and Princeton, NJ. His previous publications include *Hakkas in Power: A Study of Chinese Political Leadership in East and Southeast Asia, and South America* (CreateSpace, 2015); and *The Austerity Trap: Economic and Social Consequences of Fiscal Consolidation in Europe* (CreateSpace, 2015).